THE TRADITIONAL CHINESE CLAN RULES

MONOGRAPHS OF THE ASSOCIATION
FOR ASIAN STUDIES

VII

HUI-CHEN WANG LIU
Lecturer University of Pittsburgh

THE TRADITIONAL CHINESE CLAN RULES

Published for the Association for Asian Studies by

J. J. AUGUSTIN INCORPORATED PUBLISHER
LOCUST VALLEY, NEW YORK

The publication of this series is made possible by the generous assistance of the Council for Economic and Cultural Affairs, the Ford Foundation, Mr. and Mrs. Richard Adloff, and Mr. Charles S. Gardner

ALL RIGHTS RESERVED

PRINTED IN GERMANY BY J.J.AUGUSTIN, GLÜCKSTADT
1959

TO
MY PARENTS

TABLE OF CONTENTS

PREFACE ix

I. INTRODUCTION
   A. The Family and the Clan in Traditional China 1
   B. The Clan Rules in the Genealogies and the Present Study 7
   C. Method of Analysis 14

II. GENERAL ANALYSES OF THE CLAN RULES
   A. The Forms and the Common Characteristics of the Clan Rules 21
   B. The Titles and the Types of the Clan Rules........ 25
   C. The Subject Matter in the Clan Rules and the Value Pattern 31
   D. The Types of Clan Punishment 36

III. THE CLAN RULES ON FAMILY RELATIONSHIPS
   A. Parent-children Relationship 48
   B. Relationship between Brothers 60
   C. Heir and Adoption of Heir 70
   D. Marriage 77
   E. Wifehood and Widowhood 84
   F. Sex Segregation and Seclusion of Women 93
   G. Summary 96

IV. THE CLAN RULES ON CLAN FUNCTIONS AND RELATIONSHIPS
   A. Clan Organization 98
   B. Clan's Common Property 107
   C. Ancestral Rites and Clan Meetings 115
   D. Clan Reward and Clan Relief 126
   E. Exemplary Conduct and Intra-clan Relationships .. 132
   F. Summary 143

V. THE CLAN RULES ON SOCIAL RELATIONSHIPS AND INDIVIDUAL BEHAVIOR

- A. Relationship with Non-clan Individuals 145
- B. Neighborhood and Community Relationships 149
- C. Relationship with the Government 152
- D. Vocations and Economic Behavior 158
- E. Religions and Beliefs 166
- F. Vices and Criminal Offenses 172
- G. Summary 176

VI. THE CLAN RULES AND MODERNIZATION

- A. Limited Adjustments and Their Difficulties........ 177
- B. Clan Contribution to Modern Education........... 186

VII. CONCLUSION 190

BIBLIOGRAPHY 194

APPENDIX 209

PREFACE

THE CHINESE FAMILY INSTITUTION, through several admirable publications in recent years, has become well known to American Sinologists as well as American sociologists and anthropologists. However, the Chinese clan institution, so closely related to the family, remains largely unfamiliar, even to Chinese and Japanese scholars. It is hoped that the present attempt to study systematically a considerable number of clan rules from the standpoint of social control may serve to stimulate increasing interest in this area.

The manuscript was originally a doctoral dissertation at the University of Pittsburgh in 1956, under the title "An Analysis of the Chinese Clan Rules: A Study of Social Control," available through the University Microfilms, Ann Arbor, Number 18,242. Some minor revisions have since been made.

The author wishes to express her sincere thanks to all who have helped her. Professor Ch'ü T'ung-tsu, formerly of the National Yünnan University and now of the Chinese Economic and Political Studies, Harvard University, first suggested this research. The late Professor Ralph Linton of Yale University supported the suggestion. Mr. Howard P. Linton, the Librarian of the East Asiatic Library, Columbia University, kindly permitted the microfilming of the data and the use of reference materials to make the research possible.

Dr. M. C. Elmer, professor emeritus, University of Pittsburgh, a pioneer in the field of sociology of family, and at the time the Head of the Sociology Department, approved of the research. Professor Howard Rowland, of the same department, served as the thesis adviser and gave the author necessary help.

Professor L. Carrington Goodrich of Columbia University, the Editor of this Monograph series, has given the research and the manuscript kind considerations from the beginning to the end. Professors E. A. Kracke, Jr. of the University of Chicago and previously the Monograph editor, Arthur F. Wright, and David S. Nivison, both of Stanford University, have all encouraged her to revise the thesis for publication. Professor Lien-sheng Yang of Harvard University has most graciously spared his pressing time to give the author precious advice on the revision. My husband and colleague, James T. C. Liu, has also rendered assistance from time to time.

The inadequacies and possible errors are of course entirely the author's own responsibility.

University of Pittsburgh.   Hui-chen Wang Liu

CHAPTER I

INTRODUCTION

A. THE FAMILY AND THE CLAN IN TRADITIONAL CHINA

THE FAMILY (*chia* 家) and the clan (*tsu* 族), generally regarded as characteristic institutions in traditional China, play an indispensable part in establishing and sustaining the prevailing value system, in moulding the life of the individuals, and in shaping their social relations into an orderly and stable pattern. The social control exercised by these two institutions is the central problem of the present study. The term traditional China or traditional Chinese society refers to the society that existed in China before its rapid disintegration in the erosive process of modernization during the last few decades. Many traits of the traditional way of life have either totally disappeared or been fundamentally altered by radical changes. While many other traditional traits still remain and may well continue to linger on, the traditional society as an integral system which functioned for many centuries has definitely broken down. The term is used to emphasize the concept of the traditional pattern as distinguished from the present state of flux. What this study deals with belongs largely to the past.

In the traditional Chinese society, the family was the basic primary group in which the members had close face-to-face relations with one another in a tightly knit life. The clan was the consolidating group organized by the numerous component families which traced their patrilineal descent from a common ancestor who had first settled in a given locality. These families either lived in the same community or among several nearby communities in the same geographic region. The clan, though not as closely knit as the family, also provided occasions of face-to-face relations to many of its members and strengthened the ties of the entire group. These two groups—the family and the clan—were in many respects mutually dependent and interrelated.[1]

[1] Hu Hsien-chin, *The Common Descent Group in China and Its Functions*, p. 97.

The family institution placed the interest of the family group among the leading values. It had five essential features: (1) emphasis on the father-son relationship; (2) family pride; (3) encouragement of large family; (4) the ancestral cult; and (5) common ownership of family property.[2] The ideal of the large family was not, however, always within reach; its realization depended on the size of the family property to support all members and on their ability to attain family harmony.

Generally speaking, the traditional Chinese families can be classified into three distinctive types according to their respective sizes: the small-sized conjugal family, the large-sized joint family, and the medium-sized stem family.[3] The first type consists of the man, his wife, their unmarried children, and sometimes his unmarried brothers and sisters. This was the type of family for the majority of the people, with an estimated average size of five and one-half persons.[4] Married sons left the old family to set up their own households elsewhere. The second type, the large-sized joint family, maintained by many wealthy Chinese with pride, contains not only the conjugal unit of the head of the family, but that of his brothers, of his sons, of his grandsons, and even of his great-grandsons. These conjugal units who lived in the same household and shared the common property were not separate families but component units within one family. In celebrated, though rare, cases, a joint family spanned five or more generations along the paternal line of descent. To live together as a joint family had several advantages: to increase the total capital accumulation; to pool the social prestige earned by all its prominent members; to carry on the best family vocation and at the same time to have other members take care of the diversified family interests; and to attain social distinction as a large, prosperous family.[5] In most cases, when a joint family contained four generations,

---

[2] Lee Shu-ching, "China's Traditional Family: Its Characteristics and Disintegration," *American Sociological Review*, XVIII (1953), 272–280; and D. H. Kulp, *Country Life in South China*, p. 188.

[3] Olga Lang, *Chinese Family and Society*, pp. 12–15.

[4] Makino Tatsumi, *Shina kazoku kenkyū* [*A Study of Chinese Family*], p. 567.

[5] Shimizu Morimitsu, *Shina kazoku no kōzō* [*Structure of the Chinese Family*], pp. 510–514 (hereinafter cited as Shimizu, *Kazoku*).

it was about time to split up. The third type, maintained by many Chinese of moderate income, is the medium-sized stem family. It consists of only two conjugal units, that of the head of the family and that of one of his sons, with the latter serving as the stem of the family tree, while the other sons move away upon marriage. The estimated size of the stem family is about ten persons.[6]

The family of any size in traditional China was a patronymic, patrilineal, patrilocal, and patriarchal kinship group. The managerial authority governing its common property rested with the family head, usually the father, sometimes the eldest brother or in rare cases the ablest son by delegation. The family head had the authority to control not only the incomes of individual members and common consumption but also their conduct. When his authority came to an end, either through his death or a disruption arising from family dispute, the property would be divided into equal shares among the heirs. The inheriting members together with their conjugal units and paternal descendants then started new families of their own in separate households.[7]

Kinsmen including paternal relatives, maternal relatives, and the relatives of one's wife were regarded not so much as the relatives of an individual but as the relatives of the family. A most comprehensive nomenclature classified all relatives in precise and denotive terms and especially emphasized the rituals of the mourning circle.[8] However, maternal relatives and the relatives of the wife were never organizationally bound to the family and the clan at all. Only the paternal relatives were recognized or organized as members of the clan group, reaching beyond the mourning circle to include all who venerated the common ancestor.

The clan in traditional China does not entirely resemble that of other societies. As one authority explains, using the terms of Rivers, the Chinese clan partakes both the nature of the clan as it exists

---

[6] Makino, *Shina kazoku kenkyū*, p. 567.

[7] Martin C. Yang, *A Chinese Village, Taitou, Shantung Province*, pp. 73–85; and Shimizu, *Kazoku*, pp. 328–329.

[8] Feng Han-yi, *The Chinese Kinship System*; and A. L. Kroeber, *The Nature of Culture*, pp. 190–195.

elsewhere and the nature of the Chinese joint family.[9] This is the reason why many authors prefer to call it by its original Chinese term, *tsu*, or by the descriptive term, "common descent group."[10] The present study uses the conventional designation of clan for convenience, but with the understanding that it refers to the particular type known in China during the last ten centuries with characteristics of its own.

The simplest way to explain the characteristics of the Chinese clan is to examine briefly its historical evolution.[11] In the ancient feudal period (ca. 1122–222 B.C.), only the nobility class had clan organizations called the *shih* (氏). The rule of primogeniture gave the head of the leading lineage, called the *tsung* (宗), the control over the whole clan. After the ancient feudal period, primogeniture was no longer the practice, the sons had equal inheritance rights, and the family system became quite varied. Yet, the clan organization evolved into another form.[12] People of remote or alleged aristocratic origin found the clan institution gave them more prestige; and the pooling of their individual properties gave them more self-protection and power. Powerful clans not only dominated the local region but won from the centralized state the legal status of "esteemed clans" (*wang tsu* 望族) with special privileges in tax matters and civil service appointments. This form of clan organization reached its highest peak during the Six Dynasties (A.D. 220–589) but declined under the T'ang Dynasty (618–906) when the state abolished many of these privileges. Family welfare accordingly became more important than clan interest. The end of the T'ang empire unleashed both nomadic invasions and internal disunity so that the clan organization was much weakened.

The succeeding Sung Dynasty (960–1279) witnessed the revival of the clan organization under a different form. What the present study deals with is the clan which developed since that time. The Sung scholar-officials and their Neo-Confucian theories again stressed the

---

[9] P'an Kuang-tan, "Chia-tsu chih-tu yü hsüan-tse tso-yung" ("The Selective Influence of the Clan System"), *She-hui-hsüeh-chieh*, IX (1936), 92.

[10] Hu, *op. cit.*, p. 9; also Francis L. K. Hsu, *Under the Ancestors' Shadow*, p. 122.

[11] Hu, *op. cit.*, pp. 11–13.

[12] Moriya Mitsuo, *Kandai kazoku no keitai ni kansuru kōsatsu* (*A Study of the Chinese Family System during the Han Dynasty*), pp. 1–57.

family and its moral education. As they found that relatively few families succeeded in keeping more than three generations together, they advocated the revival of the clan in order to give the family an added measure of stability.[13] They believed the clan which upheld ethical teachings to be as necessary as the state which upheld the law.[14]

The clan in this ramified form after the Sung period differed in several respects from the clan before. The clan after the Sung period was not limited to the privileged class. It grouped together component families of various social strata: beginning with the prominent and wealthy ones and sometimes including the lowly and poor ones. As the consolidating group, it was not strictly speaking an economic unit.[15] On the one hand, it often relied upon the support and the contributions of its member families; on the other hand, the families depended on it for certain common activities, benefits, and moral well-being.[16] The essential achievement of the Sung scholar-officials was to engraft parts of the ancient heritage of the clan institution upon a broader basis of organization.

Following the Sung period, the ramified clan institution permeated the entire traditional Chinese society, though not without some qualifications. Clans were deeply rooted in rural areas and not prominent in the cities as the city was not considered to be a home town, but typically a place away from home. People loyal to their clans would send money from the city to their native places in the country.[17] Next, there was a class differentiation: the ruling class of scholar-officials cherished the clan institution far more so than those who were poor and uneducated. Third, by geographic differentiation, the clan institution was rather weak in north China, fairly well

---

[13] Shimizu, *Kazoku*, pp. 179–254; cf. Ch'ü T'ung-tsu, *Chung-kuo fa-lü yü Chung-kuo she-hui (Chinese Law and Chinese Society)*, pp. 3–4.

[14] 1926-a, "A Collection of Family Instructions," and 1930-a, "*Tsu* Standards," introductory remarks. These numeral designations refer to the genealogies; for the explanation, see the Bibliography, A. Data.

[15] Lang, *op. cit.*, p. 21; and Shimizu, *Kazoku*, pp. 203–215.

[16] Sun Pen-wen, *Hsien-tai Chung-kuo she-hui wen-t'i* [*Social Problems of Modern China*], Vol. II, p. 49.

[17] Shimizu, *Kazoku*, pp. 245–251; Lang, *op. cit.*, p. 180; and Makino, *Shina kazoku kenkyū*, pp. 568–569. Also see Max Weber, *The Religion of China*, p. 90.

developed in central China, and very strong in south China.[18] Finally, in recent decades, the clan institution has rapidly declined and almost disappeared. The modern law, for example, continues to uphold certain traditional family rights and obligations but almost neglects to mention the clan.[19]

The clan institution as delimited above has the following eight outstanding aspects which are interlocked with one another.[20] The first is group cohesion. Blood relationship on the paternal side was believed to form a natural affinity among clan members. The ancestral rites reminded the clan members that as the descendants of the common ancestor they should regard one another as if they were still members of the same family. The second aspect is the psychological security of individual members. The clan recognized the status of its members first by generation and next by age. One's status did not end with death as his name would then be included among that of the ancestors. The third of these aspects is common property for group and individual benefits. A clan, when organized, had ancestral graveyards and an ancestral hall in which the rites and other group activities took place. In addition, it kept a genealogy recording not only the descent lines but also other items of group interest. Clans that were well organized assured their members of some assistance in case of need, both from the group and from individual fellow members. A fourth characteristic is special common property for education and philanthropic purposes. Wealthy clans had common property such as clan schools and educational land to help promising but financially poor members, especially for them to take the civil service examination. The prestige of government degree-holders and other prominent individual members enhanced the standing of the clan. Fifth of these traits is the group prestige to which many prominent members contributed and from which all members benefitted. Clans often applied for official commendation on behalf of members of conspicuous virtue such as chastity or filial piety. The clan, like a savings bank, saved all the social honors and public distinctions in a common

[18] Makino, *Shina kazoku kenkyū*, p. 565.
[19] Lang, *op. cit.*, p. 118.
[20] Hu, *op. cit.*, p. 95.

pool, from which all members drew varying amounts of satisfaction. The sixth aspect is group moral well-being. As social prestige came from conspicuous virtues, a clan always tried to encourage moral behavior. On the preventive side, it sought to restrain, to discipline, and to punish misbehaving members whose social disgrace damaged the group reputation. A seventh characteristic is the clan's judiciary power, recognized by the state, for the purpose of preventing and punishing both mutual aggression within the group and aggression against other people in the community. Eighth, the clan assumed collective legal responsibility of its members toward the government and also had the right to send an incorrigible guilty member to the government for punishment under the law.[21]

At the same time, the family shared many of the clan's traits such as group cohesion, psychological security, common property, needed financial assistance, group prestige, moral well-being, disciplinary control, and other mutual responsibilities. This is one reason why the clan can be regarded as an extension of the large-sized joint family. The basic values which the family and the clan institutions cherish are much the same: stability, continuity, and perpetuation. The social control which these two institutions provide jointly lends great stability to the traditional Chinese society.

B. THE CLAN RULES IN THE GENEALOGIES AND THE PRESENT STUDY

A prominent feature of the clan institution in traditional China is the compilation of genealogy. Before the T'ang period, only the "esteemed clans" had genealogies which were filed with the government for the purpose of establishing their privileges. During the succeeding Sung period, Ou-yang Hsiu (歐陽修, 1007–1072) and Su Hsün (蘇洵, 1009–1066), two leading pioneers of the ramified clan institution, adapted the ancient form of genealogy with minor changes and set the standard for later centuries. Genealogy in this form was for the exclusive use of clan members only.[22]

[21] Ch'ü, op. cit., pp. 18–20.
[22] Yang Tien-hsün, "Chung-kuo chia-p'u t'ung-lun" ["A General Survey of Chinese Genealogies"], T'u-shu chi-k'an, n.s. III, nos. 1 and 2 (1941), 9–35 and n.s. VI, nos. 3 and 4 (1945), 17–39; P'an Kuang-tan, "Chung-kuo

Compiling a genealogy, especially a printed one, was a mark of social distinction. According to the ideal, a genealogy should be revised regularly every thirty years. Though practice often fell behind, a well organized clan usually revised its genealogy at slightly irregular intervals. The clan organization made an appeal to the sense of loyalty and honor of its prominent and wealthy members in order to raise the necessary fund. Generous contributions made it possible to have the genealogy printed and to send a copy to each component family. The appearance of a new and especially printed edition enhanced the group prestige as it was a sign of prosperity, strong organization, and ability to take care of an outstanding common interest.[23]

Simple genealogies merely record the names of members through successive generations with such essential information as birth date, marriage, offspring, death date, burial place, official title, and public honor if any. Many elaborate genealogies have a variety of other materials: prefaces paying tribute to the illustrious or the alleged aristocratic origin of the clan, essays expounding the importance of clan solidarity and permanency, articles explaining the rules on the compilation of the genealogy, and information on clan ritual. Some genealogies also have maps of the ancestral graveyard, detailed descriptions of the ancestral hall, and copied deeds of the common property. A sizeable printed genealogy often cites a variety of records in praise of the famous members in the past such as government citations, excerpts from local gazetteers and official histories, documents commemorating their worthy achievements, reputable conduct and celebrated virtues, as well as their own sayings and literary writings. These diverse materials have two common objectives. The first is social; the clan through its genealogy borrows the cumulative prestige from its past members. The second objective is moral education; the clan hopes to inspire present and future generations to live up to the high standards.

chia-p'u-hsüeh lüeh-shih" ["A Brief History of the Chinese Genealogy Discipline"], *Tung-fang tsa-chih*, XXVI, no. 1 (1933), 107–120; and Makino Tatsumi, "Mei Shin zokufu kenkyū josetsu" ["A Preface to the Study of Chinese Genealogy during the Ming and Ch'ing Dynasties"], *Tōhō gakuhō*, VI (1936), 261–288.

[23] Hu, *op. cit.*, pp. 41–52.

The compilers of the genealogies are quite conscious of social control, as evidenced by the prefaces and the rules of compilation in many genealogies. In the often quoted words of one compiler, the purpose of genealogy is "to promote the ethical teachings of mutual affinity and respect in the clan."[24] As positive measures of encouragement, the genealogies praise worthy members and record their honors. As negative measures of punishment, the genealogies put a brief note of condemnation under the name of an unbecoming member, cross the name out by red ink, or delete it entirely.[25] In fact, expurgation from the genealogy, usually combined with expulsion from the group, is a standard form of clan punishment. Many genealogies state in their rules of compilation that names of members are to be omitted if they have disregarded their ancestors, betrayed the clan, received a criminal sentence, committed a flagrant violation of ethical relations, or fallen into a socially disgraceful vocation or status.[26]

Most significant are the clan rules in many genealogies which are explicitly devoted to social control. With statements on general principles and stipulations on detailed matters, the clan rules are intended to guide the members in their attitude and behavior. In other words, a clan rule is the code of conduct for its members. It is true that verbalized sanctions, by the very fact that they are verbalized, cannot be expected to be effective to the fullest extent. It will be a mistake, however, to regard them as empty words.

Some contemporary Chinese anthropologists cast doubt on the effectiveness of the clan rules. Theoretically speaking, formal documents have a tendency of degenerating into mere formalities which call more for lip service than actual adherence. It has been observed that written clan rules rest on book shelves gathering dust. Their effectiveness is far less than that of traditional mores which permeated the society.[27] This skeptical observation is valid in the case of

[24] 1926–a, "A Collection of Family Instructions," p. 6.
[25] 1929–d, "Regulations of the Genealogy," p. 1b.
[26] Yang Tien-hsün, as in note 22; 1916–a, "The Six Omissions from the Genealogy," p. 25a; and 1933–a, "The Ten Omissions from the Genealogy."
[27] Lin Yüeh-hua, "Ts'ung jen-lei-hsüeh ti kuan-tien k'ao-ch'a Chung-kuo tsung-tsu hsiang-ts'un" ("The Study of Chinese Clan Village from the Anthropological Point of View"), *She-hui-hsüeh-chieh*, IX (1936), 129.

present-day China when the clan institution has already disintegrated, though it is a theoretical error to separate the clan rules from the traditional mores as the former was in fact a part of the latter. Plenty of evidence shows that when the clan institution was functioning well, the clan rules were often the required reading for the members.[28] Even in recent decades, some clans according to another anthropological study still read parts of their clan rules during meetings.[29] The strongest evidence are several government or government-supported surveys made between 1930 and 1945 on the actual customs adhered to by the rural communities in various parts of China.[30] Numerous customs substantially agree with the relevant provisions in these clan rules. This proves that the clan rules in their days were by no means mere formalities.

The clan rules are the data of this study. They have not received heretofore a systematic, thorough examination, for many previous works on Chinese society have used various approaches other than the intensive utilization of historical primary sources.[31] The pioneer studies in the days before World War I, such as those by Edward Alsworth Ross, Y. K. Leong, and L. K. Tao, have provided a general sketch of the Chinese society.[32] Shortly afterwards, social surveys have brought forth valuable and specific information. Leading examples are the survey of Peking by S. D. Gamble and the survey of Ting Hsien by Li Ching-han and Gamble, not to mention the numerous monographs in Chinese sociological journals. During the last two decades, anthropology has been applied to community study in China. Important contributions have been made by Chen Ta, Fei Hsaio-tung, Fei and Chang Chih-i, C. P. Fitzgerald, Morton H. Fried, Francis L. K. Hsu, and Martin C. Yang. The works of the last two

[28] 1913–b, "Family Instructions of Shih-chü-kung," p. 15; and 1914–g, "Family Instructions," p. 1a.
[29] Martin C. Yang, *op. cit.*, p. 139.
[30] *MSSHK* [*A Survey Report of the Civil and Commercial Customs in China*], *passim*. Also consult Niida Noboru (ed.), *Chūgoku nōson kankō chōsa* (*Chinese Rural Customs and Practices*), 4 vols.
[31] Morton H. Fried, "Community Studies in China," *Far Eastern Quarterly*, XIV (1954), 11–36.
[32] The works by the authors mentioned in this section are cited in the Bibliography, B. References.

authors add considerable knowledge to the study of the family and the clan institutions. Apart from these community studies, several outstanding works should be mentioned: the case study of a kinship group by Lin Yüeh-hua, a comprehensive survey of the family in Chinese society by Olga Lang, and a systematic theoretical analysis of the same subject by Marion J. Levy, Jr.

The usefulness of Chinese primary sources has been, on the other hand, demonstrated by several Japanese scholars such as Katō Jōken, Makino Tatsumi, Mitzutani Kunichi, Morohashi Tetsuji, Nishiyama Eikyu, and Shimizu Norimitsu. An equally outstanding example is the study of clan functions by a Chinese scholar, Hu Hsien-chin, who has successfully combined historical information with anthropological approaches.

The present study owes a great deal to many works by these authors, especially Hsu, Yang, Hu, Makino, and Shimizu. However, Shimizu who has dealt with the family and the clan institutions with emphasis upon the mechanism of social control has not made intensive use of the genealogies. Makino has cited more than thirty genealogies, including detailed analyses of a few taken as samples. Hu, in concentrating her attention on the functions of the clan, has somewhat left the family institution aside. Though she has extracted a variety of information from more than fifty genealogies, she has not systematically examined any one particular type of the material in them such as the clan rules.

The present study attempts to deal with both the family and the clan institutions as two closely knitted twins, the way they should be regarded, and to examine the social control in both groups. The data used are neither a few examples nor diverse information of an assorted nature, but exclusively the clan rules which, as a more or less homogeneous body of material, lend themselves to a systematic analysis.

A brief explanation on the availability of printed genealogies is in order. As many contemporary Chinese no longer care, a number of genealogies were sold as waste paper. Fortunately, some of the genealogies have found their way into leading libraries. The National Library in Peking has a good collection, but not as good as the collection of Tōyō Bunko near Tokyo, Japan. In the United States, the Columbia University library, surpassing both the Harvard University library and the Library of Congress in this regard, has more than 600 genealogies printed during the Ch'ing period (1644–1911) and more than 300 genealogies printed under the Republic of China between 1912 and 1936.

After examining all the clan rules found among the genealogies in the Columbia collection, the present writer decided to confine the data of this study to the group of genealogies printed between 1912 and 1936 for three reasons. First, many genealogies in this group, though printed in recent decades, still include the clan rules of the early days, at least as historical documents of the clans. To use the earlier editions would not materially alter the outcome of the study. Second, some of the clan rules in this group of genealogies contain significant changes. These changes not only represent the adjustments to modern social conditions but also throw a revealing light on what has been the essential features of the tradition. Third, it is highly doubtful whether any sizeable number of genealogies have been printed from 1937 on, the date marking the beginning of the long war between China and Japan. The data here probably represent the end of a long tradition.

Among the genealogies printed during 1912–1936 in the Columbia collection, slightly less than half of them have clan rules while the rest do not. Some of these clan rules happen to be either too short to be useful for analytical purposes or mere literary compositions on the generalities of ethical principles. It is desirable to limit the data further to exactly 151 genealogies which carry detailed stipulations governing specific attitude and behavior.[33]

One fundamental question on the delimitation of the source materials remains: how representative are they of the traditional Chinese society ? First, the source materials as explained above represent more of the traditional pattern in the past than the changing conditions at the time of their printing. Second, the source materials

---

[33] The full titles of the genealogies and their clan rule titles in English translation are given in the Bibliography, A. Data.

admit a regional delimitation.[34] Less than ten per cent of them have originated from southern China. Inasmuch as the clan institution has been especially strong in that region, the people there have probably refrained from parting with their genealogies. This is not a weakness of the Columbia collection alone, for the same geographic proportion is roughly true of the collections in other leading libraries. The overwhelming portion of the present data, about eighty per cent, has come from the central part of China, especially the lower reaches and the delta region of the Yangtze River, with the province of Kiangsu leading, Chekiang next, Anhui and Hupeh competing for the third. Only about five per cent of the present data have originated in northern China. This is probably because the clan institution in that area happens to be relatively weak and not many printed genealogies have been produced.

Third, an economic delimitation. Only the wealthy and well organized clans functioning at their best were able to have their genealogies printed. This is another reason why the bulk of the data has come from the rich region of the lower Yangtze River valley. Clan groups in less enviable positions and in less favorable geographic areas do not receive a fair representation in this study.

Fourth, a related delimitation in terms of class differentiation. The clan rules were compiled by members of the leading families in the clan, invariably the scholar-officials in the old days or the scholars of the old school in more recent years. It is they who exercised the indispensable leadership in promoting and reinforcing the traditional institutions. The other classes probably do not subscribe to the same ideals and values to the fullest extent.

These delimitations notwithstanding, the clan rules may be regarded as the prevailing mores in codified form, representing the idealized optimum of traditional institutions, upheld by the leading class, and followed in varying degrees with certain ramifications by the other classes.[35] The general pattern tends to be the same in most areas of China Proper and Manchuria.

[34] The geographic distribution of the 151 genealogies is given in Table 1 of the Appendix.
[35] Shimizu, *Kazoku*, pp. 250–251, has probably overstated the case in asserting that the entire Chinese society accepted the same value system without significant variations.

C. METHOD OF ANALYSIS

It is from the standpoint of social control that the present study analyzes the rules in the 151 genealogies selected from the Columbia collection. Social control may be defined as the institutions, the social forces, the group efforts, and the individual endeavors that induce individuals to conform in both behavior and attitude. Behavior is external, observable, and the overt aspect of culture; whereas attitude is largely internal, only partly observable, and the overt-response aspect of culture.[36]

The social control of the family and the clan institutions can be best understood in terms of the social structure in traditional China. Status is the basis of group structure, and the role is basis of group function. This applies to the family, the clan, as well as the entire society. The status of the members in both the family and the clan was determined by the patriarchal generation-age hierarchy. Membership was granted automatically by virtue of descent on the father's side. An old generation had a higher status than the generation which came after it. Within the same generation, one who was elder in age enjoyed a higher status than one who was younger. Sex was another differentiation of status. The status of the female was dependent on that of the male with whom she was most closely related, the father in the case of an unmarried girl and the husband in the case of a married woman. Social status conferred upon individuals by the society at large was far more complex as it came from political prominence, economic wealth, other social distinctions, and usually a combination of several factors.[37] So far as the family and the clan group were concerned, however, the generation-age order should take precedence over social status. It was the former that should determine the roles of individual members with respect to one another in group life. In accordance with roles, members granted one another specific rights in return for specific obligations.[38]

---

[36] Richard T. La Piere, *A Theory of Social Control*, p. 3; and Ralph Linton, *The Cultural Background of Personality*, p. 27.

[37] Shimizu, *Kazoku*, p. 396; and Marion J. Levy, Jr., *Family Revolution in Modern China*, p. 10.

[38] La Piere, *op. cit.*, p. 130.

For countless generations, the Chinese have conceptualized society as a complex of inter-human relations based upon proper status and sanctioned roles.[39] Confucius says in the *Analects*:[40]

If terms be incorrect, then statements do not accord with facts; and when statements and facts do not accord, then business is not properly executed; when business is not properly executed, order and harmony do not flourish, then justice becomes arbitrary; and when justice becomes arbitrary, the people do not know how to move hand or foot.

The emphasis upon status and roles received ceaseless strengthening from the social mores as well as from the written embodiments of social ethics such as the classical literature, the written regulations of the clans, and the laws of the state. All these are various forms of social control. The Chinese refer to them collectively as *ming-chiao* (名教) or *li-chiao* (禮教).

Ming-chiao, literally meaning "names and ethical teachings," denotes the entire body of social ethics based upon status differentiation which governs all social conduct. An individual has to protect his own good name or appropriate status. He is obliged on pain of group coercion to assume his roles in conformity with the mores and ethical teachings. To live up to one's status and to excel in moral behavior is to gain a good name and social esteem for oneself.[41] Hence, *ming-chiao* may be translated as status-ethics. Its significance is seen, for example, in a quotation from a clan rule:[42]

A man stands on the integrity of his name or the inviolability of his status. Do not commit shameful and unethical acts that are beneath one's status. Do not compromise one's status or fall into a disgraceful position. Such is utterly humiliating not only to himself but to his ancestors as well.

Li-chiao, an alternate term of the above, literally means "ritual and and ethical teachings." Ritual propriety specifies the relationship

---

[39] Weber, *The Religion of China*, p. 241.
[40] William Edward Soothill (tr.), *The Analects*, Book VIII, pp. 609–611.
[41] Abram Kardiner, *The Individual and His Society*, p. xiv; cf. Talcott Parsons, *The Social System*, pp. 191–192.
[42] 1922-c, "The *Tsu* Injunctions," p. 4a.

between individuals according to their respective status. It is the principal means by which individuals are reminded of their roles of subordination or superordination and what their proper conduct should be. The essence of ritual is status differentiation.[43] In the words of one clan rule, "Ritual is in the heart of man, in the human relations of all sorts, and in the daily life."[44] In the opinion of another clan rule, "No family can get along well for a single day without ritual. The disruption of ritual breeds disrespect which in turn leads to dispute."[45] In the traditional Chinese mind, ritual and ethics are inseparable. Hence, the term *li-chiao* may be translated as ritual-ethics.

The term "ritual" is well defined sociologically by Bossard in his study of family life:[46]

Ritual is a system of procedure, a form or pattern of social interaction, which has three unvarying characteristics. First, it is definitely prescribed. This is the way a thing is to be done. Ritual means exactness and precision in procedure. Second, there is the element of rigidity. The longer the prescribed procedure continues, the more binding its precision becomes. And finally, there is a sense of rightness which emerges from the past history of the process, i.e., the oftener the repetition of the prescribed procedure occurs, the more it comes to be approved. This distinguishes it from mere habit. To deviate from the procedure is wrong, not wholly on utilitarian grounds, but also because it breaks the rhythm and the rapport.

In the traditional Chinese culture, status-ethics and ritual-ethics have their deep roots in the process of socialization which begins in the primary groups of the family and the clan. An individual member learns to recognize his own status and roles as well as those of others. His attitude and behavior are conditioned by the ritual in which he has been required to participate and perform. Adjustment to his status and mastery of the ritual wins him the acceptance, the recognition, and the protection of the group. At the same time, he is taught the ethical meanings which lie behind the ritual.

[43] Weber, *op. cit.*, p. 156; Ch'ü, *op. cit.*, pp. 214–227; and Morohashi Tetsuji, *Shina no kazoku sei* [*The Chinese Family System*], p. 9.
[44] 1921–q, "Family Regulations," Preface, p. 1a.
[45] 1930–c, "Family Instructions," p. 1a.
[46] James H. S. Bossard and Eleanor S. Boll, *Ritual in Family Living*, p. 16.

Social control reaches its most effective degree when the individuals voluntarily submit themselves to it and derive satisfaction in doing so. In other words, social control is internalized and becomes the individual's self-control.[47] The emphasis upon status-ethics and ritual-ethics in traditional China is especially significant in this regard. Status stresses the rational aspect, and ritual emphasizes the emotional aspect. The term ethics implies internal voluntary self-control.[48] In fact, this self-control is an essential trait of the ideal personality to lead a life that is congenial to the cultural pattern.[49]

Social control is inseparable from value system. Effective social control sustains the value system; idealized norms of conduct strengthen it; and deviations from the norms weaken it. On the other hand, a value system places things, acts, ways of behaving, goals of action on the approval-disapproval continuum. This means that a value system also determines what kind of social control there is or should be.[50]

A similarly close relationship exists between social control and group organization. Social control has to be exercised by groups; its effectiveness depends upon the organizational strength of the groups.[51]

In analyzing the clan rules from the above frame of reference, five problem-areas emerge. First, who should exercise what kinds of social control over whom and for what kinds of conduct and misconduct? It is necessary to determine from the clan rules what conduct and misconduct are regarded as primarily the concern of the family, what others are considered to warrant the attention of the clan, and yet what others should require the action of the government, with respective rewards or punishment.

Second, on the limitations of the social control exercised by the family and the clan, to what extent are these limitations traceable

---

[47] Abram Kardiner, *The Psychological Frontiers of Society*, p. 416.
[48] Shimizu, *Kazoku*, pp. 420–421.
[49] Kardiner, *The Individual and His Society*, p. vi; and Parsons, *The Social System*, pp. 41–42.
[50] Talcott Parsons and E. A. Shils (ed.), *Toward a General Theory of Action*, p. 389.
[51] Alfred Reginald Radcliffe-Brown, *Structure and Function in Primitive Society*, pp. 9–10.

to the value system as represented in the clan rules and to what extent are they attributable to the organizational weaknesses of the kinship groups?

Third, as social control by the very fact that it seeks to control often tends to create either hidden hostility or open disobedience against it, are there evidences in the clan rules to support this proposition? If so, what hostility or disobedience is in fact anticipated by the clan rules and how do the clan rules propose to deal with it? Under this question, several alternatives can be postulated. The clan rules might seek to overcome the anticipated hostility by severe punishment, to resolve it by reconciliation and compromise, or to overlook it with an implied admission of difficulty. No matter which of these alternatives the clan rules happen to choose as the case may be, the choice will be inevitably reflected in the value system. For example, severe punishment is accompanied by the value of sternness; reconciliation and compromise, by the value of harmony; and admission of difficulty, by the value of patience.

Fourth, the assumption that the clan rules follow Confucianism is a generalization which should be accepted only with caution and qualifications. Confucianism concerns itself with general principles, whereas the clan rules as codes of conduct have to deal with concrete situations. It is legitimate to postulate that a distance exists between the two. The question thus arises: to what extent do the clan rules conform to and seek to implement the Confucian values and in what respects do the clan rules revise or depart from the Confucian values?

The fifth and final question is on the effect of modernization. From the information available in some of the clan rules, it is possible to discover some evidence pointing toward the disintegration of the traditional family and clan institutions. The question is how do these clan rules try to meet the modern conditions and to retain some degree of social control, and why have they failed in this regard.

Having outlined these five problem-areas, it is now in order to explain the procedure of the present study in analyzing the data. The analysis of the clan rules, all written in classical Chinese, has to begin with a minute scrutiny of the terms and expressions in accordance with their usages and connotations in former days. Identical terms and expressions sometimes have quite different meanings, depending on the context. On the other hand, wordings which do not look alike on the surface may actually refer to substantially the same thing. The next step is to take up the subject-matter in the clan rules topic by topic and in each case to break down the pertinent information into specific components. Having done this, a simple counting method becomes applicable.

The simple counting method has been applied mainly in three areas. First, it has been helpful in the analysis of the clan rule titles to ascertain whether some slight difference in the wordings of the titles indicate some significant difference in the nature of the clan rules. This is especially meaningful when one genealogy has several rules in it, each bearing a different title. By the use of simple counting, the wordings of the titles are related to the crucial aspects in the respective contents.

Second, the simple counting method has been useful in assessing the relative importance of various subject-matter in the clan rules. Each clan is taken as a unit, whether its genealogy contains only one, or more than one, clan rule. Each provision which its clan rule or clan rules have on given subject-matter—relationship, conduct, belief, etc. — or one of the specific components thereof is taken as one occurrence. Counting obtains the number of clans whose rules touch upon the given subject-matter or one of the components. A large number means a frequent appearance of this item among all the clan rules. It signifies that this subject-matter or this component has received more attention or greater emphasis than others which appear less frequently.

Third, the same procedure makes it possible to indicate roughly the prevailing value pattern in the clan rules. Various subject-matter can be classified into categories and the categories can be arranged into a related and meaningful composite. Comparison and intepretation are thus possible.

It must be emphasized that this simple counting method does not claim to be an exact quantification. The very nature of the data precludes such. It is not even feasible to assign weights to the counting. Nonetheless, the results of the simple counting reflect in rough approximation what is in the actual contents of the clan rules. Such representation is at least more clear than merely descriptive words. For this reason, the findings whenever convenient are incorporated into the text in lieu of lengthy accounts which would be otherwise necessary. These are itemized summaries rather than tables, whereas tabulations of considerable length and complexity are relegated to the Appendix. It should be pointed out further that the results of the simple counting do not stand by themselves but go hand in hand with the concrete excerpts from the data and the theoretical analyses.

CHAPTER II

GENERAL ANALYSES OF THE CLAN RULES

A. THE FORMS AND THE COMMON CHARACTERISTICS OF THE CLAN RULES

IN THE PRESENT STUDY, the term clan rule is a collective designation for all the rules, regulations, stipulations, and documents of such nature found in the clan genealogies that are intended to govern the attitude and behavior of the clan members. These documents are in a variety of forms, appear under a number of different titles, and contain so much miscellaneous and complicated information. They also vary in length: the shortest clan rule is no more than half a page, consisting of, for example, half a dozen injunctions against certain misconducts. The longest clan rule encompasses an entire volume. The forms vary according to the contents. Some clan rules consist of a collection of famous quotations; some merely reproduce imperial injunctions on moral conduct (*sheng yü* 聖諭) and excerpts from the penal code or other laws and statutes, while other clan rules contain essays, pieces of prose, and poems composed by leading clan members in the past as moral teachings for the clan group. However, there is a standard form, the one used most frequently. It comprises a number of articles or short paragraphs, each devoted to a specific topic frequently designated by a caption, an itemized heading, or the first sentence. These articles and short paragraphs uphold various virtues and condemn different offenses. They discuss why and how exemplary conduct should be encouraged and deviation and misconduct prohibited. They govern the clan members with regard to their individual attitude and behavior as well as their life in the family, the clan, and the society at large. Though some clan rules in this standard form confine themselves to general principles, the majority of them have either concrete details or specific provisions on punishment.

The clan rules in whatever form share many, if not all, of the following characteristics. First, these clan rules represent Confucianism in application. They uphold the moral concepts and principles and often seek to translate them into conduct befitting concrete social situations. They furnish the formalized details of status-ethics and ritual-ethics and define what the proper social relations should be between individuals under given circumstances. The words of Lü Tsu-ch'ien (呂祖謙), a Southern Sung scholar, are often quoted in many clan rules: "Scholar-officials like to talk about custom. What does custom really consist of? After all, it is no other than personal conduct in daily life."[1] This means that the clan rules should give normative orientation by directing individuals to definite goals according to the value system.[2] As another clan rule puts it, "A clan without rules leaves its members with no moral standard of conduct to follow."[3]

Second, these clan rules fulfill an important functional necessity in a closely knit group life. They are the moral codes in written or verbalized form to induce voluntary conformity without which no group can function smoothly according to its accepted ways.[4] Many societies have such codes to initiate members into group life, to get them to recognize group authority, and to make them aware of their own responsibility as required by the social mores. Violations of these rules are subject to group disapproval, punishment, and exclusion.[5] In the case of traditional Chinese society, these rules are indeed refined and rational. Claiming neither supernatural power nor divine revelation, they rest squarely on intrinsic moral authority and deal directly with the social realities of differentiated status and roles. The quotations of ancient sages are no more and no less than words of practical wisdom and experience, confirmed by countless generations and anchored in the central conception of social well-being.[6]

The third characteristic of the clan rules is their intended flexibility rather than rigid application. One clan rule explains:[7]

[1] 1928-f, "A Collection of Family Instructions," pp. 1-4.
[2] Cf. La Piere, *op. cit.*, p. 130.
[3] 1935-b, "Family Discipline Decided by *Tsu* Organization," introductory remarks, p. 1a.
[4] Shimizu, *Kazoku*, pp. 419-427.
[5] Cf. Radcliffe-Brown, *op. cit.*, p. 5 and B. Malinowski, *Crime and Custom in Savage Society*, p. 58.
[6] Tachimana Boku, *Shina shakai kenkyū* [*A Study of Chinese Society*], pp. 550-557.
[7] 1921-k, "Family Discipline," p. 2a.

In administering punishment, the clan should take into consideration the generation status and the age status. On the other hand, senior members also have due attachment and kind regard for the younger ones. All these point toward leniency. It is a common phenomenon for the members to find excuses for one another without enforcing the clan rules in earnestness.

The major emphasis of the clan rules is upon moral persuasion rather than actual punishment. Their stipulations on punishment are intended more often for preventive warnings than for actual enforcement, unless the latter becomes necessary.

Fourth, the clan rules, on the other hand, admit either explicitly or implicitly that conduct in real life always tends to fall short of ideals. In other words, certain difficulties in imposing the norms of conduct are anticipated in the clan rules. The frequency with which the clan rules mention certain misconduct and offenses shows that these are the common faults more likely to occur than others. And if the clan rules do not add due stipulations on punishment after mentioning such faults, this indicates an admitted weakness in the social control. When the same weakness is found in a large number of clan rules, it can be taken as a major shortcoming of the clan institution as a whole.

Fifth, the clan rules rely ultimately upon the authority of the state but their content is by comparison more lenient than the law. Since the beginning of the Ming Dynasty (1368–1644), the government proclaimed from time to time the imperial injunctions on moral conduct. The Ch'ing Dynasty (1644–1911), in its early days, followed the same practice with minor revisions. The original Ming injunctions consist of six points:

> Render filial piety to parents;
> Show respect to seniors by the generation-age order.
> Remain in harmony with clan members and the community;
> Teach and discipline sons and grandsons.
> Attend to one's vocation properly;
> And do not commit what the law forbids.

Many clans quoted the injunctions word for word and others cited them as the basis of authority.[8] Besides, many clan rules were for-

[8] 1914–b, "The Six Items of Village Agreement," an explanation of the Imperial Edict, pp. 1–6; and 1916–c, "The Sixteen Items of the Imperial Edict."

mally registered with the government and their binding effect approached that of the law.[9] One clan rule reads:[10]

Clan rules rely on the law of the state as their guide. The law, in turn, depends on clan rules to supplement it. In comparison, clan rules are more lenient than the law. But whoever violates clan rules will eventually find himself in violation of the law.

For example, the offense of filial impiety was often punishable under many clan rules by flogging forty times. Under the law of the Ch'ing empire, the punishment would be at least flogging one hundred times and in serious cases penal servitude or banishment.[11] The clan punishment, though punitive, is intended after all to be protective so that an offender can be spared the severity of legal sentence.

Finally, a positive and very significant aspect, the clan rules demonstrate a strong ethico-religious belief. The Chinese have long regarded ethical rationalities as being religiously valuable, not for a life "hereafter," but for the blessings of the family and descendants in this life.[12] One clan rule states the belief that "honest and kind families can rest assured of future prosperity."[13] Another says that "to establish and to abide by the clan rule is the best means of bringing about blessings for the succeeding generations."[14] In fact, the Chinese have preferred this ethico-religious belief to formal religion as the following quotation shows:[15]

Virtues have their cumulative benefits that help a family to go very far ... This does not mean that people should contribute to Buddhist activities which allegedly would bring future rewards. By virtue, it is meant that a father should discipline his sons, an elder brother should give good advice to his younger brothers and take care of their widows and orphans, a clan member should give relief to fellow members in distress, and everyone should help in settling disputes. People should extend goodwill from the ones close to them to others who are remote.

[9] 1913–b, "Officially Registered Regulations."
[10] 1921–k, "Family Discipline," p. 2a.
[11] Ch'ü, op. cit., pp. 6–21.
[12] Weber, op. cit., pp. 114 and 227.
[13] 1915–c, "Family Instructions," p. 24.
[14] 1921–c, "Regulations of the Ancestral Hall," p. 1a.
[15] 1915–g, "Ancestors' Instructions," pp. 6b–7a.

In sum, the clan rules combine moral teachings with humane understanding and integrate social ethics with religious belief. In relating ethical values and mores to the law, the clan rules partake the nature of all three and constitute a well-integrated instrument of social control.

B. THE TITLES AND THE TYPES OF THE CLAN RULES

The titles of the clan rules, set by custom and usages, do not vary a great deal and leave the impression of a stereotype. The detailed wordings of these titles, however, invite minute analysis. While some wordings are interchangeable with no significant difference in meaning and some others have no more than different shades of the same meaning, other wordings do distinguish one kind of clan rule from another. The analysis here in relating the given titles of the rules to the essential provisions in their contents makes it possible to classify the rules into types.

The application of the simple counting method proves helpful. First, words which compose the titles of the rules have been identified and their respective meanings analyzed. Next, the content in these rules have been examined in order to ascertain whether they have or they lack two crucial aspects: (1) detailed and concrete provisions on punishment of misconduct, and (2) provisions on the management of the clan's common property. These two aspects are essential indications of the strength of the clan organization. The two steps are then joined by the use of the counting method. This procedure has two objectives: first, to find out which words were used by original compilers more often than the rest in the titles of the clan rules; and second, to ascertain which type of title was generally used by the relatively well organized clan groups.

The titles are invariably composed of two parts. In such an example as "clan injunctions" or "ancestral hall bylaws," the first part of the title refers to the organization either by naming the group or by naming its most prominent organizational aspect, while the second part of the title refers to the kind of rule it is. The most frequently used words in the first part of the titles are *chia* (家), *tsu*

(族), *tsung* (宗), or *tz'u* (祠). *Chia*, in the narrow and strict sense of the word, denotes the family. Traditional usage, however, stretches its meaning to connote the clan as if the clan were still one family. *Tsu* is the proper term for clan in the form which existed after the Sung period. *Tsung*, as mentioned in the above historical sketch, is originally the term for the ancient feudal clan but kept in the genealogies after the Sung period partly in honor of the ancient institution and partly for prestige's sake. In most cases, *tsung* has the identical meaning of *tsu*. In a few cases, *tsung* has the additional connotation that the clan group branched out over a wide geographic area and the branches no longer remained in one single organization, though each branch still recognized the others as being loosely connected through a remote ancestor. Finally, the word *tz'u* means ancestral hall, a physical structure taken as a symbol of group organization where most clan activities took place.

A number of genealogies, among the 151 under study, contain more than one clan rule. It is necessary to analyze each particular rule separately, first by counting the uses of the word, *chia, tsu, tsung,* or *tz'u* and then by examining its content with regard to common property management and clan punishment. The result of the counting is presented below in itemized summary. On the extreme left-hand side, the specific wordings are given. On the extreme right-hand side, the total numbers of the titles which have these respective wordings in them are given. In between are four columns: column A indicates the number of those particular rules which mention neither common property nor punishment; column B, those which mention no common property but do mention punishment; column C, those which mention common property but do not mention punishment, and column D, those which mention both. Thus, the result appears as follows:

	(A)	(B)	(C)	(D)	*Totals*
Chia	80	27	–	7	114
Tsu	11	5	1	9	26
Tsung	15	10	–	9	34
Tz'u	2	9	4	20	35
Others	73	17	8	9	107

The counting shows that the majority of the particular rules carry the word *chia* or family, reflecting an appeal of the assimilated family sentiment in the clan group. Familism is projected to enhance clan cohesion. Only one third of such rules have, however, some kind of provisions on punishment of misconduct and they seldom mention common property. It is likely that the clans with such rules did not have sizeable common property or the subject-matter is covered in another rule of a different type. In the former case, their group cohesion probably rests more upon the sentimental appeal of kinship relationship, status-ethics, and ritual-ethics than upon organizational measures.

When the titles carry the word *tsung* or *tsu*, both meaning the clan group, more than one half of such rules have some kind of provisions on punishment of misconduct and roughly one third of them have provisions on common property. When the titles contain the word *tz'u* or ancestral hall, most of the rules have the provisions on punishment and on common property. Thus, using a word meaning clan in the first part of a clan rule title indicates a fairly strong organizational strength of the group and using the expression ancestral hall indicates an optimum organizational strength. Moreover, whenever common property is mentioned, the rules contain more detailed, concrete provisions on punishment of misconduct.

All the rest of the rules which do not fall within the descriptive analysis above are so miscellaneously titled that no significant patterns can be formulated, with the exception that a number of rules on charitable land and estates are notably concerned with both common property management and clan punishment of misconduct.

The second part of the titles consist of nouns designating the nature of the particular rules. These nouns appear either alone or in combination with one another. Most of them differ only in varying shades of meaning. Their approximate equivalents in English are given below:

Word Used to Form the Second Part of the Rule Titles	Approximate Equivalent in English	Type (see the text below)
Chang (章)	Constitution	2
Chen (箴)	Admonitions	2
Chiao (教)	Teachings	1
Chieh (誡)	Injunctions	1
Chin (禁)	Restrictions	2
Ch'üan (勸)	Advice	1
Fa (法)	Discipline	2
Fan (範)	Standards	1
Hsün (訓), (representative of type 1)	Instructions	1
I (second tone, 儀)	Etiquettes	1
I (fourth tone, 議)	Decisions	2
Ke-yen (格言)	Mottoes	1
Kuei (規), (representative of type 2)	Regulations	2
Li (禮)	Proprieties	1
T'iao-li (條例)	Articles	2
Yüeh (約)	Agreement	2

Listing the terms and their approximate equivalents in English merely serves the purpose of demonstrating their general meaning. Further analysis shows that these terms generally fall into two types: one, terms which refer in the main to moral and ethical instructions on the level of principles often without concrete stipulation on punitive measures; and the other, terms which carry the overtone of disciplinary action and frequently imply detailed stipulations on the punishment of misconduct. The former type is best represented by the word *hsün* meaning "instructions," used more often than the rest in this group. The latter type is best represented by the word *kuei* meaning "regulations" for the same reason.

The above classification greatly simplifies the task of analysis. It is sufficient to direct attention to the representative types in the second part of the titles, in combination with the word *chia*, *tsu*, *tsung*, or *tz'u* in the first part of the titles. The result is given below. Arranged in the same way as before, the titles are listed on the left-hand side and their respective total numbers on the right-hand side. The four columns in between are: column A, those which mention neither common property nor punishment; column B, those which do not mention common property but do mention punishment; column C, those which mention common property but no punishment; and column D, those which mention both. The findings appear as follows:

	(A)	(B)	(C)	(D)	Totals
Title with the word *hsün*:					
Chia hsün	47	4	–	1	52
Tsung hsün	4	1	–	–	5
Title with the word *kuei*:					
Chia kuei	16	17	–	4	37
Tsu kuei	2	5	–	6	13
Tsung kuei	3	5	–	6	14
Tz'u kuei	2	9	3	15	29

The above itemized summary shows that the rules containing the representative word *hsün* or "instructions" most likely do not have concrete and detailed stipulations on either punishment or common property management. The same is true of other rules of which the titles have a word similar in type to the word *hsün*. On the other hand, the opposite is true when the word *kuei* meaning "regulations," or words to the same effect, appear in the titles of the rules. The fact that a number of genealogies have both these types of rules, one called "instructions" and the other called "regulations," or their respective equivalents, highlights the difference.

The same procedure is repeated for all the titles in their complete wordings of various combinations. The result shows that the total number of all types of rules (316) exceeds the total number of the genealogies (151), as one genealogy often has more than one type of rule. Among the 316 particular rules, 249 of them do not have concrete, detailed provisions on common property and only 67 of them have. These rules are broken down further into those with punitive measures and those without. The result shows that 181 of the 249 rules without provisions on common property are also void of provisions on punishment. But in the minority of 67 rules with stipulations on common property, 54 of them have detailed provisions on punishment.[16] Punishment is definitely correlated

[16] See Table 2 of the Appendix.

to common property, both indicating the organizational strength of the clan.

In essence, the rule titles can be represented by two composite types: the *chia-hsün* or "family instructions" type and the *tz'u-kuei* or "ancestral hall regulations" type. All the rules, by the respective wording of their titles, can be classified as being or nearing the one or the other type. These two types represent the minimum and the maximum of the clan's organizational strength. The first type, the "family instruction," limits its major attention largely to the moral principles and ethical values. The social control which these rules exercise is likely to be mainly of ritual-ethical persuasion. The second type, the "ancestral hall regulations," on the other hand, not only upholds the moral principles and ethical values but specifies in addition the norms of conduct in a concrete, detailed manner, the punishment of deviation by appropriate penalties, as well as the regulations governing the management and protection of common property. The social control embodied in these rules is likely to be reinforced by organizational actions of both persuasion and compulsion.

Among the rules under study, the "family instruction" type far outnumbers the "ancestral hall regulations" type which means that even the clans wealthy enough to have printed genealogies are not necessarily strong organizationally. These clan groups probably rely most of the time upon the individual assertion of their leaders to maintain the desired social control. This, after all, is in essential agreement with the basic Confucian belief in the preventive influence of moral teachings, held to be more desirable than punitive measures. While the lack of emphasis upon group collective action may not imply a weakness in the clan institution as a whole, it does suggest that, within the clan institution, the organizational aspects of the clan group are weak.

The economic status of the clan is important: only the clans well endowed with common property have the "ancestral hall regulations" type of rules. These clans, economically less dependent on the support of member families, are more capable of handing out rewards for exemplary conduct and assistance in case of need as well as of punishing those who violate the rules.

C. THE SUBJECT-MATTER IN THE CLAN RULES AND THE VALUE PATTERN

The range of subject-matter in the clan rules warrants a general analysis. Many, though not all, clan rules have an orderly arrangement of dividing their contents into paragraphs, each under a caption or itemized heading. First, the essential meanings in the content are identifiable with definite values, social relations, attitudes, behaviors, and activities. Next, the counting method rates the subject-matter by the number of times it appears in the contents of various clan rules. If a clan has several kinds of rules in its genealogy and a certain category of subject-matter appears several times in these rules, only the one with the most detailed description and stipulations is counted. In other words, a clan or its genealogy as a whole is taken to be the unit. The subject-matter which has a higher rating is thus shown to have received a greater emphasis than others. This summation is, within broad limits, an approximate reflection of the value pattern of the clan institution according to the leading exponents who compiled these rules. A question may be raised here: is it possible to assign different weights to the various categories of subject-matter by the order of precedence in which they appear in the clan rules? The outstanding subject-matter or topics, such as filial piety, clan cohesion, and respect for elder clan members, seem to claim prior attention and probably receive more stress than other topics which appear later in the texts. Closer examination reveals, however, that this tendency is not generally true. Save these few outstanding instances, the order in which the subject-matter appears in the clan rules shows no definite pattern of priority or sequence.

Tabulating the diverse topics merely by the order of their respective ratings will be confusing. A more meaningful way is to classify them under six categories: intra-family relations and behavior, sex group relations and behavior, intra-clan relations and behavior, extra-clan relations and behavior, values and beliefs of individuals, and misdemeanors and criminal offenses of individuals. Each category is in turn broken down into subdivisions. A few of these subdivisions are admittedly somewhat arbitrary. For example, ancestral rites are family as well as clan ceremonies which also border upon religious belief. In the context of the clan rules, however, they concern the intra-clan relations more than the other aspects and are classified accordingly. The essential defense of this classification is the convenience of analysis within permissible limits. Many values and relationships are intermingled with one another and any classification is bound to fall short in some respects.

The resulting tabulations in Table 3 of the Appendix warrant a number of general observations with regard to the value pattern upheld in the clan rules. There is an overwhelming emphasis upon the roles of individuals within their family life. As generally known, individuals in traditional China were closely bound to the family. Though called the rules of the clan, these rules actually do not put as much emphasis upon the clan itself, as the clan is only a consolidating group comprising member families.

In intra-family relationships (see Chapter III), the relations arising from generation-age order lead the rest in importance. Filial piety significantly has the highest rating. Great attention is given to the education and discipline of children. The value of family harmony is implied in the emphasis on brotherly conduct, serious consideration of marriage matches, roles of the wife, as well as marital relations. Prominent in the area of sex group relations and behaviors are certain controls of sex segregation and seclusion of women for the purpose of avoiding embarrassing or disgraceful situations. These provisions underline the patriarchal nature of the society and emphasize the fact that the family was the center of activities.

Turning to the category of intra-clan relations (see Chapter IV), the clan rules give little attention to organizational aspects other than insisting on the selection of trustworthy and capable officers.[17] The predominant emphasis, as expected, is upon the ancestral cult which signifies clan continuity. The clan rules repeatedly stress ancestral rites, care of ancestral graveyards, building of the ancestral hall and its maintenance, and compilation of genealogy. The clan, as one author puts it, functioned under the "ancestors' shadow."[17] This

[17] Hsu, *Under the Ancestors' Shadow.*

emphasis supports the inviolability of generation-age hierarchy, for the ancestors stand at its very top. Generation-age hierarchy expresses itself in the respect due to clan members of senior status. The clan organization stresses the ascribed status by birth rather than the achieved status of social prominence and wealth. A principal means of doing so is to honor the members of high generation-age status at the ancestral rites.

For the clan group, consolidation is highly regarded. Consolidation implies common sentiment, mutual concern, and spirit of solidarity. Translated into concrete functions, it means that the clan should settle disputes between its members, provide relief and aid for the poor, commend exemplary members and punish misbehaving ones. A clan would usually take official action to reward exemplary conduct when it enhanced the clan prestige and administer formal punishment of misconduct when it damaged the reputation of the clan.

As noted earlier, many clans do not seem to have sizable common property. In fact, a large number of the clan rules urge their members to exert efforts to acquire or increase the size of common property. Others stress property protection and management. Obviously, the strength of a clan depends considerably upon the economic resources at its disposal.

On extra-clan relations and behavior (see Chapter V), the clan rules show predominantly negative attitudes. The negative attitude is especially pronounced with respect to the government, a sad commentary on the political climate in traditional China. Many clan rules forbid litigation but advise prompt payment of taxes. Litigation betrays a failure of moral coercion contrary to the Confucian ideal. Without litigation and tax arrears and settling disputes among themselves, people can enjoy a happy life immune from government intervention. These stipulations also imply the fear of government, the lack of confidence in legal justice, and helplessness with respect to tax burden.

Cordiality is the leading value in one's relationships with maternal relatives, neighbors, and community people. Cordiality does not imply an active assertion. It means proper, and even somewhat lukewarm, relations with these persons at a respectable but safe distance. Modesty, caution, and restraint are the desirable qualifying values in such relationships. This undertone of guardedness is especially pronounced in the emphasis on selecting friends carefully and on avoiding dubious persons.

In the category of personal conduct of individuals (also see Chapter V), the overwhelming stress is upon desirable vocations and economic behavior. The ideal is to earn as well as to save more, not for the individual alone but for the continuing family prosperity. There is little doubt that wealth stands high in the value pattern, though the pursuit of wealth according to the clan rules should not be at the expense of other values such as social status, morality, and personal virtue. For this reason, the clan rules express a strong preference for the vocation of scholar, for scholars were potential officials with the highest social status. As landed property was highly valued in an agricultural society, farming, especially gentleman-farming, is the next honorable vocation. It stands higher than trade and craft, though the latter two vocations are also desirable ones.

The clan rules advocate exemplary personal conduct and prohibit misconduct. The value pattern perpetuates Confucianism in stressing many ethical values such as cautiousness of speech, modesty, honesty, sincerity, and propriety. These ethical values are not abstract ones but are pointedly directed to the proper awareness one should have of his own roles and the proper regard one should have of the status of other people.

Morality is supported by an ethico-religious belief that Heaven or the way of Nature would somehow reward moral conduct by blessing the individual, his family, or his descendants. A person of high moral standard, according to the clan rules, should not boast of his moral conduct but practice unostentatious virtue. Unostentatious virtue means, in Veblen's terminology, "to be conspicuous by the very lack of conspicuousness." For the same reason, forbearance and conciliation are emphasized virtues, while complacency and arrogance are undesirable. These character traits, seemingly commonplace, have deep significance. Forbearance and conciliation are the necessary companions of the value of harmony, which is essential to the closely knit family life and the static social order in general. Complacency and arrogance, on the other hand, are ostentations which breed hostility and tension.

These values, taken together, point toward an ideal type of personality characterized not only by morality but also by modesty, caution, and self-restraint. This ideal type fits well with the stable social order in traditional China, rigid in its structure and conventional-minded in its functions. An interesting parallel exists between traditional China and the primitive Tanala society. In the Tanala culture, as Kardiner points out, the primary institutions are social prestige and social immobility. The ego structure consists of such elements as uselessness of strife, deification of the lineage cult, and property as a means of enlarging ego. And the secondary institutions are belief in fate and in morality to restrain ostentation.[18] This parallel example throws an additional light on the value system of traditional China which stresses similar qualities.

The discouragement of complacency and arrogance is especially directed toward prominent and wealthy clan members who were the mainstay of the clan organization. The clan rules express the hope that these members will exercise their leadership properly without antagonizing fellow members. The same special regard for these members is noticeable in the injunctions against misconduct. The common indulgences of the well-to-do, such as visiting prostitutes, gambling, and drinking, have ratings higher than other acts of misconduct. On the whole, the clan rules are more concerned with misdemeanors than with criminal offenses such as adultery, assault and battery. The reason is twofold: misdemeanors presumably occurred more frequently than criminal offenses; moreover, the latter, strictly speaking, were under the government jurisdiction beyond the control of the clan. The main concern of the clan rules is that their members should remain law-abiding.

The clan rules also express a negative attitude toward organized religions and religious profession. What the religions preached and practiced often did not agree with Confucianism, the ancestral cult, ritual-ethics, or status-ethics. Religious groups did not, for example, stress filial piety, social status, or seclusion of women. To join them is,

[18] Kardiner, *The Individual and His Society*, pp. 326–327.

in the opinion of the clan rules, a disregard of moral order. Furthermore, unorthodox and secret religious sects were likely to be politically dangerous. In any event, the clan rules cherish few values in the relationship outside the family and clan.

In summing up, the value pattern as revealed by the general content of the clan rules displays a strong moral character. The outstanding values are personal integrity, family prosperity, family harmony, and, by the extension of family interest, clan cohesion. Contacts with people and groups outside the two kinship groups are to be held at a proper minimum. This general characteristic of the value pattern contradicts a cardinal assumption in the Confucian theory that personal integrity and moral life in the family are sufficient conditions for a well-ordered community and a well-governed nation. What the clan rules aim at is an ideal type of personality so closely and even exclusively orientated to the family and the clan that he can hardly be expected to play an active role in community life, let alone political matters. In fact, the concept of community does not occupy a prominent place in the value pattern at all; and politics is generally regarded by the clan rules as undesirable. In other words, personal integrity and moral life in the kinship groups are not likely to contribute directly to either community or national well-being as Confucianism assumes.

D. THE TYPES OF CLAN PUNISHMENT

Numerous clan rules have detailed stipulations on appropriate punitive measures to cope with deviations from the norms of conduct, though many other clan rules as noted before rely merely upon moral teachings and ethical appeals. Punitive measures constitute a salient instrument of social control and warrant a general analysis here.[19]

[19] For the primary sources on Chinese law, see *Ta Ch'ing lü-li* and *Ta Ch'ing hui-tien*. For secondary sources on Chinese law and the legal position of the clan organization, see the following authors: Ch'iu Han-p'ing, Chu Ch'eng-hsün, Ch'ü T'ung-tsu, Hsü Ch'ao-yang, and Wu Ch'i. For secondary sources in English language on law and punishment in many other societies for comparative purpose, see the works by Arthur Sigismund Diamond, Georges Gurvitvh, L. T. Hobhouse, Edward Adamson Hoebel, Robert Harry Lowie, Bronislaw Malinowski, W. I. Thomas, and Edward A. Westermarck.

The kinship groups in ancient China, as in many primitive societies, had the power to punish their own members. After the establishment of the centralized empire in the third century B.C., this power was sharply curtailed by the legal system. Nevertheless, the lack of rapid means of communication over vast territory rendered direct control by the state of minor local matters exceedingly difficult. No government official sitting in court and removed from the actual scene of offense was capable of looking into the case thoroughly and taking all relevant factors into due consideration as a clan group was. The government therefore allowed the clan groups to take care of the order within themselves by defining and recognizing their limited punitive power under government supervision. From the viewpoint of the clan, punitive power was a logical extension of its moral disciplinary function. The ability to deal with intra-group disputes, misdemeanors, and minor criminal offenses helped the elimination of these misconducts and the protection of group reputation.

One clan rule, typical of many others, stresses that the family needs discipline, punishment, and reward:[20]

Ancient people have said, no family can afford to dispense with instructions and punishment. A family should reward good behavior of the members with gifts and praise them from time to time in order to encourage them. Likewise, a family should punish its misbehaving members so that they will become afraid of misbehaving again.

What was needed in the family was also needed in the clan; though it was not so easy for the clan to discharge the same function. As one clan rule admits: "Putting these regulations in the clan rules into effect depends on persuasion. Resorting to punitive measures is more easily said than done."[21]

The legally defined limitations of the clan's judiciary power were several. First, the state recognized that the clan had quasi-autonomous authority to deal with minor cases only among its members. A case involving another clan would have to be decided otherwise, by a mutually satisfactory settlement, by arbitration in the community, by resorting to a brutal feud (which the law forbade but sometimes

[20] 1936-b, "Miscellaneous Statements of Family Instructions," p. 27a.
[21] 1935-d, "Family Standards," p. 4a; 1915-d, "Family Regulations," p. 30a.

overlooked), or by submitting the case to government litigation. Second, the quasi-autonomous judiciary power of the clan did not cover serious cases. Though what constituted a serious case was subject to flexible and arbitrary interpretation, both the government and the clan groups recognized the essential line of demarcation. Under the law, treasonable acts, murder, cases involving loss of life, and criminal offenses liable to penal servitude fell under government jurisdiction.[22] The law, in maintaining the inviolability of ethical relationship, also required legal trial for such flagrant violations as harming the parents by the son or adultery between relatives.[23] The clan rules generally observed the same principles. For example, one clan rule states: "Cases involving death and flagrant violation of ethical relationship should be sent to the government for due punishment under the law."[24] Another clan rule makes a clear demarcation: "The clan head shall administer corporal punishment at the ancestral hall to a member who commits an illegal offense which is punishable under the law by flogging. However, if it is a criminal offense subject to penal servitude, the guilty member shall be sent to the government."[25] On the other hand, a few exceptionally stern clan rules exceed the legal limitations. One clan, so states its rule, would order the death of a member who harbored criminals or who was himself guilty of serious crimes "so as to avoid legal trial which brings shame upon the ancestors."[26] However, such cases must be regarded as rare exceptions. While a clan might compel one of its members to commit suicide, the law did not permit the clan to put him to death. Third, the judicial decision of the clan had no final binding effect. When a culprit or a plaintiff felt that the clan decision had done him injustice, he could appeal to the government. More often, a clan would

---

[22] *Ta Ch'ing hui-tien*, p. 114.
[23] Sir George Thomas Staunton (tr.), *Ta Tsing Leu Lee*, pp. 26–27; also Hsü Ch'ao-yang, *Chung-kuo ch'in-shu fa su-yüan* [*The origin of Chinese Kinship Law*], pp. 1–4. Hereinafter cited as *Ch'in-shu fa*.
[24] 1924–e, "Family Mottoes," item on avoidance of litigation, p. 3a.
[25] 1922–f, "Regulations of the Ancestral Hall," item on offenses and punishment, p. 10a.
[26] 1919–d, "The Ten Admonitions," item on harbouring criminals, p. 3a; also 1914–h, "Family Instructions," item on theft and robbery, p. 4b.

ask for government approval in order to make the decision official and binding. Finally, the clan assumed toward the government collective responsibility for the misbehavior of its members and had to, under coercion of penalty, report a serious crime to the government. This was partly the reason why a clan would often punish its misbehaving member by expunging his name from the genealogy or by formally expelling him from the group so that the clan would no longer bear the legal responsibility for him.

Several minor points ought to be clarified: who had the authority in the clan to decide on punishment and who administered the punishment to whom? Generally speaking, the judiciary power of clan was vested in the hands of clan heads and leading officers. But it was not entirely so. Clan heads often settled a case by calling a clan meeting at the ancestral hall to ascertain the consensus of opinion among the clan members. The opinion of influential members such as scholar-officials naturally carried weight. Nor was the administering of punishment necessarily done by the clan officers themselves. In minor cases, the decision would call upon the family head to punish the offender, confirming the principle that the primary responsibility of discipline rested with the family. When a serious offender received corporal punishment at the ancestral hall, ordinary clan members might also take a hand in it. Punishment was not necessarily administered to an offender himself. The family was in turn held collectively responsible by the clan. A father who allowed his son to commit misdemeanors might have to take the punishment himself. A husband was generally liable to punishment for the misconduct of his wife, and a son likewise for that of his widowed mother.

A crucial question remains: what are the various types of punishment in these clan rules? In order to answer the question, it will be necessary to examine the data in detail.[27] The language of the clan rules poses a number of difficulties. Many clan rules use loose terms whose meanings are often flexible, ambiguous, and literary, rather than specific, clear-cut, and exact. Even vigilant and thorough analysis cannot reach an exactness that will remove all traces of doubt. Elucidation is the best that can be expected.

[27] For detailed information, see numerous tables in the Appendix.

To classify the punishment in the clan rules into types, it is necessary first of all to distinguish what constitutes punishment and what does not. In the clan rules are a large number of injunctions prohibiting various misbehaviors but which do not mention any specific punishment. Presumably such stipulations were to be enforced by informal disciplinary steps such as a word of warning, an oral disapproval, or a threat of possible punishment, usually at the discretion of the family head or sometimes clan officers. The present study classifies them as *prohibition* which does not amount to punishment.

The most lenient punishment is *oral censure*. The clan rules have a number of terms referring to it such as *ch'ih* (斥), *chieh* (誡), or *yü* (諭). These terms have obvious meanings and their identification presents no difficulty. Oral censure was an official act of the clan. The clan officers either reprimanded the offender personally or declared his censure at a clan meeting in the ancestral hall. Sometimes, the clan ordered the family head to reprimand the offender. In a few clan rules, censure might take the written form of having a public notice of condemnation posted in front of the house of the offender or on the wall of the ancestral hall. However, written censure was seldom an isolated act but frequently taken in conjunction with other more severe measures of punishment. It is therefore not classified as mere oral censure.

The clan rules use a number of terms to designate the various forms of punishment which fall within the range between oral censure and corporal punishment. These terms are most confusing as their dictionary meanings seem more or less similar to one another. Translated into English, they roughly mean the equivalents of "discipline," "chastisement," or "infliction." The comparative degree of their severity can only be ascertained by reading the context critically, by comparing these terms whenever they appear in the same clan rule, and then by comparing various clan rules which use the same terms.

The term *fa* (罰), comes next after oral censure in the order of severity. One clan rule defines *fa* as "bowing, kneeling, or donation of incense and candles to the ancestral hall."[28] Another clan rule

[28] 1916–c, "Additional Family Discipline," item on reward and punishment, p. 3a.

defines it as "bowing, kneeling, or donation of silver or rice" to the clan.[29] In short, *fa* is either a formal ritualistic apology, a monetary fine, or material fine. The present study classifies it as *penalty*. Ritual penalty takes various forms: kneeling before ancestral tablets for the duration of a burning incense stick, bowing and kneeling in apology before the offended party, or chanting a liturgy for a designated number of days. Material penalty also varies in form, such as a monetary fine of from a hundred copper coins to the sizable amount of one tael of silver or a material donation of candles, incense, or bogus money to be used for burning at the ancestral rites, depending upon the seriousness of the offense. A utilitarian redemption by material donation is to make the offender provide a feast at the home of the person to whom a formal apology should be due, a banquet at the ancestral hall with the participation of clan officers, or a stage show at the ancestral hall for the enjoyment of all clan members.

Corporal punishment is the next severe type of punitive measure. The clan rules use a great variety of terms referring to it. Some of these terms are easily identified. *Chang-tse* (杖責) means punishment with a stick; *ch'ih-tse* (笞責), punishment with a bamboo tool; and *ch'ui-tse* (箠責), punishment by beating. The term *tse*, the common denominator in these expressions, denotes corporal punishment in one form or another. One clan rule defines *tse* as "beating, flogging, or chaining the offender to a stone," usually a decorative stone in front of the ancestral hall.[30] Other terms are not so readily identifiable. *Chia-fa* (家法), literally meaning "family discipline," alludes to the tool a family keeps for the exclusive use of administering bodily discipline. One clan rule explains that *"chia-fa* is made of small bamboo sheets." *Fa-ch'ui* (法箠), literally meaning "beating in accordance with family discipline," alludes to the same. *Li-p'u* (禮撲), literally meaning "ritualistic beating," denotes corporal punishment as sanctioned by ritual-ethics.

Another group of terms is especially baffling. *Ch'eng* (懲), *chih* (治), *chiu* (究), and *ch'u* (處), all have the same general meaning of "punishing," "meting out punishment," or "dealing with the offense

[29] 1919–e, "Family Discipline," item on reward and punishment, p. 11a.
[30] 1930–a, *"Tsu* Standards," item on *chia-fa*, p. 18a.

in a severe manner." Though many clan rules use these terms frequently, none of them gives any precise definition for them. Judging from the content, they generally have a connotation of indefiniteness and flexibility, rather than an exact denotation. In comparison with what has already been ascertained, these terms evidently represent a type of punishment more severe in nature than penalty in the present classification scheme. And judging from the kind of offenses to which they are applicable, they approach corporal punishment in severity but not quite to that extent. Hence, the present scheme classifies them as *castigation*, defined here as a type of punishment with some physical coercion or a threat of physical coercion. It may include some corporal punishment but is not meant to be entirely such. Or it may combine a light amount of bodily disciplining with another more lenient form of punishment such as oral censure or ritual penalty.

Four types of punishment have been established thus far: oral censure, penalty, castigation, and corporal punishment, in the ascending order of severity. Yet, a number of compound terms present even greater difficulties in identification and classification. *Tse* which means corporal punishment is often used in a compound expression together with a term already classified as penalty or as castigation. Examples are: *tse-fa* (責罰). *ch'eng-tse* (懲責), and *ch'ih-tse* (斥責). These compound terms, coined out of rhetoric convenience, border upon ambiguity. Without digressing into a philological discussion, a few examples will serve to clarify their varying shades of meaning.

In the compound expression *ch'eng-tse*, *ch'eng* has been classified under castigation and *tse* is definitely corporal punishment. *Ch'eng* and *tse* together imply either the one or the other. Since castigation in this classification scheme means physical coercion which may well include some corporal punishment, this compound expression still falls within the definition and is classified accordingly. Another compound term, *tse-fa*, with *tse* meaning corporal punishment and *fa* meaning penalty, indicates a flexible range between the two. Since castigation lies between the two on the scale of punishment, it will also cover this particular compound term.

The word *tse*, however, has both a specific denotation meaning corporal punishment and a loose connotation referring to punishment in general. When used in this loose sense, its meaning is on the lenient side. For example, *ch'ih-tse*, in which *ch'ih* means oral censure, actually means "oral censure and punishment," except there is an added shade of meaning indicating that it is somewhat more severe than ordinary oral censure. The present classification scheme, which does not claim to be quantitative, nor exact, may regard it as the same as oral censure.

The classification scheme here cannot be exact because the data are not meant to be. As offenses in a similar category may well differ in their seriousness under varying circumstances and complications, rigid stipulations on punishment will in effect defeat justice. There are reasons to believe that the compilers of many clan rules deliberately made their stipulations flexible. First, the intended flexibility is explicitly stated. Many clan rules use such expressions as *i-fa* (議罰) which means penalty to be considered and *i-tse* (議責) which means corporal punishment to be considered. These clan rules do not state how much the amount of fine should be or how many times an offender should be flogged as some other clan rules do. Second, the intended flexibility is indicated by descriptive qualifications. For instance, instead of stipulating the exact amount of punishment, the clan rules read that an offender should be *"heavily* penalized" or *"lightly* beaten." Third, the intended flexibility lies in a stipulated choice between two types of punishment. Many clan rules maintain that a minor case of a certain offense should be punished leniently by oral censure but a serious case of the same offense should be punished severely by flogging. Filial impiety, for example, should be punished according to a large number of clan rules by either corporal punishment or legal sentence by the government, depending upon how offensive the misconduct has been. Fourth, the differentiation between initial and repeated offense indicates another flexibility. A considerable number of clan rules in stipulating the distinctions between first offense, repeated offense, and persistent or incorrigible offense provide progressively severe punishment in that order. Such flexibilities do not, however, affect the classification scheme.

The classification scheme becomes simpler once it gets beyond corporal punishment. Next to corporal punishment in the ascending order of severity is forfeit of clan privileges, such as permanent disqualification from holding clan office, no ration of sacrificial food normally distributed to members after the ancestral rites, denial of the privilege of taking part in the ancestral rites either for a number of years or permanently, and formal exclusion from the ancestral hall. Forfeit of clan privileges means, in addition, a serious depreciation of status. An offender excluded from the ancestral hall is no longer recognized as a senior by other members whose generation-age status is originally junior to his. An offender permanently expelled from the ancestral hall loses his good standing in the clan group. He cannot be buried in the clan cemetery or the ancestral graveyard, the posthumous tablet bearing his name cannot be placed in the ancestral hall to partake the sacrificial rites, nor can his descendants be admitted into the ancestral hall.[31]

The most severe form of punishment which the clan rules impose is cancellation of clan membership and expulsion from the clan organization. This type of punishment is implemented in several ways: expurgation of an offender's name from the genealogy, formal expulsion from the clan, complete severance of relationship with him and even with his descendants, and in rare cases his compulsory removal from the community.[32] In other words, an offender so punished loses all his status in the clan, a punishment comparable to ex-communication in a religious organization or in a society dominated by an organized religion.

The classification scheme of clan punishment is now complete. More serious than clan punishment is punishment by law under government jurisdiction. As mentioned earlier, the dividing line between the judiciary competency of the clans and the juridiction of the government, though not always clear-cut, was generally understood and observed. When a clan could not settle a case itself, either because the case was far too serious or because the offender

---

[31] 1919–e, "Family Discipline," p. 11a and 1922–e, "Family Instructions of Ancestor Tan-ya-kung," p. 60a.
[32] 1915–a, "Family Regulations," item on unorthodox religious sects, p. 28b.

refused to obey the authority of the clan, the clan had the right to invoke the state power by petitioning the government. Punishment under the law usually included beating, flogging, and chaining. Criminal offenses often resulted in penal servitude, banishment, condemnation into government slavery, as well as capital punishment. Whatever the legal service was, the convict suffered from the stigma for the rest of his life. His clan often would compound it by cancelling his membership. In any event, he would lose much social prestige, if not his clan privileges and status also.

In summing up, the types of prohibition and punishment in the clan rules are as follows:

(A) Prohibition, without mention of punishment.
(B) Clan punishment:
    (1) Oral censure (admonition or reproof);
    (2) Penalty (monetary fine and ritual penalty);
    (3) Castigation (physical coercion probably including some corporal punishment);
    (4) Corporal punishment (usually flogging by bamboo tools);
    (5) Forfeit of clan privileges;
    (6) Expulsion from the clan and exclusion from its genealogy;
    (7) Death or order to commit suicide (in a few exceptional clan rules only).
(C) Government punishment under the law.

Prohibition is a moral injunction, basically relying upon moral pressure and the individual's self-control. Oral censure and penalty are the punishment at the lenient level, largely in the realm of ritual-ethics. Monetary fines may be regarded also as a ritual token. The implication behind the lenient level of punishment is that ritualistic control is sufficient to maintain the inviolability of ethical standard. The clan rules usually stipulate these for relatively minor offenses that do not compromise or threaten another member's status, the family generation-age hierarchy, the clan generation-age order, the clan's reputation, or its vital interest.

Castigation and corporal punishment constitute the medium level of punishment. The use of physical coercion indicates that ritual-ethical control is no longer regarded as sufficient to restrain or to correct the offender.[33] Such punishment subjects the offender to a physical indignity or an extreme ritualistic humiliation. The offender suffers a loss of personal prestige, but not yet a degradation of his status. It is significant to note that the medium level of punishments are the ones most frequently mentioned in the clan rules.

Forfeit of clan privileges, expulsion from the clan, and exclusion from the genealogy are the severe level of punishment. They involve the suspension or cancellation of the status of the offender. Such punishment is used when physical coercion or medium level punishment is unable to rectify or remedy the situation, when the status of another member is threatened or violated, when the offender compromises his own proper status, or when he disgraces the clan group. These punishments represent the enforcement of status-ethics: a retaliation in status as punishment of misconduct that flagrantly violates status.

In short the various clan punishments form a continuum of moral, ritual, and status punishments. This continuum agrees in broad outline with the value pattern which emphasizes moral appeal, ritual-ethics, and status-ethics.

[33] Levy, *op. cit.*, p. 27.

CHAPTER III

THE CLAN RULES ON FAMILY RELATIONSHIPS

THE GENERAL ANALYSES of the clan rules in the preceding chapter are subject to further substantiation and qualification through a closer examination of the data. The principal attention of the clan rules is given to family relationships and the individual roles in them. The relationships in a traditional Chinese family, numerous and complex, can be grouped into two main sets.[1] The first set is the generation-age hierarchial relationship between senior members and junior members with particular emphasis upon the males. It includes the parent-children relationship, the relationship between brothers, and the need of a male heir. The significance of these relationships extends into the clan. Parent-children relationship provides the foundation of the generation-age order in the clan; relationship between brothers sets the norm for clan members of the same generation; and an heir is essential not only for the continuation of the family's line of descent but for keeping the place of the family in the clan organization.

The second set of family relationships concerns sex status governing such matters as marriage, wifehood, widowhood, sex segregation, and seclusion of women. The roles of women, though subordinate to those of men, are indispensable to family harmony and solidarity. Control over married women aims at their proper adjustment, the lack of which often leads to domestic troubles and even a decline of the family prosperity and prestige.

These two sets of family relationships are closely interwoven. The parent-children relationship involves the sons and the daughters-in-law as well. Relationship between the brothers is inseparable from those between their wives and dependants. In a large household, some rules on sex segregation are necessary to regulate the daily

---

[1] Chia Yuan-i, *Chung-kuo chia-t'ing chung ch'in tzu kuan-hsi chih yen-chiu* [*A Study of the Parent-child Relationship in the Chinese Family*], pp. 7–15; and Levy, *op. cit.*, pp. 165–207.

contact between male members and their aunts-in-law, sisters-in-law, daughters-in-law, and nieces-in-law. The presence of an heir or an adopted one enhances the status of his widowed mother. In short, a well-ordered family regulates its relationships with regard to all three key factors: generation, age, and sex.

The clan is concerned lest a family should have serious conflicts between members, disputes over inheritance settlement, or misbehaving members. The well-being of the component families in turn contributes to the better functioning of the clan.

A. PARENT-CHILDREN RELATIONSHIP

The chief control within the family rested with parental authority. The father, as the family head, had the right to dispose of the family property, to punish, to reward, and to give orders to the family members as well as the responsibility to guide them and provide for them.[2] The colloquial language calls him *yeh* (爺) which has the connotation of 'lord,' indicating his dominant status. The classical language often describes the father as 'stern' (*yen* 嚴) in referring to his disciplinary role. The ideograph father (父), in its archaic forms (𠂇, 又, and 乂), depicts the picture of a hand raising a rod or stick to discipline someone.[3] However, parental authority did not reside with the father alone. The mother, whose status was next only to the father, shared his authority to a certain extent or by his delegation. Her role was to assist him generally in domestic matters and especially in rearing children.[4]

Parental control, to be effective and lasting, demands from the children the virtue of filial piety which is more than a mere passive obedience, but an active devotion to the parents.[5] The main stress is placed upon the sons, for they remain in the family, whereas daughters are married off into other families. Among the intra-family relation-

---

[2] 1917-c, "Family Instructions of Ancestor San-feng-kung," p. 15a; Lang, *op. cit.*, pp. 26–27; and Hsü Ch'ao-yang, *Ch'in-shu fa*, pp. 71–73.

[3] Ch'ü, *op. cit.*, p. 5 citing *Shuo-wen*.

[4] Hsu, *Under the Ancestors' Shadow*, p. 59.

[5] Lang, *op. cit.*, p. 25 and 1925-e, "Family Instructions," item on filial piety and brotherly conduct, pp. 4–5.

ships covered by the clan rules, filial piety stands above the rest with the highest rating.[6] The Confucian scholars advocated it with utmost vigor. They advised emperors "to rule the country by upholding filial piety" in the belief that a man who respected parental authority would respect the law and one who accepted filial responsibility would honor his social obligations. While the logic of this contention is open to question as shown at the end of the preceding chapter, there can be no denial of the importance of filial piety to the family and as a concern of the clan.

Filial piety was first cultivated by discipline of the mother, who made it clear to the child that the ultimate authority in the family rested with the father. A boy soon came under the direct control of his father.[7] The recognition of where authority lay taught the child the technique of ingratiation. He learned to please his parents, especially his father, in exchange for security and reward.[8] But ingratiation is hardly filial piety. It is only a submission based on fear and not infrequently accompanied by hidden hatred. Parental authority cannot be secure by relying on the inadequate control of coercion and reward.[9]

Filial piety must be a self-control by which the children respect their parents with deep, voluntary, and lasting affection.[10] It relies essentially upon ritual-ethics. The Chinese classics taught that as soon as a child became old enough to grasp the meaning of social relations, he should be taught the proper rituals and their moral justifications.[11] The child then learned to respect the superior status of his parents, to assume his proper roles toward them, and to derive satisfaction in doing so.

For this reason, many clan rules explain the need of filial piety by numerous moral justifications. These moral justifications given in the rules of 68 clans are summarized as follows:[12]

---

[6] See Table 3 in the Appendix.
[7] Martin C. Yang, *op. cit.*, pp. 126–128; and Lang, *op. cit.*, pp. 239–240.
[8] Cf. Kardiner, *The Individual and His Society*, pp. 301–318.
[9] Lang, *op. cit.*, p. 24, note.
[10] Shimizu, *Kazoku*, pp. 414–416.
[11] *KCTSCC, Chia-fan tien, ts'e* 627, *chüan* 39, especially pp. 12–17.
[12] The items in total exceeds the number of clans, because a clan rule may

	Number of Clans
Parents have taken much trouble in rearing children	52
Filial piety is in human nature as well as an eternal principle	20
Parents are like heaven and earth to children	9
Other justifications	3

The leading justification for filial piety is significantly naturalistic and humane. Since parents have done so much in rearing their children, it is only reasonable for the children to express their gratitude in return. A typical clan rule states the case thus:[13]

A child comes into life after about ten lunar months of pregnancy. He grows up after some three years of feeding in arms. Even when he does his utmost in his mature life to please his parents, he cannot possibly repay more than a small fraction of what his parents have done for him.

Other clan rules regard filial piety as an eternal principle of the universe, inherent in the nature of man.[14] Some clan rules emphatically equate parents with the universe itself:[15]

Since a person derives his very life from the principles of heaven and earth as embodied in his father and mother, he should be forever grateful to them for having brought him into life as much as he should be grateful to heaven and earth.

All these moral justifications for filial piety stress two points: profound gratitude and deep respect. Emotionally, it is a feeling of both warmth and solemnity. A son should revere his parents not because he has to, but because he wants to.

Filial piety may be defined in terms of concrete attitudes and behavior, as revealed in the rules of 77 clans:

mention several of these moral justifications. This clarification also applies to many other itemizations hereafter.

[13] 1918-a, "Family Instructions," item on filial piety, p. 2a.
[14] 1915-e, "Family Instructions," item on filial piety, p. 2; and 1921-1, "Family Instructions," item on filial piety, p. 1a.
[15] 1925-c, "Family Instructions," item on filial piety, p. 2a.

THE CLAN RULES ON FAMILY RELATIONSHIPS

	Number of Clans
To please parents, especially with a pleasing expression even under trying circumstances	49
To support parents with material provisions	48
To remain pious toward parents, even though they might be unkind	32
To bury parents properly and to perform ancestral rites for their spirits thereafter	22
To cause parents no worry	11
To give personal attention to ailing parents	10
To bring parents public honor through official career	10
To require the wife to be equally pious toward parents	10
To have no quibbling between brothers with regard to filial responsibility of providing for parents	6
To have no argument with parents but to advise them gently	5
To please a stepmother as one's own parent	4
To follow father's wishes after his death	1

Generally speaking, filial piety means to take care of the need of parents in their daily life and to give them psychological satisfaction. Between the two, the latter is more important. Confucius laments that "filial piety of the present day merely means to feed one's parents," hardly a virtue.[16] The essential test is whether or not the parents are happy.[17] Other clan rules point out that filial piety is to please parents in more ways than one. In essence, it is to anticipate and to follow their wishes, always in great earnest.[18] According to another clan rule, "The essence of filial piety is to understand and to meet the wishes of parents, during their life as well as after their death. Good food and elaborate sacrificial rites are really secondary."[19] What parents usually cherish is the well-being of the son himself. Therefore he should do nothing to cause them worry.[20] Another wish

---

[16] Soothill (tr.), *The Analects*, Book II, p. 157.
[17] Shimizu, *Kazoku*, p. 420.
[18] 1924–b, "Family Instructions," p. 14b; 1919–b, "Family Instructions," p. 12a.
[19] 1914–d, "Family Regulations," p. 2a.
[20] 1929–c, "Family Regulations," p. 3a; 1930–a, "Family Instructions," item on filial piety, p. 2.

of parents is to enjoy lasting respect, from their son and his wife, during their lifetime and even after their death.[21] If a son through his official career can bring his parents public honor, it will please them no end.[22]

The clan rules by no means underestimate the difficulty of achieving filial piety. Some of them agree realistically that a son's lack of filial piety is not necessarily his own fault; the mistake of his parents may have caused his antagonism.[23] An uncooperative stepmother frequently complicates matters: the father, partial to her, behaves harshly toward the sons by previous marriage who can not help losing some of their filial piety.[24] Parents who become senile and act foolishly can hardly retain the respect of their children.[25] Yet even when parents are hard to please, the clan rules insist that a son should always "endeavor to make his parents happy by bending his own inclination in deference to theirs." He should realize that after all "his parents do not have much time left in this world."[26]

The most difficult part of filial piety, many clan rules agree, is for a son to remain respectful under the trying circumstances when the parents themselves act improperly. A son should offer appropriate advice to keep his parents from making mistakes, yet he can do so only with utmost tact, mild language and pleasing manners, when parents are in a good mood to listen.[27] If the fault of parents is none too serious, he might as well overlook it.[28] The highest ideal of filial piety is to defer to parents without visible displeasure and even without mental reservation.[29]

The second important element of filial piety is to take care of the daily material needs of the parents. The clan rules do not require a

---

[21] 1928–d, "Family Instructions," item on filial piety, p. 1b; 1930–e, "*Tsu* Regulations," p. 1.

[22] 1933–i, "Family Instructions," item on filial piety, p. 2b; 1929–a, "Family Instructions," p. 1a.

[23] 1922–b, "Miscellany of Family Proprieties," p. 2b.

[24] 1930–c, "Family Instructions," p. 1a.

[25] 1920–c, "Standards for Succeeding Generations," p. 4b.

[26] 1919–b, "Family Instructions," p. 2b; 1918–b, "Family Instructions," p. 2a; 1921–q, "Family Instructions," p. 14a.

[27] 1922–b, "Miscellany of Family Proprieties," p. 2b.

[28] 1916–b, "An Epitome of Family Regulations," p. 2a.

[29] Lang, *op. cit.*, p. 25.

son to provide his parents with luxuries, but he should give them the best that the family can reasonably afford within its means.[30] This obligation rests equally on all the sons and none should evade or leave the burden to his brothers.[31] The responsibility also lies with the daughters-in-law, who wait upon the parents.[32] When parents become ill, filial piety takes on an added measure of seriousness. The son himself should be at their bedside as constantly as possible.[33]

The ancestral cult extended filial responsibility beyond the lifetime of parents. The traditional Chinese believed that delay or neglect of burial would cause discomfort to the spirit of deceased parents.[34] To be miserly and fail to bury one's parents with due dignity required by the ritual propriety is a serious offense in the clan rules,[35] often punishable by castigation. Filial piety also requires regular visits to the grave of one's parents and to offer sacrifices to their spirits at customary occasions.[36] On the whole, however, the clan rules are realistic enough in placing more emphasis on what happens during the lifetime of parents than on what should be done after their death.

One clan rule sums up the definition of filial piety extremely well:[37]

Filial piety consists of providing for and attending to the needs of parents everyday. A son should obey their commands, relieve their anger, and remove their worries. When parents are in error, he should give them proper advice, but only with a pleasing countenance. When parents become ill, he should give utmost care and personal attention. A son who does not distinguish himself socially should work hard enough in farming so as to assure his parents of adequate livelihood. A son in an official career should earn good reputation so as to bring his parents public glory. When parents die, a son should not be

[30] 1934–a, "Family Regulations," p. 6b.
[31] 1915–j, "Ancestors' Instructions," item on filial piety, p. 2a.
[32] 1915–h, "Mottoes of *Tsung* Instructions," p. 46b.
[33] 1928–d, "Family Instructions," p. 2a.
[34] 1924–b, "Family Instructions," p. 14b; 1914–d, "*Tsung* Restrictions," p. 2b; 1928–c, "Family Regulations," p. 1b.
[35] 1934–a, "Family Regulations," p. 6b; 1921–c, "Family Regulations," pp. 1b–2a and 1924–a, "Family Instructions," p. 30; 1916–a, "Regulations for Controlling a Family," p. 7a.
[36] 1924–f, "Proclaimed *Tsu* Regulations," p. 2b; 1914–g, "Family Instructions," p. 12a.
[37] 1918–f, "New Family Regulations," p. 12b.

miserly in arranging a proper funeral with good clothing and a coffin for burial. Burial should follow without undue delay at a well chosen site. He should visit the grave of his parents at regular intervals and remember them through memorial service.

Wanton lack of filial piety or misconduct diametrically opposite to it was known in traditional China as the impermissible offense of filial impiety. While many clan rules refer to this offense without defining it, some of them have various specifications:

	Number of Clans
Filial impiety (with no specification)	51
To favor one's wife and dependants to the neglect of parents	13
Offensive contravention of parents	6
Non-support or inadequate support of parents	5
To maintain separate household away from parents	3
To insult and curse parents	3
Battery of parents	2
Neglect of parents' burial and memorial service	2
To hurt parents' feelings	1

Filial impiety essentially means denying one's parents either material provision, or dutiful respect, or both. Providing for parents in a disrespectful manner is hardly different from treating parents like paupers.[38] One clan rule condemns a son for "being partial to his wife, neglectful of his parents, being arrogant to them, and using abusive language to them."[39]

When parents have little control over their sons, the discrepancy between status and reality causes family instability. A few clan rules are flexible enough to advise the dissolution of such a family by allowing the disrespectful son to move away and set up his own household.[40] Most clan rules, however, prohibit such a dissolution. The ideal is to keep a family together as long as feasible, at least while the parents are living. The generation-age hierarchy recognizes no "retirement" of parents from either their status or their authority.

[38] 1921–a, "*Tsung* Regulations," p. 1a; and 1914–a, "*Tsung* Regulations," item on filial piety, p. 1a.
[39] 1914–h, "Family Instructions," item on filial piety, p. 1a.
[40] 1914–e, "Regulations for Controlling a Family," p. 7a.

The fact that some parents are incapable of exercising authority makes no difference. The clan should exert pressure to protect their status by punishing the unfilial son.[41]

Parents who are afraid of their powerful son may suffer him out of their lingering love rather than appeal to the clan for help or bring a formal charge of filial impiety. However, the clan rules regard filial impiety as such a serious clan concern that the clan should act on its own initiative.[42] On the other hand, the rules also protect an innocent son from false charge of filial impiety, for example, by his malicious stepmother or his father under her evil influence.[43] If the clan finds the allegation groundless, it should censure the accuser instead.[44]

Many clan rules arm themselves with definite punitive measures against filial impiety. Punishment varies, depending upon the seriousness of the case and upon whether it is the first time, a repeated offense, or a persistent, incorrigible one.[45] Generally speaking, severe punishments are stipulated at two levels: (1) corporal punishment by flogging or castigation which probably includes some flogging at the ancestral hall; and (2) government punishment under the law. For example, one clan rule stipulates:[46]

A son who contravenes his parents in violation of the clan instruction and neglects to provide for them shall be severely castigated by the clan officers. If he proves to be incorrigible, he should be sent to the government for due punishment under the law. A son, who is partial to his wife and fails to instruct her to respect his parents shall be punished likewise.

Another clan rule proclaims: "Serious cases of filial impiety, so charged by the father or the elder brother, should be sent directly to

---

[41] 1916–c, "Family Instructions," p. 3b; 1919–e, "Family Discipline," p. 11b.
[42] 1926–a, "Instructions of Ancestor Ch'ing-yin-kung," item on filial piety, p. 6b; 1919–e, "Family Discipline," p. 12a.
[43] 1921–j, "Mottoes," words by Shih Chin-ch'en on step-mother under the subject of marital relations.
[44] 1922–g, "Tentative Regulations of the *Tsung*," item on filial piety under the subject of human relationship, p. 4b.
[45] See Table 5 in the Appendix.
[46] 1921–a, "*Tsung* Regulations," p. 1a.

the government. Even light cases of filial impiety should be punished by flogging at the ancestral hall."[47]

It is impractical to punish filial impiety by forfeiting clan privileges or expelling the guilty son from the clan organization. These measures will not help the distressed parents. Nor can the clan take over the responsibility of supporting them. The son must be compelled to fulfill his duties; otherwise, appeal to the government is the last resort.

Since the traditional Chinese society took such a serious view of filial impiety, how did it ever arise? Part of the reason has been mentioned: a son may take over power from his aged parents and turn against them. Some contemporary authors interpret filial impiety in terms of the Freudian father-son antagonism.[48] This is doubtful for the lack of evidence and certainly cannot explain a son's disrespect toward his mother. More applicable, perhaps, is Kardiner's interpretation in the case of the Tanala culture that in the basic personality development there is a trait of hidden hostility against both parents.[49]

The clan rules seem to have anticipated the possible existence of hidden hostility in the children. For instance, according to one clan rule, the disciplinary role of the father should be tempered with kindness, understanding, and forgiveness, and further compensated by the tender love of the mother.[50] Field investigations confirm that when a son comes to age and marries, the parents recognize his status as an adult and a full family member. Henceforth, the father generally refrains from disciplining or scolding him but prepares him to take over family matters. After a son takes over, the parents will avoid excessive interference so as not to irritate him. For the aged parents to retain their authority, they should generally rely more on their own personality than actual power.[51] In the opinion of one clan rule, the best way to sow harmony between parents who have the authority by

---

[47] 1922-g, "Tentative Regulations of the *Tsung*," p. 4b.
[48] Lang, *op. cit.*, pp. 27–28.
[49] Kardiner, *The Individual and His Society*, pp. 301–306.
[50] 1915-g, "Ancestors' Instructions," p. 1a and Lang, *op. cit.*, p. 29.
[51] Martin C. Yang, *op. cit.*, p. 129; Lang, *op. cit.*, pp. 163–164; and Shimizu, *Kazoku*, pp. 426–427.

status and the son who holds real power is for each to be mutually aware of the other's temperament and inclination.[52] Conceivably, hidden hostility may thus be reduced to a minimum and kept under control.

Another reason why filial impiety emerges is the neglect of the parents themselves. In the best Chinese tradition, parents should give the young children proper training in respectful speech, careful manners, and dignified gestures until such become a habit.[53] During meals, children should reach for food only after their elders. This is a necessary and effective training in deference to and recognition of generation-age order.[54] A child should be loved, but not spoiled.[55] One clan rule states that "if a child does not have a proper upbringing while young, he will grow up with neither filial piety nor respect for other elders."[56] By that time, "it will be too late to correct him."[57] The rules of 119 clans give one or more of the following pieces of advice:

	Number of Clans
Male youngsters should be provided with education or schooling	111
Male youngsters must be trained properly (unspecified)	87
Sons, especially, should be subject to strict discipline without being spoiled	43
Male youngsters must be provided with proper vocational training	28
Girls should also be provided with some schooling or knowledge of reading	14
Girls should also be disciplined to know proper manners and household work	7

---

[52] 1920–c, *op. cit.*, pp. 1a–1b.
[53] Cf. Francis L. K. Hsu, *American and Chinese: Two Ways of Life*, pp. 79–83; 1915–g, "Ancestors' Instructions," p. 1b; cf. Ch'en Hung-mou, *Yang-cheng i-kuei* [*Rules on Proper Upbringing*] (*Ssu-pu pei-yao* ed.), *ts'e* 159, *chüan* 1, pp. 3–17.
[54] 1924–a, *op. cit.*, p. 1b.
[55] 1920–c, *op. cit.*, p. 2b.
[56] 1914–d, "Family Regulations," p. 2a.
[57] 1916–c, "Family Instructions," p. 1b.

According to some clan rules, education and proper training of children are considered so important that fathers and elder brothers who fail to discharge this responsibility should suffer due chastisement.[58] One clan rule asks if parents fail to impress upon their offspring the inviolability of the generation-age order, how can they spare themselves eventually the humiliation of filial impiety?[59] The strict discipline of children contributes not only to family order but also to community peace. It has been observed that Chinese parents abhorred fighting and brawling among children far more than the parents in Western society.[60]

To prevent filial impiety, the clan rules urge the father to exercise his parental authority without abuse and only for the well-being of family members.[61] As one clan rule explains:[62]

Filial impiety and parent-child disputes are often caused by a father who favors his concubine and neglects his wife, who does not treat his sons equally well, or who shows special favor toward the younger sons by giving them a better portion of the family property. It is up to the parents themselves to realize these mistakes and avoid them.

Some clan rules accordingly stipulate punishment for a father who allows his children to be mistreated by their stepmother.[63]

The discussion of both filial piety and impiety underscores the significance of mutuality. Parental authority, though supreme over children, is not absolute. Parent-child relationship is not simply a superordinate-subordinate relationship, but one which is characterized by mutual obligations with both sides observing their defined roles. Mutuality is in fact at the root of such traits known as forbearance, conciliation, toleration, and patience, governing many other relationships. A celebrated case was the Chang family who lived together for nine successive generations during the T'ang Dynasty. When questioned by the emperor as to the secret of this unusual family harmony and continuity, the head of the family, instead of

---

[58] 1922–b, "Family Regulatios," p. 1b; see also Table 6 in the Appendix.
[59] 1919–e, "Family Teachings," p. 6a.
[60] Lang, *op. cit.*, p. 239.
[61] *Ibid.*, p. 26.
[62] 1929–a, "The Twelve Injunctions," p. 1a.
[63] 1930–a, "*Tsu* Standards," p. 19. See Table 7 in the Appendix.

giving an oral reply, wrote the word patience (*jen* 忍) a hundred times. This case has been quoted by many rules as the model of "hundred patience."[64] In the closely knit structure of the Chinese family, mutuality between parents and children, as well as between all other members, is a necessary condition.

Mutuality is also emphasized in the rules of no fewer than 30 clans which regard the following serious default of parental responsibility as punishable offenses:[65]

	Number of Clans
Selling children into servitude	15
Infanticide of daughter by drowning	10
Giving away children to Buddhist or Taoist temples	4
Mistreating children by inflicting bodily harm	3
Mistreating patrilocal fiancée of the son[66]	3
Marrying daughter off as concubine	2
Selling daughter into prostitution	2
Giving away son to another family	1

The clan regards the child as a member of the group. Reducing a child to a disgraceful social status reflects unfavorably upon the clan. One clan rule even considers some of the above offenses as humiliation of the ancestors.[67] Some clan rules stipulate that the offending father should be excluded from the ancestral hall, expunged from the genealogy, or expelled from the clan.[68]

Giving away children to religious organizations is regarded as "a very regrettable custom,"[69] as it denies the children their due place in the society and the clan its potential manpower. A far worse custom is infanticide, "a deplorable offense which is forbidden by law and should also be punished by the clan."[70] Several clan rules condemn its cruelty and inhumanity.[71] "Human life is sacred. To kill is

---

[64] 1919–e, "Family Discipline," p. 12b; 1914–h, "Family Instructions," p. 3a; and 1916–c, "Family Instructions," p. 2a.
[65] See Table 7 in the Appendix.
[66] It was a custom for a girl from a poor family to come and live with the family of her fiancé and render domestic help.
[67] 1916–a, "Regulations for Controlling a Family," item on ancestral hall, p. 2a.
[68] 1934–f, "*Tsu* Regulations," item on selling children, p. 2b.
[69] 1916–c, "Family Instructions," p. 2a.
[70] 1919–e, "Family Discipline," item on infanticide, p. 9a.
[71] 1929–a, "The Twelve Injunctions," item on infanticide, p. 5a.

an unforgivable crime. People even call for help when they see the lives of other people in danger. How can one possibly kill his own infant ? ... It is as guilty as murder."[72] Another clan rule states: "If all infant girls are to be sacrificed, mankind will soon come to an end."[73] Some clan rules try to dissuade infanticide by offering some hope: "The parents should realize that the family may yet manage to get along without killing the child."[74] Besides, "who can tell whether the victim girl, if she grows up, might not have a better destiny ?"[75]

The stipulated punishments for the default of parental responsibility has an interesting feature of retaliation.[76] For parents who let their children fall into disgraceful social status, the clan in retaliation should deprive the unworthy parents of their status in the clan group. The fact remains, however, that many parents were forced by poverty to give up their children and thereby also their clan status.[77] In other words, the security of one's status depends on the minimum economic solvency of a man or his family, in which situation the clan is not particularly helpful.

B. RELATIONSHIP BETWEEN BROTHERS

The clan rules generally mention brotherly love immediately after filial piety, in accordance with the Confucian tradition. However, primogeniture had long been abandoned, and every son had an equal right of inheritance, the eldest one had no more than a pre-ëminence among equals, rather than predomination over his younger brothers. Senior status by age carried far less weight than senior status by generation. As the succeeding head of the family, he had a limited authority over his younger brothers so long as they were willing to

---

[72] 1914–f, "Family Instructions," p. 7a.
[73] 1929–a, "The Twelve Injunctions," p. 5a.
[74] 1931–c, "Instructions and Regulations," p. 22b.
[75] 1914–g, "Family Instructions," p. 4a.
[76] See Table 7 in the Appendix.
[77] *MSSHK*, pp. 788, 794, and 961; and 1917–b, "Existing Regulations of the Charitable Estate," p. 1b.

remain in the same household and to cooperate with him by deference.[78] The tendency during and after the Sung period was for the majority of families to split up among the brothers upon the death of the father.[79] Nonetheless, the clan rules do uphold the value of brotherly love in order to discourage this tendency and to promote family harmony between married brothers and their dependants.

The cooperative nature of brotherly relations is shown in the rules of 63 clans, which offer the following reasons as its justifications:

	Number of Clans
Brothers have a natural affinity	56
No love between brothers is as bad as filial impiety	8
Brothers share much common interest	7
Brotherly love prevents outsiders from taking advantage	6

The sentimental appeal for brotherly love is mingled with the realistic persuasion that brothers will find it advantageous to cooperate with each other. One clan rule states: "The dispute between brothers over family property usually plays into the hands of outsiders who take advantage of them."[80] Another clan rule explains that "brothers are joined naturally like limbs of a body. They should be united in sentiment, defend themselves against others, and help each other in distress."[81] When the clan rules appeal to authority in order to maintain brotherly love, it is to the parental authority.[82] Nothing is said at all about the elder brother having a predominant authority over his younger brother. As one clan rule puts it, "To mistreat a brother is to mistreat the parents."[83]

The cooperative nature of brotherly love is further demonstrated by the way the rules of 43 clans define this virtue:

---

[78] Levy, op. cit., pp. 159–161; and MSSHK, p. 702.
[79] KCTSCC, Chia-fan tien, ts'e 613, chüan 3, p. 2; Shimizu, Kazoku, p. 446; and Ch'ü, op. cit., p. 17.
[80] 1913–e, "Regulations of the Ancestral Hall," item on brotherly conduct, p. 2b.
[81] 1914–h, op. cit., p. 2b.
[82] Shimizu, Kazoku, pp. 454–455 and Hsu, Under the Ancestors' Shadow, p. 61.
[83] 1923–c, "Regulations and Instructions," item on brothers, p. 9a.

	Number of Clans
Affection from elder brother and respect from younger brother	24
Sharing property in common with one's brother	10
Taking care of widow and orphans of one's deceased brother	8
Harboring no grievances and resentment against one's brother	3

The standard definition for brotherly love is affection from the elder brother and respect from a younger brother. "By affection, it is meant kindness with due regard; and by respect, it is meant deference and cooperation."[84] Brotherly love is thus an attitude of mutual cordiality which composes differences between brothers in the interest of family harmony. The essential point is "not to argue with one another."[85] Frequently, "troubles develop because brothers are incensed at each other and neither side will yield. Troubles will subside if one side suppresses his anger and makes up with a few kind words."[86]

Unbrotherly conduct is the commission of aggressive act against one's brother or his dependants or the omission of certain acts that are required by the social ethics. In the rules of 97 clans, the following types of misbehavior are considered unbrotherly:

	Number of Clans
Dispute over family property	56
Yielding to wife's influence against one's brother	56
Lack of brotherly love (with no specification)	27
Quarreling and fighting	12
Mistreating or taking advantage of a younger brother	6
Contravening or disobeying an elder brother	5
Insulting or cursing an elder brother	3
Beating an elder brother	1

Lack of brotherly love, while not specified in many rules, is defined in others as a total lack of cooperation making it impossible for the brothers to remain in the same household. No family can go on if

---

[84] 1921-j, "Mottoes," p. 7a.
[85] 1920-c, *op. cit.*, pp. 3b, 9b, and 10b.
[86] 1916-c, "Family Instructions," p. 3a.

"the brothers curse and insult each other, particularly when the younger offend their elder brothers and their wives."[87] On the other hand, younger brothers deserve fair treatment from their elder brothers "who should not seize the best part of the family property."[88] The clan rules also require an equal treatment between one's own dependants and that of his brothers.[89]

Punishment for unbrotherly conduct generally follows the same pattern as that for filial impiety, though it is not nearly so severe.[90] The types of punishment most frequently stipulated are castigation and corporal punishment. The next frequent type is to send the offender to the government for punishment. However, light cases and first-time offenders are subject only to oral censure, ritual penalty, or monetary fine; while serious cases of repeated and incorrigible offenders should suffer more severe punishment.[91] Sometimes, the clan rules advise such punitive measures as denial of clan privileges and expulsion from the clan organization. When an individual infringes upon his brother's status, he should be deprived of his own status in the clan.

The rules of 97 clans mention the following causes of unbrotherly conduct:

	Number of Clans
Craving for family property or inheritance	56
Influence of a selfish wife	56
Friction between the brothers' wives	19
Jealousy caused by a brother's obtaining wealth from sources outside the family	9
Favoritism of parents in not treating sons equally, especially between sons of a wife and sons of a concubine	4
Gossip of domestic servants	3
Difference in temperament of brothers	2
Refusal to let a son be the heir of a brother	1

[87] 1923–c, *op. cit.*, p. 9a.
[88] 1921–a, "*Tsung* Regulations," p. 10a.
[89] 1920–c, *op. cit.*, p. 12b.
[90] See Table 9 in the Appendix.
[91] 1920–a, "*Tsung* Discipline," item on punishment, p. 10b; 1916–a, "The Six Omissions from the Genealogy," p. 25a; and 1918–c, "*Tsung* Restrictions," p. 1a.

As one scholar points out, it is no easy task for the brothers in a large household to maintain harmony.[92] One clan rule describes the difficulty clearly: "The reasons why brothers do not get along well are always the same. They crave wealth and each favors his own wife and dependants."[93] Another clan rule warns: "Brothers should not dispute over money and property, nor listen to their wives whose bad influence usually sows discord."[94] Besides property disputes and the divisive influence of wives, there are other causes. The lack of fair treatment from parents and the disparity of achievement between brothers both contribute to the disappearance of brotherly love.[95]

The fundamental cause of friction between brothers is in the family organization. First, the pooling of income is required by many families. As a typical clan rule states the ideal: "One should turn over to his parents his salary, income, land, and house. When he needs money, he should ask his parents for it."[96] What he has contributed becomes the common family asset and his brothers have an equal right to it as he does. This ideal principle was not, however, rigidly followed in reality. Sons usually contributed to the family only a share of their income from sources outside the family such as salary and business profit and kept the rest as their own.[97] The disparity between the ideal and the practice points toward argument between brothers. Second, brothers and their dependants enjoy common consumption from the common family asset. This creates additional difficulty. Third, inheritance of equal shares frequently leads to dispute. An aggressive brother may take advantage of his younger brothers, weak brothers, or orphaned nephews, without giving them a fair portion.[98]

These frictions are seen in the living conditions of a large joint family. It is easier for a struggling family to cooperate because whatever the family saves benefits all members. With a relatively well-to-

---

[92] Martin C. Yang, *op. cit.*, p. 68.
[93] 1929–c, "Family Regulations," p. 1a.
[94] 1914–h, *op. cit.*, p. 2b.
[95] 1920–c, *op. cit.*, pp. 7–14.
[96] 1922–b, "Miscellany of Family Proprieties," p. 1.
[97] Lang, *op. cit.*, p. 17.
[98] 1914–j, "Family Regulations," p. 3b.

do family, some of its members prefer better enjoyment of life while others wish to keep on saving.[99] Common consumption becomes a problem, especially when the brothers have varying earning power. One who earns more from sources outside the family may wish to give his dependants some extra goods and services in addition to their common share in the family. This arouses the jealousy of other family members. Also, the earning members who value industriousness and frugality resent their unproductive brothers who live off the common pool of family income.[100]

Three viewpoints are possible on the question of common consumption. The first is the viewpoint based on self-interest that each brother and his dependants should receive the amount of goods and services in the family commensurate with what he contributes to the family.[101] However, the clan rules generally reject this viewpoint in favor of the second viewpoint, a more idealistic one, which holds that all family members should share the goods and services with neither disparity nor discrimination. From the parents' standpoint, their love for their children should be equal. As one clan rule says:[102]

If the earnings of the sons vary, there is all the more reason for parents to maintain a balance between them. Parents often help a low-income son by giving him more food and clothing and by turning over to him what a well-to-do son has contributed to the family. This is because parents love their sons equally well. The well-to-do son must not complain thoughtlessly. He should realize that if he were the poor one, his parents would do the same for him.

The third viewpoint admits the difficulty of equal common consumption and advises that each conjugal unit should take care of its own consumption separately:[103]

It will be ideal for several generations to live together. However, this is sometimes impossible. Many unproductive sons are burdens upon others. Some members are frugal, others are extravagant. It will be better under these circumstances to appropriate money for

[99] Martin C. Yang, *op. cit.*, pp. 80–81.
[100] 1920–c, *op. cit.*, p. 9b.
[101] Lang, *op. cit.*, p. 160.
[102] 1920–c, *op. cit.*, pp. 7b and 8a.
[103] 1930–c, "Family Instructions," p. 4b.

daily consumption to each of the sons and let them take care themselves of the expenses of their own conjugal units. This will avoid disputes.

Another clan rule openly advocates the dissolution of disharmonious joint family: "When brothers and their conjugal units quarrel with one another, why not let them live separately and yet maintain cordial relations? Even when parents are still living, brothers may set up families of their own."[104]

The problem of common consumption in the family is vividly illustrated by meal arrangements. In a harmonious family, members all eat the same meal provided from the common kitchen, "without permitting members to enjoy private meals by themselves."[105] In a less harmonious family, brothers "live together but have separate meals with their own dependants in their apartments."[106] This is done in no less than three different ways: either the conjugal units receive the same meal from the common kitchen and feel free to add whatever they like on their own, or they take turns using the common kitchen and each unit prepares its own meal, or they have little kitchens in their own apartments. None of these arrangements eliminates jealousy and friction entirely.

A large number of the clan rules puts the blame for unbrotherly conduct on the wives. They hold that women are by nature "uncooperative and jealous."[107] Unfortunately for the wives, they are the first ones to get into daily friction over common consumption.[108] One clan rule gives the further explanation that since the sisters-in-law come from different family backgrounds, "the ones from rich families despise the ones from poor families and the smart ones make fun of the slow ones."[109] Another clan rule points out that "sisters-in-law, being selfish and jealous of one another, sow discord between their husbands . . . Their domestic servants, in maneuvering their respec-

---

[104] 1914–e, *op. cit.*, p. 7a.
[105] 1921–q, "Family Regulations," p. 7a; 1916–c, "Family Instructions," p. 3b.
[106] 1921–l, "Family Advices," pp. 4b–5a.
[107] 1922–f, "Family Instructions," p. 4a; 1920–c, *op. cit.*, p. 14.
[108] Hsu, *Under the Ancestors' Shadow*, p. 121; Lang, *op. cit.*, p. 31; and Martin C. Yang, *op. cit.*, p. 67.
[109] 1930–e, "*Tsu* Regulations," p. 2a; 1921–q, "Family Regulations," p. 11a.

tive masters against one another, complicate the situation even more and cause a great deal of friction."[110] Gossip leads to domestic disputes:[111]

When family members repeat what is said of one another behind the back, many disputes will arise. Even sages would be helpless ... What is said behind another's back should not be repeated to him. Since he does not know, no dispute will ensue ... When words get repeated back and forth, especially with distortion by either addition or omission, the resulting misunderstanding is often beyond repair. Wise persons will simply refuse to listen to family gossip.

The wives, not being originally members of the family, have fewer bonds between them to sustain the accumulated tension of trivial frictions over what one has and what one does not have.[112] But most rules have probably over-stressed or exaggerated the non-cooperation between wives. Some rules point out that husbands have the responsibility to dissuade their wives from quarreling or to refuse to share the prejudice of the ladies.[113] The root of the question is whether brothers themselves, independent of their wives' influence, have real affection for one another. The answer in many cases is likely to be in the negative.[114]

Difference between brothers is also caused by parental favoritism.[115] One clan rule reads:[116]

The father who dislikes the mother and favors the concubine, the parents who lack fairness in treatment of their various sons, the parents who fail to allot equal shares of family property to their sons: all cause dispute among the brothers.

Another commonly known cause is the stepmother who mistreats the children of the previous wife.[117]

[110] 1930–c, "Family Instructions," p. 3b.
[111] 1920–c, *op. cit.*, p. 14a.
[112] 1918–e, "Instructions for Succeeding Generations," p. 24a.
[113] 1914–d, "*Tsung* Agreement," p. 1b.
[114] Hsu, *Under the Ancestors' Shadow*, p. 129.
[115] 1914–b, "The Twelve Injunctions," p. 3a.
[116] 1929–a, "The Twelve Injunctions," p. 1a.
[117] 1920–c, *op. cit.*, p. 8b.

Psychologically, sibling rivalry is probably connected with the hidden hostility toward the father. Since the father is too powerful to be antagonized, the hostility is reflected upon the brother.[118] This is very likely when the parents shift their love from an elder son to a younger son.[119] Kardiner in his study of the Tanala culture considers sworn brotherhood as a compensating institution for sibling rivalry.[120] To a certain extent, the same may well apply to China. One clan rule, for instance, wonders why "people do not care much for their own brothers and yet pledge their friends as sworn brothers."[121]

The psychological factor which underlies unbrotherly conduct is inseparable from the socio-economic factor. Personal attainments outside the family often drive the brothers apart.[122] According to one clan rule, "When a person attains wealth and social prominence, he becomes the object of jealousy to his brothers." It is not easy "to disregard the disparity as of no consequence."[123] Since brothers themselves dislike one another, the friction between their wives is either a consequence or no more than a contributing factor.

A strained relationship between the brothers enters into a crisis when the time comes to divide the family property. A father with foresight sometimes allots the inheritance before his own death. One clan rule records what a father said on such an occasion:[124]

Three of you are the offspring of my first wife and two of you, of my second wife. Since you are not willing to cooperate with each other, I have now divided the family property among you. From now on, you should each take care of your own livelihood but remain cordial with one another.

Cases similar to the above were relatively few.[125] In dividing family property, it was customarily necessary to decide who among the brothers would assume the responsibility of supporting the living or

[118] Kardiner, *The Individual and His Society*, p. 315.
[119] 1920–c, *op. cit.*, p. 8a.
[120] Kardiner, *The Individual and His Society*, pp. 326–327.
[121] 1928–c, "Family Regulations," p. 4.
[122] Levy, *op. cit.*, pp. 152–159.
[123] 1930–c, "Family Instructions," p. 3b.
[124] 1934–f, "Family Instructions," p. 1a.
[125] Shimizu, *Kazoku*, pp. 164–167; Fei Hsiao-t'ung and Chang Chih-i, *Earthbound China*, p. 115.

surviving parent. The custom in some regions was to choose this son by drawing lots at random and to give him a slightly larger share of inheritance.[126]

The principle of giving each son an equal share of inheritance varied somewhat with local custom. In some places, the eldest son received a double share of inheritance either on the ground of his having more grown-up offspring than his younger brothers, or in partial imitation of the ancient feudal rule of primogeniture. Sons of the wife usually got more than the sons of a concubine. But many localities allowed none of these deviations from the principle.[127] The major difficulty in implementing the principle is the question of equal value. As real property does not always lend itself conveniently to exactly equal shares by size and by quality, "brothers often get into quarrels over inheritance by choosing land of better quality and refusing land of inferior quality."[128]

When brothers did not agree among themselves on the division of property, it was customary to submit the case to arbitration by the clan officers. The clan rules warn that neither should the elder brother trespass upon the inheritance right of the younger ones, nor *vice versa*.[129] Yet arbitration requires the consideration of many complicating factors. A son may claim that a certain piece of property, having come to him from his wife's dowry or entirely from his personal career, should not be regarded as a part of the common property. Other sons would retort that whatever he earns himself is not entirely his own fortune, as his personal fortune begins with the initial help of the family. The brothers feel that their sacrifice has made an indirect contribution to his personal success and should share what he mistakenly alleges to be his personal property.[130] If clan officers are unable to settle inheritance disputes to the satisfaction of the parties involved, the case often goes into court.[131]

---

[126] *MSSHK*, pp. 52, 633, 864, and 885.
[127] Shimizu, *Kazoku*, pp. 135–176; and *MSSHK*, pp. 649–655.
[128] Martin C. Yang, *op. cit.*, p. 83 and 1914–d, "*Tsung* Agreement," p. 2b.
[129] 1921–a, "*Tsung* Regulations," p. 10; and 1914–d, "*Tsung* Restrictions," p. 3a.
[130] 1920–c, *op. cit.*, pp. 10–11.
[131] 1931–a, "Family Regulations," p. 1a.

The clan rules invariably deplore litigation, principally because it is costly to all.

The various causes of unbrotherly conduct reflect an inherent weakness and instability in the family organization. Only parental authority can keep under control the dissatisfaction resulting from common consumption, the friction between the wives living in the same household, the conflict between brothers because of differences and jealousy, and the disputes over inheritance. Once parental authority declines or disappears, no other control is powerful enough to maintain family harmony. The sentimental appeal of the clan rule is hardly enough to overcome the substantive difficulties. Ritual-ethics and status-ethics are helpful only within limits, for the pre-eminent status of an elder brother does not give him a controlling authority. The best that the clan can do is to reduce the conflicts between brothers in some measure, to punish undue aggression, to prevent mistreatment, to disallow unfair settlement of inheritance, and to facilitate a smooth dissolution of one family into several. The clan cannot really instill the spirit of brotherly cooperation to keep a family together. In fact the average family in traditional China did not succeed in keeping more than three generations together but underwent a perpetual splitting process.[132] What the clan institution seeks to achieve is a cordial bond among the descendants of a family after its dissolution.

C. HEIR AND ADOPTION OF HEIR

A male heir was necessary "to keep the incense smoke burning" for the ancestral rites and to continue the family descent line.[133] One who left behind him a son and some property felt that he had made a lasting contribution to the future family prosperity. Having no heir was believed to be a terrible misfortune and, as Mencius said, a failure in filial piety toward the ancestors.

Concubinage was justified for the purpose of begetting an heir. One clan rule permits an heirless person over thirty years old to take a concubine,[134] but many other clan rules give such permission only to

[132] Cf. Ch'ü, *op. cit.*, pp. 3–4.   [133] 1914–j, "Family Regulations," p. 5a.
[134] 1934–a, "Family Regulations," p. 6b.

an heirless person over forty.[135] A few rules even encourage such persons to do so and stipulate financial aid for those who need it.[136] The main provisions on concubinage in the rules of 14 clans are summarized here:

	Number of Clans
Concubinage permitted:	
When an heirless man is over forty years old	8
When an heirless man is over thirty years old	1
Concubinage opposed:	
When one already has a son	3
When one is too old	2
When one already has a concubine but wants another	2
When one is still under forty years of age	1
When one's real motivation is the beauty of the woman	1
Concubinage forbidden for status and morality reasons:	
Taking an indentured servant as concubine	5
Taking a prostitute as concubine	2
Taking a woman as concubine after adultery	1
Categorical opposition to concubinage	1

Most rules prefer not to discuss concubinage, admittedly an indulgence of the wealthy.[137] Only a few rules mention it and lay down certain injunctions: he who takes a concubine before he is forty years old should be punished by monetary fine and he who takes a concubine when he already has a son should be punished more severely by flogging.[138] Aged men should take no concubine.[139] Nor should one take two or more concubines as it would "cause endless family disputes."[140] One modernized clan rule categorically condemns concubinage as "being inhumane and disturbing proper family relations."[141]

[135] 1921–i, "Family Instructions," p. 5a.
[136] 1923–b, "Regulations of the Charitable Estate," p. 21a and 1924–d, Regulations of the Charitable Estate," p. 4b.
[137] Lang, op. cit., pp. 220–221.
[138] See Table 13 in the Appendix; 1921–q, "Miscellaneous Instructions for Controlling a Family," p. 19 and 1930–d, "*Tsu* Regulations," p. 3a.
[139] 1914–g, op. cit., p. 15b.
[140] 1914–e, op. cit., p. 6b.
[141] 1930–b, "Regulations," p. 8b.

On the whole, these rules show no adequate control over this upper class abuse and laxity of Confucian morality. In fact, they betray a double standard in forbidding the giving away of a daughter to be a concubine while expressing no disapproval of taking a concubine.[142]

Heirs have to be so recognized by the clan according to the rules. A son by a marriage unknown to the clan should have neither status in the group nor the privilege to enter the ancestral hall or take part in the rites.[143] An illegitimate son born out of wedlock is similarly rejected.[144] However, the clan after due consideration may agree to confirm such a person as a legitimate heir.[145]

One who has no son should adopt someone in the clan as his heir. However, the rules of 60 clans differ considerably on how to choose an heir properly. The difference is summarized as follows:

		Number of Clans
(a)	One should adopt an heir only from one's clan	43
(b)	One should adopt an heir among his closest available kin of the next generation in the clan	22
(c)	One may select as heir any one of the next generation in the clan whom he likes	13
(d)	One must abide by (b) and desist from (c)	4
(e)	The clan shall take care of the ancestral rites for an heirless person after his death	6
(f)	The clan shall not allow dispute over adoption motivated by coveting the property involved	6
(g)	The clan shall select an heir for a surviving widow	4
(h)	The clan shall require an adopted heir to be pious toward the adopting parents	3

The generation-age order dictates that an heir should be selected from one's next generation.[146] Under this principle, the ideal is to adopt an heir very close to the original descent line. Many clan rules advise the adoption of a nephew who is the nearest kin.[147] In case one brother

[142] 1915-d, "*Tsu* Regulations," p. 1b.
[143] 1931-d, "*Tsung* Regulations," p. 3b.
[144] 1934-f, "*Tsu* Regulations," p. 7a; see also Table 8 in the Appendix.
[145] *MSSHK*, pp. 698–699 and 828.
[146] 1930-c, "Regulations of the Ancestral Hall," item on adoption, p. 1b.
[147] Hsu, *Under the Ancestors' Shadow*, p. 250; Martin Yang, *op. cit.*, p. 83.

has no son and his brother has only one, they may share the same heir. When the heir in turn has several sons, he shall designate one of them to be the next heir of his adopted father in reinstituting a separate descent line.[148] Yet adoption of nephew as one's heir is not always feasible if one is not on good terms with the brother; either he or his brother will be unwilling. Moreover, the adopting person may prefer a bright, handsome, and promising boy in the clan, though not closely related to him. Conflict develops between the ideal on the one hand and either availability for adoption or individual preference on the other.

The conflict calls for a flexible compromise.[149] For instance, one clan rule states:[150]

When a sonless person adopts an heir, he must choose from the proper generation group in the clan. Within this group, he should prefer those who are closely related to him. However, he is also permitted to choose the one whom he likes best. When he finds no closely related kin is available for adoption, he may then select an heir among distant kin.

On the other hand, closely related kin with an eye on the property of the adopting family would often force their son upon it.[151] Therefore, some clan rules not only permit the choice of a distant kinsman by preference but also forbid other clan members from disputing the choice.[152] But other clan rules warn that adoption which ignores the criterion of close blood relationship easily leads to dispute.[153] Jealous or disappointed kin would frequently denounce such an adoption as the result of flattery or deception.[154] In order to prevent disputes from arising, many rules advise that adoption by preference should be formally recognized by the clan organization.[155] Some rules require a

---

[148] 1916–d, "Additional Rules of Genealogy," item on adoption, p. 1b.
[149] *MSSHK*, pp. 841–842.
[150] 1925–a, "Family Regulations," p. 1a.
[151] 1913–b, "Officially Registered Regulations," p. 2b.
[152] *MSSHK*, p. 643.
[153] 1918–g, "Family Instructions," p. 2b; *MSSHK*, p. 780.
[154] *MSSHK*, p. 718.
[155] 1930–c, "Regulations of the Ancestral Hall," p. 1b.

financial contribution in connection with such adoption so that other members will have less ground for complaint.[156]

When someone died without adopting an heir, the clan officers had the right to choose one for him. According to one clan rule, "If a widow is pregnant before the death of her husband, she should report her condition to the clan so that if it is a son there will be no doubt or question of heir."[157] In general, a widow should not decide on adoption by herself; certainly not to dispose of the family property without the knowledge of the clan.[158] When the clan officers consider the adoption on behalf of a family, blood relation proximity should prevail.[159] But they should see to it that the adopted heir will be obedient and respectful to the widowed mother.[160]

The clan rules stipulate the punishment for improper adoption. Some rules, while disapproving adoption by preference, impose no punishment for it. But when adoption confuses the generation-age order, the adopting father should, according to a few rules, suffer some lenient punishment. No fewer than twenty rules forbid the adoption of a non-clan member. He who so adopts should suffer castigation, flogging at the ancestral hall, or the denial of clan privileges.[161]

Objections against adopting non-clan members are numerous. In the first place, the law prohibited a man from assuming a family name other than his own.[162] Second, for an outsider to come into the clan through adoption violates patrilineal homogeneity.[163] Third, several generations henceforth, the descendants of this improperly adopted heir might unknowingly marry someone of his original clan and such marriage would be a violation of clan exogamy forbidden by the law.[164] Fourth, an outsider adopted as heir might move away and take the family property with him, which would be a loss in resources for the

[156] 1918–c, "New Regulations of the Ancestral Hall," p. 3a.
[157] 1920–c, *op. cit.*, p. 19b.
[158] 1930–d, "*Tsu* Regulations," p. 2b; also see Table 8 in the Appendix.
[159] 1913–b, "Officially Registered Regulations," p, 2b.
[160] 1929–a, "The Twelve Injunctions," p. 2a; and Table 8 in the Appendix.
[161] See Table 8 in the Appendix.
[162] 1916–d, "Twenty-one Rules of the Genealogy," p. 3a; 1921–f, "Abridged Statements from the Law of Adoption," p. 1.
[163] 1919–a, "Family Regulations," p. 2b.
[164] 1920–c, *op. cit.*, p. 18b.

clan group.[165] One clan rule, for example, has the stern injunction that in case of such an improper adoption the clan should not only refuse to recognize the heir but should confiscate the property of that family.[166] The rules of no fewer than 51 clans, as shown in the following summary, have a negative attitude toward adoption of an outsider as well as toward that of a member by another clan:

	Number of Clans
Adoption of a non-clan member as heir:	
Ban with punishment	22
Ban with no punishment mentioned	21
Conditional acceptance	9
Adoption of a matrilocal son-in-law as heir:	
Ban with punishment	3
Ban with no punishment mentioned	6
Conditional acceptance	4
Clan member as heir in another clan:	
Ban with punishment	9
Ban with no punishment mentioned	4
Conditional permission	1

Adoption of non-clan members was sometimes inevitable under abnormal conditions. For example, many families disrupted during the T'ai-p'ing rebellion (1850–1865) took abandoned or refugee boys to be their heirs.[167] "Such an adoption deserves sympathy," as one rule admits, "and to nullify it after long lapse of time would discontinue the descent line."[168] While the adoption should be recognized as legitimate, it should not be used as a precedent. Some clan rules permit such adoption only when there is no one available in the clan.[169] In any event, clan approval is necessary. Upon granting approval, the clan may, according to some rules, record the boy's family name by birth so that his future descendants are clearly separated. None of them is eligible to be the clan head.[170] Other clan rules require those

---

[165] 1918–g, *op. cit.*, p. 2a.
[166] 1919–a, "Family Regulations," p. 2b.
[167] 1933–d, "Regulations of the Eleventh Edition of Genealogy," p. 1a; and *MSSHK*, pp. 843–846.
[168] 1916–d, "Additional Rules of Genealogy," p. 3a.
[169] 1925–e, "*Tsu* Agreement," p. 1a; and 1930–d, "*Tsu* Regulations," p. 3a.
[170] 1934–f, "*Tsu* Regulations," p. 1b; *MSSHK*, p. 866; 1920–d, "Additional Family Regulations," p. 6b; and 1915–d, "*Tsu* Regulations," p. 1a.

who so adopt to make a contribution to the ancestral hall as if to compensate the clan for having allowed the property of a component family to be inherited by an outsider.[171]

A matrilocal son-in-law is a special case, for he lives with the family of his wife and formally changes his surname into that of the family.[172] A few rules look upon the practice with disfavor and insist that he should not succeed as the heir.[173] If the parents like him, he might share some portion of the family property. A proper heir would still be required.[174] One modernized rule in advocating the equality of sexes gives the property to the daughter, but states nevertheless that if the daughter dies without a son, the clan should choose an heir for her. If her husband remarries, he should return to his own clan.[175]

By the same logic, the clan rules generally disallow their members to become heirs in another clan, for the clan would suffer the loss of this member and whatever advantage it might derive from his future success. Some rules stipulate that the father or the elder brother responsible for the act shall be castigated at the ancestral hall as if guilty of filial impiety.[176] If the family needs the boy to be its own heir, the clan officers should, after flogging the guilty party, cause the adoption to be nullified. Even if the adoption should be allowed to take place, the clan would not relinquish its claim on the boy and still keep his name in the genealogy. Should his family by birth need an heir later on, the clan has the right to order his return.[177]

Disputes of adoption are in reality disputes of inheritance and frequently develop into costly litigation.[178] A number of rules warn

[171] 1918–c, "New Regulations of the Ancestral Hall," p. 3a.
[172] *MSSHK*, pp. 770–771.
[173] 1921–i, "Mottoes of Former Scholar Lu Ch'ing-hsien," p. 4b; 1924–f, "Additional Regulations," p. 2b; *MSSHK*, p. 703.
[174] 1921–f, "Abridged Statements from the Law of Adoption," p. 2; 1930–d, "*Tsu* Regulations," p. 3a.
[175] 1914–e, *op. cit.*, p. 8.
[176] 1924–h, "Family Decisions" (1860), p. 3a.
[177] 1921–c, "Regulations of the Genealogy," p. 1b; 1929–d, "Regulations of the Genealogy," p. 6b.
[178] 1930–e, "Contemporary Acupuncture," p. 1a; and 1921–a, "*Tsung* Regulations," p. 3.

that no one should force his son upon a wealthy family as its heir; though few rules mention punishment for making such an attempt, unless it becomes a dispute.[179] A poor family, on the other hand, was often unable to get an adopted heir; nor could a clan force someone to be its heir against his own wishes. One clan rule offers a compromise: "One should not refuse to become the heir of a closely related family because it is poor. He shall be permitted to retain his inheritance in his family by birth. However, heirs adopted by families with property shall not cite this provision as a precedent."[180] When a family found no one to adopt, the clan had the responsibility to take care of the ancestral rites for that family lineage, such as a separate room in the ancestral hall reserved for the disrupted descent lines.[181] Other clans, not so well situated, would assume this responsibility provided it took over whatever family property there was.[182] Some clans would perform the rites for an heirless family if it had previously donated some land to the clan.[183] These measures reveal the practical limitations of the clan institution.

The content of the clan rules on heir and adoption seems to be primarily concerned with proper status and only secondarily with the family property involved. The clan has no direct control over the property of the individual families so long as there is neither question of status nor dispute between clan members.

D. MARRIAGE

As mentioned at the beginning of this chapter, the first set of family relationship concerns the generation-age hierarchy, while the second set involves the female members such as marriage, conduct of wife, status of concubine, status of widow, and seclusion of women. Marriage as the beginning of an incipient family unit receives considerable attention in the clan rules.

---

[179] 1913–b, "Officially Registered Regulations," p. 2b; 1935–e, "Family Regulations," p. 16b.
[180] 1915–d, "*Tsu* Regulations," p. 1a.
[181] 1921–c, "Regulations of the Ancestral Hall," p. 1b.
[182] 1915–a, "Family Regulations," p. 29a.
[183] 1924–f, "The Eight Instructions of Ancestor Chih-ssu-kung," p. 7b.

The traditional Chinese culture, like many other pre-modern cultures, played down the sex factor.[184] Many rules take the view that "without due control, the ever-present sexual desire in both men and women could lead into adultery and violation of morality."[185] The institution of marriage is for the solemn promise of "perpetuating the descent line."[186] Some rules go so far as to authorize the use of a common fund to help poor members get married. One clan rule, which originally provides "four taels of silver at the engagement and ten taels of silver at the wedding" of such a member, later on revises its stipulation in terms of modern currency: three *yüan* or silver dollars for a man's first marriage, one and half for a second marriage, and one silver dollar and forty cents for a girl's marriage. To remain a bachelor is an unfilial behavior.[187] Another rule threatens to punish a confirmed bachelor by excluding him from the ancestral hall.[188]

Traditionally, marriage was a family rather than an individual concern. According to the rules, the family should give a marriage proposal careful consideration with regard to personal fitness, family happiness, and social standing.[189] In the words of one rule, "Marriage as the beginning of the human relationships deserves the utmost caution."[190] In fact, families on both sides want to make sure that the bride would be well received in her new environment. The social prestige of a family is also at stake. It will be enhanced by marriage relationship with another family of a higher social standing and impaired by having relatives of inferior status. For these reasons, the parents usually made the decision for the marriage of their children.[191] Under the law in traditional China, the father had the right to decide.[192]

[184] Kardiner, *The Individual and His Society*, p. 296.
[185] 1930–a, "Family Instructions," item on sex misbehavior, p. 16b.
[186] 1915–b, "Instructions of Ancestor Mien-wu-kung," item on marriage, p. 3a; and 1924–d, "Regulations of the Charitable Estate," p. 3b.
[187] 1919–c, "Regulations of the Charitabel Estate," item on aid for marriage, p. 9a and "Revised Regulations of the Charitable Estate," item 2 on aid for marriage and funeral.
[188] 1914–f, "Family Instructions," item on prohibition of bachelorhood, p. 6b.
[189] 1928–g, "Ancestors' Instructions," item on marriage.
[190] 1934–a, "Family Regulations," p. 6b.   [191] Martin C. Yang, *op. cit.*, p. 67.
[192] Hsü Ch'ao-yang, *Ch'in-shu fa*, pp. 79–83.

The rules of 64 clans set forth a number of criteria for desirable marriage:

	Number of Clans
Spotless family background	41
Virtue of prospective daughter-in-law	34
Ability of prospective son-in-law	25
Matching social status of the two families	22
Hypergamy for girl and hypogamy for boy	14

The foremost consideration is the social standing of the other family, consisting of both status and prestige. Many rules prefer families of equal status and prestige or as the common saying goes, "matching gates and doors."[193] Prominent urban families usually abided by this principle.[194] There is a practical advantage, for the bride from a family of matching situation readily makes the adjustment in her new home.[195] Precisely for the same reason, many other rules follow the suggestion of a Sung scholar in advocating hypergamy for girls and hypogamy for boys: "A daughter-in-law should preferably come from a family of somewhat lesser social standing, but a daughter should be married off to a family of somewhat higher social standing."[196] In either case, the bride is delighted by her "social promotion."

Moral prestige also helped social standing in traditional China. A number of clan rules have advised that in considering marriage proposal, one should choose a family of good reputation.[197] Families in rural communities were not too keen about status but still preferred a family of good name, at least a family without a bad name.[198] Notoriety in a family is regarded as an indication of its moral laxity. Family with spotless background implies "virtue and good upbringing."[199] In evaluating a family, one should, according to some rules, "observe its ways in domestic life and the personal conduct of

---

[193] 1920–d, "Additional Family Regulations," p. 5a.
[194] Martin C. Yang, op. cit., p. 107.
[195] 1922–b, "Miscellany of Family Proprieties."
[196] 1913–a, "*Tsung* Instructions," p. 4a.
[197] 1918–b, "Family Instructions," p. 3b.
[198] Martin C. Yang, op. cit., p. 107.
[199] 1914–j, "Family Regulations," p. 5a.

its members."[200] Furthermore, the traditional Chinese believed that moral conduct led to prosperity. This ethico-religious belief is not superstitious but realistic, for high moral standards help produce promising individuals.

Nor should the personal qualities of the eligible young man and young woman be neglected. The rules value the integrity and ability of a young man more than his family wealth.[201] The desired qualities of a bride should be her virtues, especially "her willingness to serve her parents-in-law."[202] Yet, the preference for a family with high status and prestige often conflicts with the desire for a young man or young woman of these qualifications, because socially superior families frequently spoil their children. One rule summarizes the considerations well:[203]

> In looking for a daughter-in-law, parents should select a girl with commendable behavior and graceful manners . . . They should consider spotless family background as an essential condition and should not covet the wealth and influence of her family. Wealthy and influential families often produce conceited and quarrelsome girls. In looking for a son-in-law, parents should choose a young man of sagacity who is not spoiled by his family.

A number of injunctions against certain undesirable marriages are found in the rules of 63 clans:

	Number of Clans
Marriage motivated by craving for the wealth and influence of the other family	60
Betrothal in childhood	12
Marrying a girl only for her beauty	3
Cross-cousin marriage	3
Marriage at the instigation of a match-maker without proper consideration	2

Many rules consider the moral prestige of a family as more essential then the wealth or the lack of it.[204] Nor is a marriage relation with a wealthy family necessarily advantageous. One has to keep up with

---

[200] 1934–a, "Family Regulations," p. 6b.
[201] 1924–e, "Family Mottoes," p. 4a.
[202] 1929–b, "Family Regulations," p. 8b; and 1919–b, *op. cit.*, p. 14a.
[203] 1921–c, "Family Regulations," item on marriage, p. 1a.
[204] 1919–b, *op. cit.*, p. 14a; and 1922–b, "Family Instructions," p. 8a.

that family or "suffer humiliation from it."[205] Yet, the majority of people did in fact prefer to have their children married to members of wealthy families.[206] It is interesting to note that only two rules among the present data threaten to punish those who decide upon the marriage of their children on account of wealth at the expense of other considerations. One rule states: "The clan should severely castigate a member who arranges marriage with a family of inferior social status just because it has wealth."[207] The other stipulates that "the clan should consider due punishment of a member who breaks an engagement with another family because it has become poor and promises the marriage to a third family who is wealthy."[208] In both instances, the offense is really not the craving for wealth but the degradation of one's social status or the breaking of a solemn betrothal. There is no objection to members marrying their children to wealthy people so long as the match does not violate status-ethics or propriety.[209]

A few rules require marriage of eligible boys and girls without undue delay, usually shortly before the age of twenty for girls and twenty-five for boys.[210] Prompt marriage is regarded as desirable partly because of the anxiety to secure offspring for the family and partly because of the fear that illicit relations might otherwise occur. On the other hand, the clan rules condemn the poor custom of early betrothal during childhood. One clan rule observes that such a promise is often made with an ulterior motive and lacks sincerity. It is lightly agreed upon and later on as easily broken when the wealth and influence of the other family declines.[211]

Some rules hold the opinion that a beautiful girl does not make a good wife. She probably lacks moral fortitude and is likely to cause trouble.[212] Other clan rules disapprove of cross-cousin marriage. A

---

[205] 1915–b, *op. cit.*, p. 4a; and 1921–1, "Family Instructions," p. 2.
[206] *MSSHK*, p. 764 and Ch'en Ku-yüan, *Chung-kuo hun-yin shih* [*A History of Marriage in China*], pp. 94–100.
[207] 1935–d, "Family Standards," p. 1b.
[208] 1916–a, "Regulations for Controlling a Family," p. 6a.
[209] 1929–b, "Family Regulations," p. 8b.
[210] 1914–e, *op. cit.*, p. 6b.
[211] 1921–c, "Family Regulations," p. 1a.
[212] 1934–c, "Family Standards," p. 5a; and 1914–g, *op. cit.*, p. 4.

cross-cousin marriage should lead to easy adjustment.[213] But some rules take a different view. First, the wife may capitalize on her former status as a cousin to claim special favors in the family over her sisters-in-law, thus creating domestic friction.[214] Second, cross-cousin marriage is rather similar or comparable to a violation of clan exogamy.[215] One rule states:[216]

A cardinal principle of marriage is to avoid persons of close blood relationship; hence, the rule of clan exogamy and of not even marrying a person who happens to have the same surname. Cross-cousin marriage, though nominally a marriage between two persons of different surnames, is in reality in contravention to this principle and therefore a serious mistake in social custom.

An undesirable marriage is not necessarily a punishable offense. But marriages which involve violation of generation-age order or serious degradation of status such as the following are forbidden with punishment according to the rules of 42 clans:

	Number of Clans
Marrying a person of disgraceful low class	19
Marrying a person with the same surname (even when not of the same clan)	17
Marrying the widow of a brother	9
Other incestuous marriage between family or clan members	7
Marrying a fiancée of an elder brother	4
Marrying a widow or girl by elopement	1

The rules usually insist upon nullification of such disreputable marriages or denying the guilty party of his clan privileges or clan membership. Sometimes, it was required that the offender be sent to the local government for punishment.[217]

The principle of clan exogamy is stated in the ancient classics in the belief that marriage within the clan would hinder reproduction.[218] The

---

[213] Hsu, *Under the Ancestors' Shadow*, p. 79.
[214] 1914–j, "Family Regulations," p. 5a; and 1920–c, *op. cit.*, p. 23a.
[215] 1914–j, "Family Regulations," p. 5a.
[216] 1928–f, "A Collection of Family Instructions," p. 3a.
[217] See Table 16 in the Appendix.
[218] 1922–e, "Family Instructions of Ancestor Tan-ya-kung," p. 60.

same principle applies by extension to people of the same surname or family name, as there is the possibility that they might be the descendants of an unknown paternal ancestor.[219] Since China has fewer than 500 surnames, a rigid application of this prohibition is rather hard sometimes. In northern China and parts of central China, marriage between unrelated persons of the same surname was permissible.[220] But marriage within the same clan was forbidden throughout the land as "beastly misconduct in flagrant violation of ethics."[221]

Marriage within a family is condemned as incest. As a matter of fact, many poor families for the sake of convenience and saving expenses married the fiancée or the widow of a deceased member to his brother.[222] The rules hold that "proper family relationship cannot tolerate such abhorrent arrangement."[223] Even a fiancée has a status as inviolable as that of a wife. Her marriage to a brother of her deceased fiancé should be nullified.[224]

The rules generally condemn marriages with persons whose social statuses are disgracefully low, such as "the descendants of prostitutes, theatrical players, indentured servants, government slaves, government runners, and convicts, even when such persons have become wealthy."[225] The rules require the group to dissociate with such persons by not recognizing either the marriages, or the violaters as clan members in good standing. Similarly, the rules forbid marriages resulting from adultery, elopement, or disreputable misconduct which cast an unfavorable reflection upon the clan's reputation. Taking an indentured girl as concubine, especially after adultery, is considered disgraceful.[226] Some rules do not permit their members to marry off their daughters as concubines in return for a sum of money as it is a degradation of the girls and a humiliation for the clan. As

[219] 1915-a, "Family Regulations," p. 28a.
[220] *MSSHK*, pp. 630, 740, 738 and 788.
[221] 1928-a, "Family Regulations," p. 8a.
[222] 1921-f, "Officially Sanctioned Regulations," p. 2b; and 1935-e, *op. cit.*, p. 16b.
[223] 1925-a, "Family Regulations," p. 1a; and 1933-c, "Family Regulations," item on marriage, p. 3b.
[224] 1918-c, "*Tsung* Restrictions," p. 1a.
[225] 1921-n, "Regulations of the Ancestral Hall," p. 57a.
[226] 1928-d, "Family Instructions," p. 4b.

mentioned earlier, such prohibition on the one hand and permission given their members to take concubines on the other hand constitute a double standard.[227] This is not inconsistent, however, from the standpoint of status. The man who takes a concubine, especially for the legitimate purpose of begetting an heir, does not in any way compromise his own status.

It is clear that status is the chief consideration of the clan rules with regard to marriage. Proper observance of status makes a desirable marriage; and disregard of status, an objectionable or forbidden marriage. Yet, a marriage which is desirable in terms of status does not necessarily insure domestic harmony.

E. WIFEHOOD AND WIDOWHOOD

With characteristic patriarchal prejudice, the clan rules blame the women as the major cause of domestic friction for "women are by nature ignorant, narrow-minded, sly, and jealous."[228] Paradoxically, the same clan rules express the hope that a wife will somehow achieve the virtues of womanhood in abiding by ritual propriety, in being kind to other family members, in fulfilling her obligations toward them, in enhancing family harmony, and in pursuing neither her selfish interest nor that of her husband and children.[229]

The wife had a subordinate status in the family. Soon after her marriage, the parents-in-law would exercise their control by telling her what to do and what not to do.[230] An ideal wife was supposed to have "three subordinations" and "four virtues." The "three subordinations" are subordination to her father before her marriage, subordination to her husband after marriage, and subordination to her son who succeeds the father.[231] The "four virtues" are fidelity, cautious speech, industriousness, and graceful manners.[232] An ideal

---

[227] 1930–a, "*Tsu* Standards," item on concubinage, p. 19a, and item on marrying a daughter, p. 21a.
[228] 1914–j, "Family Regulations," p. 4b.
[229] 1922–f, "Family Instructions," pp. 3b and 4a; *KCTSCC, Chia-fan tien, t'se* 613, *chüan* 2, p. 2; Fei and Chang, *Earthbound China*, p. 115.
[230] 1921–j, "Mottoes," p. 9; Levy, *op. cit.*, pp. 34–35.
[231] Martin C. Yang, *op. cit.*, p. 59.
[232] Hsu, *Under the Ancestors' Shadow*, p. 147.

wife should assist her husband in the interest of family prosperity and harmony. She should never speak in a loud voice and never say much, for neither would be conducive to good feeling.[233] Her manners should be impeccable and respectful. In the words of one rule, "when a good wife sits, she sits gracefully without crossing her knees; when she stands, she does not plant her feet wide apart."[234]

Her subordinate status notwithstanding, a wife has important roles. One rule, for example, requires that a wife should wait on her parents-in-law with filial piety, help her husband in respectful obedience, treat her sisters-in-law with kindness, take care of her children with love, and attend to domestic matters with industriousness and thrift.[235] In short, her roles are to serve everyone else in the family.

On the negative side, the rules of 57 clans comment on numerous faults of the wife:

	Number of Clans
Failure in her roles toward husband:	
Usurping the roles of her husband	16
Meddling with matters outside the family	13
Jealousy especially in not letting the husband take a concubine for the sake of begetting an heir	11
Disobedience to husband	9
Failure in her roles toward seniors:	
Lack of filial piety toward parents-in-law	21
Disrespect of seniors in family or clan	11
Being a termagant, without respectful manners	8
Failure in her roles toward family members in general:	
Discord with sisters-in-law	27
Repeatedly and deliberately keeping family members divided	15
Keeping family property to herself	3
Quarreling with family members	1

[233] 1930-c, "Family Instructions," pp. 6-7.
[234] 1912-a, "Admonitions for Women," p. 10a.
[235] 1930-c, "Family Instructions," p. 6b; and 1921-q, "Regulations for Married Women," pp. 16-17 and "Miscellaneous Instructions for Controlling a Family," p. 22b.

	Number of Clans
Failure in personal morality:	
Licentiousness	6
Incest or adultery within family or clan	2
Elopement	1
Guilty of one or more of "the seven traditional grounds for divorce" (this overlaps with some of the above items)	6

Power in the family goes with the superior status of man. One rule advises:[236]

The proper way is for the husband to set the pace and for the wife to follow. A family in which the wife usurps power inevitably declines. It all begins with the mistake of the husband who in loving his wife gives her the power. Soon afterwards, he will find himself becoming afraid and in no position to rectify her usurpation.

It is considered shameful for a husband to leave family decisions to his wife and equally disgraceful for the wife to usurp power.[237] The rules assume that an average wife has little interest in the family as a whole; when she has power, she may favor her own conjugal unit, ignore the interest of other family members, and even give benefits to her own family by birth.[238] In the opinion of many rules, one abnormality will lead to another. When a husband cannot control his wife, the wife would soon mistreat her parents-in-law or turn the husband against them.[239] She would also become disrespectful toward the other senior family members. Usurping power, she might even become a termagant who disregards all proper manners.[240] The generation-age hierarchy would be undermined and the family helplessly divided. A divided family certainly has no hope of attaining prosperity. This is the realistic reason why the rules are so overwhelmingly against the wife's having power. On the other hand, a husband should not ignore the good advice of his wife. The general principle upheld by the rules is for the wife to assist the husband but not to dominate him.[241]

[236] 1917–c, "*Tsung* Standards," p. 5a; cf. 1914–d, "Family Regulations," p. 3b.
[237] 1918–e, "Instructions for Succeeding Generations," p. 24a.
[238] 1920–c, *op. cit.*, p. 23b; and 1921–j, "Mottoes," p. 9b.
[239] 1918–f, "New Family Regulations," p. 21a.
[240] 1919–i, "Family Regulations," p. 4.
[241] 1936–b, "Miscellaneous Statements of Family Instructions," p. 4b; and 1916–a, "Regulations for Controlling a Family," p. 4b.

The tremendous emphasis upon generation-age hierarchy was not without bad effects. Mistreatment of a wife by her mother-in-law was commonplace in the traditional days. Sometimes, it resulted in the suicide of the wife.[242] Such mistreatment has a psychological root in the mother who feels resentful when the son transfers his love from her to his wife.[243] The rules are, however, singularly silent on this point; only one of them states: "A wife should not take rash action on account of quarrels and minor disputes. If she is very unhappy and falls into illness or even takes her own life, it is her own fault."[244]

Another important aspect of wifehood is to get along with sisters-in-law, previously discussed in connection with brotherly relations. One rule advises the wife:[245]

Wives come from families of different background. Living together in one household, they should learn to be cordial with one another. The poor ones should not flatter, the rich ones should not be conceited, and none of them should be selfish. When a wife gets a gift from her family by birth, she should take it to her mother-in-law. When a wife wants to use something, she should ask for the permission of her mother-in-law.

Inasmuch as the family holds property in common, no wife should keep money and things to herself or improperly regard family goods as her private possession.[246]

The punishment of a misbehaving wife is, in many instances in the clan rules, administered to her husband for his fault in not restraining her. A typical rule reads: "If a wife fails to wait on her parents-in-law, quarrels with her sisters-in-law, or otherwise infringes upon status-ethics, her husband shall suffer due punishment."[247] Punishment, generally speaking, is at the level of castigation which probably includes some flogging. It depends on how much of the fault really lies with the husband. For example, if the wife offends a senior member in the clan, the husband is subject to monetary fine. If he should take

---

[242] Lang, *op. cit.*, p. 48.
[243] Martin C. Yang, *op. cit.*, pp. 58–61.
[244] 1912–a, "*Tsung* Regulations," p. 5.
[245] 1918–e, "Instructions for Succeeding Generations," p. 24a.
[246] 1922–b, "Miscellany of Family Proprieties," p. 1b.
[247] 1917–d, "Family Regulations," p. 3b.

his wife's side in this misconduct, then he should be flogged. If he is the instigator behind the wife, then his punishment should be exclusion from the ancestral hall.[248] On the other hand, if the husband is ascertained to be blameless, the punishment should be directly administered to the misbehaving wife. The punishment may vary from mere oral censure to legal punishment by the local government.[249]

Traditionally, the most severe punishment for an unworthy wife was divorce by dismissal. The seven offenses which constitute the legitimate grounds for dismissing a wife were: (1) offensive contravention of the parents-in-law; (2) failure to bear children; (3) adultery; (4) extreme jealousy; (5) repulsive diseases; (6) being garrulous; and (7) theft. The first offense is equivalent to filial impiety.[250] The second offense underscores the wife's procreative role, while the fourth offense refers to an heirless and jealous wife who prevents her husband from taking a concubine or mistreats the concubine.[251] The third offense, adultery, is especially serious if it is incest.[252] The sixth offense refers to a wife whose discord with other members threatens family stability.[253] By custom a dismissed wife was sent back in utter disgrace to her family by birth.

A wife was subject to family punishment. As one rule puts it, "The corrective punishment of a wife by her husband, with the exception of wanton mistreatment, admits no interference from her own family by birth."[254] This principle holds true even in serious cases:[255]

When a married woman, after the discovery of her disreputable misconduct, commits suicide by hanging herself, taking poison, or drowning herself, her own family should not come with their fellow clan members like a mob, make trouble for her husband's family, or demand money as a compensation for her death. Only when a married

---

[248] 1919–e, "Family Discipline," p. 9a.
[249] See Tables 10 and 11 in the Appendix.
[250] 1922–f, "Family Instructions," p. 3b.
[251] 1916–a, "Regulations for Controlling a Family," p. 4b; 1914–j, "Family Regulations," p. 4b.
[252] 1918–e, "Instructions for Succeeding Generations," item on discipline of wife; 1919–g, "*Tsung* Regulations," p. 1b.
[253] 1933–c, "Family Regulations," p. 4b.
[254] 1930–a, "*Tsu* Standards," p. 21b.
[255] 1921–f, "Additional *Tsu* Regulations," p. 4a.

woman has done no wrong and yet has been driven into suicide by intolerable mistreatment can her father, her brother, or her close relatives appeal to the government in order to correct a grave injustice.

Normally, however, a wife received due protection; divorce by dismissal seldom happened.[256] It must be based on one of the seven legitimate grounds and substantiated by concrete evidence acceptable to her family or clan by birth who would otherwise feel compelled to take steps in protecting not only her but also its group reputation.[257] Moreover, the traditional mores forbade the dismissal of a wife who previously mourned for her parents-in-law, endured poverty with the family, or had no family of her own to go back to.[258] According to the rules, one cannot dismiss his wife merely because she is not good looking and her family by birth has become poor.[259] A poor husband who abandons his wife or sells his wife into servitude should be expelled from the clan or have his name deleted from the genealogy.[260]

The rules also protect a wife from her misbehaving husband. A husband who mistreats his wife is according to one rule punishable by monetary fine, denial of clan privileges, or expulsion from the ancestral hall.[261] A husband who favors his concubine and humiliates his wife should be publicly punished by the clan head.[262]

In summing up, so long as a wife fulfills her roles and remains on good terms with the family members, especially her parents-in-law, her status is assured. Her best hopes are for the parents-in-law and her husband to treat her well, for her husband to succeed in his career so that she also gains in prestige, and for her to have a son so that in time her own status as a mother will rise high in the generation-age order. On the other hand, if she fails to take up her roles but compromises her status, she is in danger of punishment and even dismissal.

---

[256] Lang, *op. cit.*, p. 49.
[257] 1921–f, "Additional *Tsu* Regulations," p. 3b.
[258] Lang, *op. cit.*, pp. 40–41; and 1921–k, "Family Discipline," p. 3a.
[259] 1921–f, "Additional *Tsu* Regulations," p. 3b.
[260] 1921–k, "Family Discipline," p. 2; also see Table 12 in the Appendix.
[261] 1930–d, "*Tsu* Regulations," Article 9, p. 1b.
[262] 1916–a, "Regulations for Controlling a Family," p. 4b–5a.

A concubine's status is inferior. She ranks below the youngest sister-in-law or everyone else of the same generation.[263] Some rules permit concubines neither a record in the genealogy nor a tablet in the ancestral hall, not even those who have given birth to sons.[264] Other rules are more tolerant: a concubine honored by official commendation may have her tablet included in the ancestral rites; a concubine who has children and observes widowhood may be so recorded in the genealogy, but her children are entered under the name of the legal wife.[265] A concubine should neither assume the status of wife, nor become the second wife after the death of the first one.[266] Status once determined admits no improper change. Although the rules cannot prevent a husband from favoring his concubine, at least they insist upon due respect to the wife and her status.[267]

A widow is entitled to financial provision and protection. Normally, the family assumes this responsibility. "Brothers should respect and take good care of their widowed sisters-in-law who remain in chastity. It is forbidden to re-marry her against her will."[268] The clan should intervene when the family fails to take care of a widow or when other clan members try to take advantage of her. The provisions in the rules of 64 clans are summarized here:

	Number of Clans
Protection of a widow:	
No mistreatment of and insult to a widow	16
No plotting to take over a widow's property	10
No pressure to force a widow to re-marry	7
No slandering of a widow	3
No selling of a widow into servitude	1
No seduction of a widow	1
No persecution causing a widow to commit suicide	1

[263] 1923–c, op. cit., p. 11a.
[264] 1915–h, "Regulations for the Ancestral Hall and Graveyard," p. 71b.
[265] 1927–a, "Additional Regulations of the Charitable Estate" (1885), p. 18b; 1928–b, "Rules of Genealogy," p. 118a; 1929–d, op. cit., p. 6a.
[266] 1915–f, "Family Instructions," p. 26a; 1921–c, "Regulations of the Genealogy," p. 1b. See also Table 13 in the Appendix.
[267] 1923–c, op. cit., p. 11a.
[268] 1921–a, "Tsung Regulations," item on protection of widows, p. 8.

Assistance to a widow: *Number of Clans*

   Assistance (no specification, meaning voluntary contribution as a moral obligation)   30

   Request for government commendation of a celebrated chaste widow, with the clan paying the expenses   16

   Public commendation of a widow at the ancestral hall and in the genealogy   14

   Fixed amount of assistance to a widow from the clan fund   12

A widow without the help of a male adult in her family is vulnerable to aggression. The clan should prevent unscrupulous members from slandering her, violating her chastity, or forcing her into re-marrying so that they can take over her family property.[269] According to one rule, for example:[270]

The clan should go to the government to indict an offender who trespasses on the property of a widow, who conspires with non-clan members to seize her property, or who in pretending to help her and her orphans maneuvers them with ulterior motive.

The clan punishment for these types of misconduct are, however, relatively lenient. It is either monetary fine or castigation.[271] As few rules advise petition to the local government for the purpose of punishing an aggression, adequate protection for widows seems to be lacking.[272]

Nor is there adequate help for widows in financial need. Most rules merely ask "the close kin to help them now and then." Only a few rules of the wealthy clans with charitable estates stipulate definite amount of assistance to poor widows.[273] The general lack of adequate

---

[269] 1922–d, "Old Regulations of the *Tsung-tsu*," item on protection of widows, p. 12b.

[270] 1929–a, "The Twelve Injunctions," item 6 on protection of widows, p. 2b.

[271] 1930–a, "*Tsu* Standards," item on protection of widows; and 1928–a, "Family Regulations," item on protection of widows, p. 2b; and see Table 15 in the Appendix.

[272] 1934–a, "Family Regulations," p. 8a.

[273] 1919–c, "Regulations of the Charitable Estate" (1859), p. 17b; 1923–b, "Regulations of the Charitable Estate" (1876), p. 19b; and 1924–d, "Regulations of the Charitable Estate" (1847), p. 4a.

protection and provisions for helpless widows discloses that the clan rules fall short of the Confucian ideal in this respect. Nonetheless, the clan rules betray great interest in borrowing prestige from the chaste widows. These points will be discussed further in the following chapter.

Neo-Confucian morality after the Sung period regarded remarriage of a widow almost as disreputable as adultery. However, poor families frequently married off their widows. and even collected money from the men who took them.[274] Only a few rules adopt a realistic and kind attitude in allowing a poor widow to re-marry and, if necessary, providing a gift from the clan fund to send her off. She must leave, however, her son and family property with the clan. The closest kin should be appointed to take care of the orphan.[275] One rule eloquently argues in favor of permitting re-marriage:[276]

Chastity of a woman requires her to remain forever faithful to her husband after his death. Such cannot be expected of, nor imposed upon, every widow. When a widow wants to re-marry herself, let her do so. But when she re-marries, she cannot retain her place in the clan, nor the control of the family property of her former husband. She should leave the property to worthy clan members to take care of the orphans. Re-marriage itself need not be condemned. Though it is disgraceful, it is far less shameful than adultery.

Those who remain widows must behave properly. A number of clan rules stipulate the punishment by oral censure of "quarrelsome, riotous, unreasonable, or unbecoming widows."[277] If a widow secretly disposes of the family property, she should be fined.[278] If she takes a second husband by matrilocal marriage, the clan should take over the family property, exclude her from the ancestral hall, and delete her name from the genealogy.[279] If she refuses to give up the family

---

[274] *MSSHK*, pp. 723–762, 896, 906, and 945–946.
[275] 1914–e, *op. cit.*, p. 7a.
[276] 1915–b, *op. cit.*, p. 4b.
[277] 1928–b, "Rules of Genealogy," p. 2a; also see Table 14 in the Appendix.
[278] 1930–d, "*Tsu* Regulations," p. 2b.
[279] 1922–d, "Old Regulations of the *Tsung-tsu*," p. 12b; and 1914–e, *op. cit.*, p. 7a.

property, the clan should ask the local government not only to recover it but to condemn her into servitude for her licentious misconduct.[280] When a widow commits adultery, the clan should erase the shame by ordering her to be re-married formally and thus remove her from the clan group.[281]

F. SEX SEGREGATION AND SECLUSION OF WOMEN

The clan rules place another control over women, namely, sex segregation and social seclusion. The purpose is to keep the women from coming into undue or improper contact with the opposite sex which might lead to illicit relations.[282] The ideal is to "keep suspicion from arising so that people cannot possibly slander the family."[283] Many rigid stipulations in the rules are intended only for upper class families living in large households.[284] Farming families whose female members have to work outside the house and on the farm cannot follow the same standards; though the general principle of sex segregation and seclusion of women was commonly accepted by all classes.

Sex segregation according to the rules applies mainly to the females from their 'teens to the time when they reach fifty years of age. One rule which segregates girls as early as seven years old is an exceptional case in imitation of an ancient feudal formality.[285] In most rules, 'teen-age means from ten years old to sixteen years old; in other words, around the time of puberty.[286] Women over fifty are considered to be above suspicion.[287]

Sex segregation restrains the activities of women in three major areas: domestic life, the use of services from outside the home, and social activities. The rules uphold the principle of avoidance between sexes in domestic life. Male servants are not permitted in inner

---

[280] 1929–a, "The Twelve Injunctions," p. 2a.
[281] 1919–g, "*Tsung* Regulations," p. 4a.
[282] 1915–b, *op. cit.*, p. 4a; and Hsu, *Under the Ancestors' Shadow*, p. 61.
[283] 1912–a, "Admonitions for Women," p. 10b.
[284] 1917–c, "Family Instructions of Ancestor San-feng-kung," p. 17a.
[285] 1922–b, "Miscellany of Family Proprieties," p. 4a.
[286] 1921–e, "*Tsu* Regulations," p. 5b.
[287] 1930–d, "*Tsu* Regulations," p. 4b.

chambers.[288] Male family members should not enter the bedroom of a young woman. Separate toilets should be provided for both sexes.[289] During banquets, men and women should not be seated at the same table.[290] A few rules even disallow a married woman to sit down at the meal with her father-in-law or brothers-in-law.[291] One rule shows how sex segregation helps to avoid embarrassing situations:[292]

Quarrels between a male member and a female member of the family is forbidden. An elder brother who finds his sister-in-law at fault should speak to her husband about it. An uncle who finds his niece-in-law in the wrong should mention it to the nephew. It is the responsibility of the husband to correct his wife in private . . . Few women have the proper upbringing to refrain from offending their elders in the family. If an elder member scolds a female member, he will suffer her retort which is an insult he inadvertently brings upon himself.

Male members should supervise when the female members use goods and services brought in from outside the house. Even doctors should treat a lady patient in the parlor rather than in her chamber.

The seclusion of women also discourages contacts with outside females of inferior status or character who are presumably bad influences. Gossiping neighbors are highly undesirable. Beauticians should not be summoned as female members of the family can help one another.[293] Numerous rules suspect the "three nuns" and the "six service women" of immoral influence. The "three nuns" are Buddhist nuns, Taoist nuns, and female fortune-tellers. The "six service women" are brokers, match-makers, soceresses, "bewitchers," medical women, and midwives.[294] These persons know little about ritual

---

[288] 1924–a, "Family Instructions," item on sex segregation.
[289] 1916–a, "Regulations for Controlling a Family," p. 9a.
[290] 1916–b, "An Epitome of Family Regulations," p. 2b; and 1921–c, "Family Regulations," p. 3a.
[291] 1921–c, "Family Regulations," p. 6b.   [292] 1923–c, *op. cit.*, p. 12a.
[293] 1918–g, *op. cit.*, p. 9b; and 1921–q, "Miscellaneous Instructions for Controlling a Family," p. 23a.
[294] Traditional China had female brokers whose occupation was to engage the service of maids, female cooks, singing and dancing girls for the upper-class families. "Bewitchers" did not have a definite vocation; the term refers to those women who by their sugar-coated words induce people to do things which they normally would not do.

propriety and are likely to spread indecent gossip to defame people.[295] Sometimes they are agents of romantic intrigues.[296] When they come into a household to perform some needed service, they should not be allowed to closet themselves with female family members.[297]

Women should be strictly confined to the home. Various social contacts and activities are prohibited in the rules of 44 clans as undesirable:

	Number of Clans
No visits to temples, especially in mixed company	26
No outing for lantern festival, boat festival, or theatrical gatherings	16
No spring outing or sight-seeing of public celebrations	10
Not leaving the house at night without escort and lamp	12
Not to stay away from home overnight	3
No loafing around neighborhood families	3
Not to have or visit any sworn sister	3
Not to befriend a re-married woman	2
No visit to family of a sister-in-law	2
No visit to a wife's family by birth after death of her parents	2
No visit to a wife's family by birth in case one of its members has joined a religious order	2

Women in traditional China liked to visit temples for offerings and praying, partly as a form of recreation.[298] This is precisely where the objection arises. "Women shall not visit temples and stay overnight in the mountain shrines. Such bad custom, though prevailing among ordinary people, cannot be tolerated in well-educated families of the official class."[299] For women to be in the crowd during festivals of any kind, religious or otherwise, is a violation of sex segregation.[300] A lady with self-respect certainly should not allow herself "to brush shoulders" with strangers.[301] "She should not make many visits, not even

[295] 1912–a, "Admonitions for Women," p. 11a.
[296] 1930–c, "Family Instructions," item on seclusion of women, p. 7a.
[297] 1924–a, op. cit., item on seclusion of women, p. 30.
[298] Hsu, Under the Ancestors' Shadow, pp. 25–26.
[299] 1934–f, "Tsu Regulations," p. 3a.
[300] 1925–e, "Family Instructions," p. 6.
[301] 1912–a, "Admonitions for Women," p. 10b.

to the families of close relatives."[302] It is feared that while visiting she might hear gossip detrimental to family harmony or come into undue contact with the opposite sex. Gambling in mixed company during occasions of celebration is also forbidden.[303]

Strict seclusion of women is in agreement with their roles. Since a woman's status is ascribed to her by that of her father, her husband, or her son, there is no need for her to be socially active. What might be termed social life according to modern standards may cause women to become less obedient to the family control. However, punishment for the violations of sex segregation and women's seclusion is no more than oral censure or monetary fine. Corporal punishment is seldom advised. Moreover, the punishment should be normally administered to the husband, or to the son in the case of an unbecoming widow, rather than to the woman herself.[304]

The seclusion of women causes the neglect of their education. A few exceptional rules object to the common saying that "a woman's lack of talent is her virtue." One of them points out that ignorance is no virtue, whereas reading good books, especially the biographies of righteous women in history, is a desirable training.[305] Another one holds that this common saying is responsible for "turning millions of women, generation after generation, into useless human beings."[306] Extremely rigid sex segregation is really not one of the original ideals of Confucianism.

G. SUMMARY

The provisions of the clan rules on family relationships have definite objectives of social control. These objectives are well summarized in the following quotation:[307]

A family in governing itself has four objectives. The first objective is education to raise the family's social standing through the official careers of its members. The second objective is thrift so that the family can accumulate more wealth through saving. The third objective is harmony for the purpose of maintaining a well-ordered domestic life. The last objective is to follow ethical teachings which keep the family from declining.

[302] 1921–j, "Mottoes," p. 14b. [303] 1934–f, "*Tsu* Restrictions," p. 3a.
[304] See Tables 17 and 18 in the Appendix. [305] 1930–c, "Family Instructions," p.10a.
[306] 1917–c, "*Tsung* Standards," p. 5a. [307] 1928–f, *op. cit.*, p. 1a.

The first objective is not always within reach, for official career depends a great deal on chance and opportunity in the government. The second objective or thrift cannot be realized unless the family members cooperate. Thus, the third objective or harmony is really the most important of all, while the fourth objective or the upholdings of moral teachings mainly serves to reinforce the same.

Considering the complexity of family relationships, harmony is not easily attainable. The family relationships have to be regulated in accordance with the status-ethics, the ritual-ethics, and their required precedence of one relationship over another. In essence, they rest upon voluntary and mutual respect as well as affinity.[308]

In the daily life of a well-regulated family, harmony can best be achieved through patience and conciliation.[309] The family head in exercising his control over other members cannot really be strict on everything. As stated in one clan rule, "He should leave small faults alone as if he does not notice them, but he should keep a sharp eye on important matters and serious mistakes."[310] In the closely knit family life, everyone has his respective roles and responsibilities. The family structure is not a strict authoritarian one, but a diffused one which requires integration.[311] Integration means harmony. The way to attain harmony is to defer to each other and not to insist on one's privileges unilaterally. In the opinion of another rule, "When the family members dispute, nothing is ever enough for them all; when they yield to one another, there will be plenty for everyone."[312] This is the reason why the rules, after stipulating all kinds of regulations on the family relationships, always come back to the values of harmony, patience, and conciliation.

Moral conduct in the family is interrelated with that of the clan. Members of a harmonious and prosperous family usually have a strong clan consciousness, while members of a declining family often care little for clan cohesion.[313]

[308] Levy, *op. cit.*, pp. 15–16.
[309] 1916–c, "Family Instructions," p. 2a.
[310] 1929–c, "Family Regulations," p. 1b.
[311] Levy, *op. cit.*, pp. 232–246.
[312] 1936–a, "Disciplinary Codes by Common Decision," p. 13a.
[313] Martin C. Yang, *op. cit.*, pp. 133–134.

CHAPTER IV

THE CLAN RULES ON CLAN FUNCTIONS AND RELATIONSHIPS

THE CLAN is the consolidating group which maintains an organizational bond between members of common descent who are no longer in the same family. It should go on forever, though the fact is often otherwise. One clan rule reports:[1]

In looking over the history of many clans, one finds that they have not lasted very long. Either their line of descent has become disrupted, or their descendants have dispersed far away from the native place. In the latter case, nine out of ten clans no longer enjoy prosperity.

A clan can last as long as it functions properly with an effective organization, some amount of common property, regular observance of ancestral rites, activities to take care of the clan welfare including reward and relief, necessary control of its members' conduct toward one another. The clan rules express serious concern with all these functions and relationships.

A. CLAN ORGANIZATION

The clan organization results from natural growth. The descendants of a common ancestor generally recognize one another as kin, even though there is as yet no formal organization. The influential ones, by their age, generation, popularity, social prestige, and wealth, exercise an informal leadership in taking care of the group's common interest. With increasing common activities, formal organization becomes both necessary and feasible. The initial step is to keep a register recording the births, the marriages, and the deaths in the group. The formal organization comes into being with the compilation of a genealogy, regular meetings, selection of officers, and building of an ancestral hall which is the physical site of the organization and the center of its activities.

[1] 1922–g, "Tentative Regulations of the *Tsung*," p. 5b.

The clan organization varies according to its size. A relatively small clan forms one integral unit, whereas large and populous clans frequently have several subdivisions within it, known by various terms: *fang* (房) or "house," *hu* (戶) or "household," *men* (門) or "gate," *chih* (支) and *fen* (分), both meaning "branches." For the sake of convenience, the present study refers to them collectively as branches or sub-branches as the case may be. Usually, each son of the founder is the beginning of a separate branch. In time, some branches become disrupted through migration, poverty, or deaths in large number during disasters, while other branches grow in both size and prosperity. The latter branches are then divided into several sub-branches. In structure and function, there is practically no difference between a branch and a sub-branch, for a sub-branch merely steps into the vacancy of a defunct branch; the purpose is to have each branch and sub-branch assume an equal share of responsibility, especially with regard to ancestral rites, common welfare activities, and control of the members' conduct.[2]

The clan rules reveal that leadership in the clan organization is both formal and informal. The formal leaders are the selected officers. The informal leaders are mostly scholar-officials whose civil service examination degrees, government positions, and official ranks "command the respect of the whole clan."[3] They are given special honors at the ancestral rites.[4] Many of them exert no small effort to promote the common welfare of the clan and help the clan organization deal with other clans in the community and with the local government.[5] These informal leaders generally do not serve as formal clan officers. Besides scholar-officials, there are sometimes other informal leaders. According to one rule, for example, one who has helped other members financially should be honored as an "esteemed member" and one who has exemplary virtue should be designated as a "sagacious member." These are, however, only honorary titles.[6]

---

[2] Hu, *op. cit.*, pp. 18–20; and Levy, *op. cit.*, pp. 50–51.
[3] 1924–f, "The Eight Instructions of Ancestor Chih-ssu-kung," p. 6b.
[4] See Section C below.
[5] Hu, *op. cit.*, pp. 22–26.
[6] 1918–c, "New Agreement of the *Tsung*," p. 1.

The clan officers who assume the formal leadership have, according to the rules, various titles which indicate their respective roles. Their titles generally fall into five categories: (1) titular leader; (2) clan head; (3) branch or sub-branch heads; (4) coordinating officers; and (5) assistant functionaries.

The titular leader of a clan is the *tsung-tzu* (宗子). Following the ancient feudal principle of primogeniture, he should be the heir of the eldest line of descent in the whole clan.[7] He has some prestige and influence but little executive power. His functions are largely the performance of ritual formalities.[8] Some rules, without abiding by the traditional qualification of *tsung-tzu*, assign this title to a member of senior generation-age status who has "moral character and ability."[9]

The general trend after the Sung period vested the executive power of clan organization in a selected clan head. As one rule explains:[10]

In ancient times, *tsung-tzu* governed the entire clan . . . Since people have long departed from the ancient system, the clan shall now select a clan head. The clan members, through public deliberation, shall nominate several candidates who have both senior status by the generation-age order as well as respected qualities of virtue. After having offered prayer to the ancestors, the members shall draw at random the name of one of the candidates. He shall be the clan head.

Some rules in keeping with the ancient tradition call the clan head by the title *tsung-chang* (宗長).[11] Most clan rules designated the office as *tsu-chang* (族長), meaning precisely clan head. In both cases, the word *chang* implies executive power. A number of rules mention both the titular leader and the clan head. Presumably, they share the executive power.[12]

A clan does not necessarily have a clan head. A relatively large clan with several subdivisions has according to its rule merely the

[7] 1923–c, "Regulations and Instructions," p. 3a.
[8] 1932–a, "Regulations of the Ancestral Hall," p. 9a; Shimizu, *Kazoku*, pp. 529–530; *MSSHK*, p. 721; and 1916–a, "Regulations for Controlling a Family," p. 1a.
[9] 1919–e, "Family Teachings," p. 5a.
[10] 1921–n, "*Tsung* Agreement," p. 45a.
[11] 1916–b, "Management of the Ancestral Hall," p. 1a.
[12] 1929–f, "*Tsung* Regulations," p. 2a.

branch heads or sub-branch heads. They exercise the executive power jointly in matters concerning the entire clan, either by general agreement or by rotation.[13] Some rules of these clans require, in addition, the appointment of a clan arbiter whose duty is to coordinate and to settle possible differences between the branch heads.[14]

Many rules of large clans provide a number of assistant functionaries to help the titular leader or the clan head. Being the heir of the leading descent line, the titular leader frequently happens to be a very young person, who needs some guidance from the assistant functionaries in performing his ritual duties. A clan head, on the other hand, is likely to be old and feeble, which makes it desirable sometimes to have a vice-head or a clan arbiter to assist him.[15] In many clan rules, the helping role is assumed by the branch heads or the sub-branch heads in which case they control the executive power and the clan head carries no more weight than the titular leader. One clan rule which does not appoint any assistant functionary simply calls upon the fair-minded members to help the clan head.[16]

The titles of the various officers in the rules of 64 clans are summarized as follows:

	Number of Clans
Titular leader, *tsung-tzu*	15
Clan head:	
With the title *tsung-chang*	7
With the title *tsu-chang*	42
Branch or sub-branch heads, with no clan head:	
With the title *hu-chang* (戶長)	5
With the title *fen-chang* (分長)	3
With the title *fang-chang* (房長)	2
With the title *chih-chang* (支長)	1
Coordinating leader, clan arbiter, *tsu-cheng* (族正) or *tsung-cheng* (宗正)	4
Assistant to the titular leader with the title *tsung-hsiang* (宗相) or *tsung-fu* (宗輔)	3

---

[13] 1921–k, "Family Discipline," p. 4a; 1933–c, "Family Regulations," p. 7a.
[14] 1915–e, "Family Regulations," p. 5a.
[15] 1925–c, "Regulations of the Genealogy," p. 4a; 1930–c, "Regulations of the Ancestral Hall," p. 1a.
[16] 1919–f, "*Tsu* Regulations," p. 2a; 1921–c, "Regulations of the Ancestral Hall," p. 1b; and Hu, *op. cit.*, p. 21.

Assistant to clan head:	*Number of Clans*
Vice-head of the clan	4
Coordinating leader as assistant with the title *tsu-cheng* (族正) or *tz'u-cheng* (祠正)	8
Branch or sub-branch heads as assistants to clan head:	
With the title *fang-chang*	14
With the title *fen-chang*	3
With the title *men-chang* (門長)	3
Fair-minded members to serve as occasional assistants	1

This summary shows the general pattern that the branch heads and the sub-branch heads often hold the executive power in a large clan organization. Presumably, the subdivisions wish to guard their own particular interest as well as to share the burden equally with one another.

The clan rules reveal that the criteria for the selection of different clan officers vary. The two leading criteria are the ascribed generation-age status and the achieved standing of the individual candidate. A titular leader, more often than not, is automatically designated by his birth status as the heir of the leading descent line. A clan head, in addition to his qualification of being senior both by generation and by age, should have such realistic qualities as fairness, honesty, integrity, wisdom, maturity, capability, and experience that command the respect and trust of the clan members.[17] Ideally, he should be a model personality in the entire group.[18] The selection of a branch or sub-branch head follows the same standards. In the words of one rule, "He should have senior status and integrity of character which are looked up to by the branch members."[19] The role of the assistant functionaries is to help the titular head or the executive officers. Their selection stresses capability, rather than generation-age status.[20]

[17] 1918–f, "Family Instructions," p. 6b; 1922–b, "Family Regulations," p. 2b; 1931–a, "Family Regulations," p. 1b; 1935–b, "Family Discipline Decided by *Tsu* Organization," p. 1b; and *MSSHK*, p. 661.

[18] 1935–d, "Family Standards," p. 3b.

[19] 1922–d, "Regulations of the *Tsung-tsu*," p. 19; and 1924–g, "*Tsung* Agreement," p. 1a.

[20] 1925–c, "Regulations of the Genealogy," p. 4a.

Some other considerations are often added. One rule, for instance, prefers the choice of an executive officer with a government career or official rank. Such a person is eminently qualified to deal effectively with other clans and with the local government.[21] Another rule wants a wealthy member to be its executive officer.[22] Some clan rules stipulate that even assistant functionaries should know how to read and write so that they can handle rituals and documents properly.[23]

In sum, the rules do not rely upon the generation-age or birth status alone on the matter of selecting clan officers, with the sole exception of titular head. They aim at the strongest possible combination of desirable qualities: generation-age status, moral fortitude, ability, education, and, if available, personal wealth and prominent social status.[24]

Most clan rules, compiled long before the modern changes, give little attention to the procedure of selecting clan officers. They usually use such expressions as "to select carefully," "for the members to choose publicly," and "for the members to recommend unanimously." These expressions indicate a selection controlled by group opinion in which the scholar-official members presumably exercise considerable influence. According to some rules, the clan head, once chosen, holds his office for life.[25] The terms of other offices are often fixed at one, three, or five years. In case an officer betrays the trust, the clan members may get together and remove him from the office.[26] If an officer discharges his responsibilities in an improper manner, such as receiving bribery, playing favoritism, or embezzlement, he is subject to serious criticism, dismissal, or permanent exclusion from conducting clan affairs.[27] Above all, no clan officers should infringe upon the clan property or use it for their private purposes.[28]

---

[21] 1924–g, "Abridged Constitution of *Tsu* Self-governing Association," p. 3a; and *MSSHK*, p. 871.
[22] 1921–b, "*Tsu* Regulations," p. 3a; and *MSSHK*, pp. 954–955.
[23] 1918–c, "New Agreement of the *Tsung*," p. 1a; and 1921–c, "Regulations of the Ancestral Hall," p. 1b.
[24] Hu, *op. cit.*, p. 29.
[25] 1922–d, "Regulations of the *Tsung-tsu*," p. 19.
[26] 1918–f, "Family Instructions," p. 6b; 1930–c, "Regulations of the Ancestral Hall," p. 1a.
[27] 1931–a, *op. cit.*, p. 1b.
[28] 1919–f, *op. cit.*, p. 1a; 1916–c, "Additional Family Discipline," p. 1b.

The power of the executive officers is comprehensive. It governs the clan interest in general and three specific areas in particular. First, the rules give the clan head or the branch heads, the titular leader, and the scholar-official members the power to regulate the rites in the ancestral hall, which are ceremonies that exercise socio-psychological control.[29] Second, the executive officers have the power to deal with mutual aggression, inheritance issues, adoption controversies, transfer of property titles, disputes over property rights and misconduct in general.[30] Finally, the clan officers jointly control the management of common property.

The management of common property and its financial details is sometimes taken care of by the clan's executive officers but, more often than not, by appointed managers who work under their supervision.[31] The following is a summary of the various types of management in the rules of 75 clans:

	Number of Clans
Management under the clan head:	
With assistants	2
With auditors	1
Management by the branch heads:	
Joint management	20
Annual rotation	11
Management by appointed managers under supervision:	
Managers appointed for one to three years term	25
Managers appointed for indefinite term	11
Separate management for the charitable estate	5

The rules show a number of ways to choose management personnel. One way is to let clan members select among themselves two or three "able, honest, and scrupulous persons" to be managers. The term of these managers is sometimes three years.[32] A second way is for the clan group to ask its honest and wealthy members to serve as the

[29] *MSSHK*, p. 761 and Shimizu, *Kazoku*, p. 540.
[30] Lang, *op. cit.*, pp. 177–179 and *MSSHK*, pp. 392–393, 632, and 768–769.
[31] 1921–n, "*Tsung* Agreement," p. 45b; and 1919–e, "Family Proprieties," p. 1a.
[32] 1922–d, "Regulations of the *Tsung-tsu*," p. 19; 1921–n, "*Tsung* Agreement," p. 45b; and 1917–a, "Regulations for the Management of the Property of the Ancestral Hall," p. 1a.

managers by annual rotation.[33] A third way is to empower the clan head to appoint a number of trustworthy members to take charge of the common property by monthly rotation.[34] A fourth way is to have branch heads submit the names of six to eight candidates and, after praying to the ancestral spirits, ask the clan head to draw two names at random. The managers selected by this method should serve one year or so with pay. In addition, two elders in the clan should be asked to be the supervisors to check the management.[35]

A charitable estate is a special kind of common property. Many rules require a separate management, for example, a salaried manager and one or two assistants.[36] Some rules leave the selection of this separate management to the descendants of the original donor; but other rules forbid them to monopolize or interfere with the management of the charitable estate.[37]

The selection of rotating or salaried managers differs from that of the clan officers in giving particular emphasis to honesty. Some rules prefer personal wealth as a guarantee of financial honesty. One rule states: "If a wrong person becomes a manager at the ancestral hall, he will omit the scheduled rites, fail to pay the taxes on the common property, and get the whole clan into financial trouble. The clan should therefore select only wealthy persons to take charge."[38] In case of embezzlement, the clan can always confiscate their personal property as restitution.[39] Other rules have a different opinion: "Members who are personally wealthy are not necessarily trustworthy for they are often motivated by selfish interest rather than by sense of justice."[40] An opium addict or a gambler, for example, should be

[33] 1919–a, "Officially Sanctioned Regulations," p. 2a.
[34] 1921–o, "Additional Regulations of the Ancestral Hall" (1903), item on ancestral hall management, p. 14a.
[35] 1921–c," Regulations of the Ancestral Hall," item on selection of managers, p. 3a.
[36] 1923–b, "Revised Regulations of the Charitable Estate" (1923), p. 29b.
[37] 1917–b, "Existing Regulations of the Charitable Estate," chapter on selection of managers, p. 3b; and 1924–g, "*Tsung* Agreement," p. 1b.
[38] 1921–b, "*Tsu* Regulations," items on selection of managers, p. 3a.
[39] 1916–c, "Additional Family Discipline," p. 1.
[40] 1921–n, "*Tsung* Agreement," p. 45b.

automatically disqualified.[41] The ideal qualifications are, in the order of general preference, "honesty, wealth, and capability."[42]

Supervision is necessary to prevent possible embezzlement and improper management. Most rules require an annual account to be published at the ancestral hall.[43] A few rules regard the supervision to be a regular responsibility of the executive officers.[44] Other rules add the stipulation that they should check upon each other.[45] Some rules consider it desirable to check upon both the executive officers and the managers by appointing someone else to audit the accounts independently.[46]

The supervision of common property management tends to be ineffective. This is suggested by the lenient punishment which the rules provide for embezzlement.[47] Most rules emphasize the restitution of the loss incurred, rather than such punitive measures as monetary fine, ritual penalty, dismissal from office, denial of clan privileges, or permanent non-participation in clan affairs.[48] Only a few rules give the stern warning that the guilty officer should be sent to the government for punishment.[49] The general tendency towards leniency is probably because of the likelihood that a clan officer or manager was someone of considerable status and influence. Instead of antagonizing him too much, the clan would be well satisfied just to recover the losses and would appeal to the government for settlement only as a last resort.[50] At any rate, infringement upon common property, though immoral, is not regarded as a violation of the ethical relationship with which the rules are mainly concerned.

[41] 1919–c, "Regulations of the Charitable Estate," p. 23a.
[42] 1921–o, "Regulations of the Ancestral Hall" (1779), p. 9a.
[43] 1913–c, "Regulations of the Ancestral Hall," p. 4a; 1921–c, "Regulations of the Ancestral Hall," p. 2a; 1930–c, "Regulations of the Ancestral Hall," p. 1b.
[44] 1933–h, "*Tsu* Organization," p. 2b.
[45] 1925–b, "*Tsung* Regulations," p. 6b.
[46] 1931–a, *op. cit.*, p. 2b; 1933–b, "Regulations of the Ancestral Hall," p. 1a.
[47] See Table 19 in the Appendix.
[48] 1923–b, "Regulations of the Charitable Estate" (1876), p. 18a; and 1913–b, "Officially Registered Regulations," p. 3.
[49] 1916–d, "*Tsung* Regulations," p. 10; and 1919–a, "Officially Sanctioned Regulations," p. 3a.
[50] 1927–a, "Record of the Charitable Estate," p. 15b.

The controlling leadership in the clan organization tends to be a power structure consisting largely of those members who have achieved some measure of individual power through their achieved political, social, and economic status, such as scholar-officials who exercise the informal leadership, the branch heads whose influence in their respective sub-groups is already established, and the managers who have personal wealth. The major problem in the clan organization seems to be whether the controlling leadership will be loyal to the ideals of the clan institution. The rules in following the Confucian principle invariably place their hope in the good conduct of these leaders. The special honors and the deference which the clan group accords them is an inducement. The moral persuasion of status-ethics and ritual-ethics is also to a significant extent an effective control. On the other hand, the rules fail to provide severe punishment to correct these leaders when they abuse their leadership and betray the trust placed in them. Their abuses, in turn, undermine the strength of the clan organization and the clan cohesion.

B. CLAN'S COMMON PROPERTY

The common property of the clans may be classified into two kinds: essential property and additional property. The essential properties are those dedicated to the ancestral cult such as the ancestral hall, ancestral graveyard, and ritual land. The importance of ritual land is seen in the following quotation:[51]

Ritual land is necessary to bring the clan members together. When the clan is consolidated, the young members will respect their elders. Their moral conduct will be encouraged and their benevolent feeling will be cultivated so that they will help those members who cannot afford to get married and those members who cannot afford to bury their deceased.

Additional properties are those devoted to welfare functions such as charitable land, school land, educational land to help the schooling of young members and to assist the civil service examination candidates, as well as charitable estates and charitable grana-

[51] 1915-i, "Regulations of the Ancestral Hall," introductory note, pp. 1–2.

ries, both for the relief of poor members. An extremely wealthy clan was able to maintain, in addition, a hostel at the provincial capital for the convenience of its members who took the civil service examination there.[52] However, such cases were very rare; most of the clans which had the essential property did not have charitable estate or granary.[53]

The kinds of common property owned by 116 clans as revealed in their rules are summarized as follows:

	Number of Clans
Essential common property:	
Ancestral hall	95
Ancestral graveyard	76
Ritual land	57
Additional common property:	
Charitable school	15
Charitable estate	12
Charitable cemetery	11
Charitable granary	6
School or educational land	6
Clan house in the city	5
Examination hostel in the city	3

The summary shows three major emphases in the order of their importance: first, the emphasis upon the ancestral cult; second, the emphasis upon promotion of education; and last, the emphasis upon the relief of poor members.

Land is the most prominent form of clan property, though a small number of clans own, in addition to land, houses and store buildings in the city for rental income. The information available in these rules indicates that in most cases the clan held common land of modest size, 100 *mou* or less.[54] Only twelve clans had large charitable estates. One charitable estate had 55 *mou* at the beginning, 195 *mou* in the year 1838, 255 in the year 1874 and finally 616 in the year 1915.[55] The largest charitable estate recorded in the present data started with 100

---

[52] 1931-b, "Record of the Examination Hall" (1821), p. 16a.
[53] 1930-c, "Family Instructions," p. 5b.
[54] *Mou* varies somewhat in different regions; however the ratio generally speaking is about 6.6 *mou* to one acre.
[55] 1915-d, "Record of the Charitable Estate," p. 1.

mou in 1831 and grew into 3,412 *mou* in 1906.[56] According to another rule, compiled in the year 1917, one *mou* of its charitable land gave the clan an annual rent of one picul of rice.[57] This indicates that the sizable charitable estates did have considerable income.

Common land property is acquired either through large endowment or by gradual acquisition. The following summarizes the information in the rules of 39 clans:

	Number of Clans
Large endowment:	
By a few generous members	21
By a single generous member	2
Gradual acquisition:	
Through surplus income from existing property	18
Through surplus income from miscellaneous items	15
From membership donations in general	14
Mainly by the donation of scholar-official members	9

In an exemplary case, 500 *mou* of land was donated by a single member.[58] Such generosity often inspired a descendant to follow suit:[59]

Five generations ago, his ancestor established the charitable estate. His great-grandfather added another 300 *mou* to it. He himself again contributed 1,000 silver dollars which added another 1,040 *mou*.

Sometimes, several prominent members set the example with large donations and other members followed with modest contributions.[60]

The rules disclose that the clan organization had various ways to raise funds: occasional solicitation, appeal to the entire clan, encouragement of contributions by granting clan privileges in return, and certain required contributions.[61] One rule stipulates that a member who contributes five *mou* of land is entitled to the privilege of having his posthumous tablet in the ancestral hall.[62] In another rule,

[56] 1927-a, "Record of the Charitable Estate," p. 16a.
[57] 1917-b, "Regulations for the Establishment of the Charitable Estate," p. 1a.
[58] 1924-d, "Regulations of the Charitable Estate" (1847), p. 3a.
[59] 1923-b, "Regulations of the Charitable Estate" (1876), p. 16a; cf. 1934-f, "Common Welfare," p. 1b.
[60] 1913-c, *op. cit.*, p. 1a; 1914-i, "Regulations of the Ancestral Hall" (1750), p. 1a; and 1921-b, "Articles for the Affairs of the Ancestral Hall," p. 6b.
[61] 1914-j, "Record of the Charitable School."
[62] 1915-d, "*Tsu* Regulations," p. 1b; also 1933-g, "Regulations of the Ancestral Halls throughout Kiangsi Province" (1933), p. 1b.

members of a family who have donated land should be invited to the commensal banquet after the ancestral rites and the family should receive one catty of sacrificial meat for each *mou* of land donated.[63] On the other hand, those who have made no donation whatsoever are often excluded from the clan's welfare benefits. One rule reports an interesting case: a branch of the clan, having been disconnected with the organization for nearly two centuries, applied for re-admission; the application was approved, except that no member of this branch was entitled to the clan's welfare benefits on the ground that it had made no donation during the interrupted period.[64]

A number of rules require each adult male member to pay a small annual fee such as a few hundred copper coins either to build or to maintain the ancestral hall.[65] Some rules require a small contribution when a member registers with the clan the birth of a son, a death or a wedding in the family, adoption of an heir, the division of family property, or departure from the native community in connection with government service.[66] A rather exceptional rule stipulates that five per cent of an inheritance settlement of a member family should be set aside as the common fund of all the family descendants to be used for the observance of sacrificial rites.[67]

The major source of clan income is the contribution of scholar-official and wealthy members. One rule makes a rather typical appeal to scholar-official members:[68]

A scholar-official member should realize that his successful career owes much to the protective influence of the ancestors and to their lasting virtues. He should be honest in government service; but he should also be grateful enough to save from his salaries in order to make a generous contribution to the clan.

Another rule, in recalling that scholar-official members often begin their careers with financial assistance or gifts from the clan, requires them to refund the amount they have received three years after their

---

[63] 1917-a, "Regulations for the Spring and Autumn Sacrifices," p. 2a.
[64] 1918-k, "Regulations of the Genealogy," p. 21a.
[65] 1925-e, "Common Decisions of the *Tsu*" (1894), p. 1a.
[66] 1925-b, *op. cit.*, p. 6b; and 1921-e, "*Tsu* Regulations," p. 7b.
[67] 1921-e, "*Tsu* Regulations," p. 7a; cf. Hu, *op. cit.*, p. 65.
[68] 1922-g, "Tentative Regulations of the *Tsung*," p. 8a.

official appointment, preferably with some additional contribution.[69] A third rule, which is very exceptional, requires every member in government service or other occupation with an annual income over five hundred silver dollars to contribute two per cent each year to the clan.[70]

The rules seek to control not only the contributions but the good management of common property. They give much attention to five problems: how to rent the common land; how to use the surplus income; how to protect the common property from trespassing and abuses; how to keep the common property; and how to prevent embezzlement and mismanagement.

The first problem is that of tenancy. The rules of 36 clans have the following provisions:

	Number of Clans
Choice of tenants of common property:	
No specification of tenants	18
Only non-clan members as tenants	6
Clan members permitted as tenants but required to observe the terms strictly	6
Gradual shift from clan member to non-clan member tenants	1
Treatment of tenants in general:	
Punishment of tenants for their default	12
Lenient treatment of tenants	12
Use of standard measures in receiving rent in kind	5
Deferment of rent when justified	3
Change of tenants only after long default	3

Many clans prefer non-clan persons to be tenants on their common property or forbid members from renting it, for it is difficult to deal with the latter in case of default.[71] Several clan rules require the

---

[69] 1918–k, "Regulations of the Genealogy," p. 21a.
[70] 1921–e, "*Tsu* Regulations," p. 7b.
[71] 1918–f, "New Family Regulations," section on ancestral hall, p. 19; 1919–c, "Regulations of the Charitable Estate (1859)", p. 19a; 1922–d, "Regulations of the *Tsung-tsu*," p. 17a; 1924–d, "Regulations of the Charitable Estate" (1847), p. 5a; 1930–a, "Regulations of the Ancestral Hall," p. 12; 1933–b, *op. cit.*, p. 3a; 1913–c, *op. cit.*, p. 4b; and 1914–j, "Family Regulations," p. 10a.

eviction of a defaulting member tenant in favor of an outsider.[72] According to a number of rules, tenants should be well treated.[73] An appeal for kindness and against undue exploitation is found, for example, in the following quotation:[74]

Tenants work so hard and we enjoy the profit. How can we fail to treat them with kindness? When they need some money during the farming season, we should help them out. If they are hard up owing to flood or drought, we should look into the situation and consider a reduction of rent. We should never demand from them the performance of labor service in addition to the rent. Nor should we increase the rent just because prices have gone up somewhat, change tenants because of small faults, allow our servants and young members to abuse them, or charge them heavy interest on loans and rent arrears.

Good management has two major objectives: surplus accumulation and investment in more land. The optimism in one rule maintains that three consecutive years of good harvest should produce enough surplus to buy additional common property.[75] The rules differ, however, on the management of surplus accumulated before it is used to buy land. The following summation shows their varying opinions:

	Number of Clans
Depositing and loaning of the surplus permitted:	
Depositing and making loans in general	9
Depositing in bank or post office accounts	4
Entrusting a wealthy and honest member	4
Making loans to members in need	2
Investing in industrial enterprises	1
Surplus to be kept by the clan organization:	
Against depositing and loaning in general	3
Against making loans to members especially	3

Those rules in favor of using the surplus to earn interest are comparatively of more recent date than those which are not. They stipulate further that the rate of interest should be between ten and

---

[72] 1922–g, "Tentative Regulations of the *Tsung*," p. 10b.
[73] *MSSHK*, p. 416; 1920–c, "Standards for the Succeeding Generations," p. 1; and 1929–c, "Family Instructions," p. 4a.
[74] 1930–a, "Family Instructions," item on treatment of tenants, p. 5.
[75] 1919–c, "Regulations of the Charitable Estate" (1859), p. 15b.

THE CLAN RULES ON CLAN FUNCTIONS AND RELATIONSHIPS   113

thirty per cent annually but never in excess of the legal limit.[76] Several rules permit small loans at ten per cent interest or less to trustworthy members in need for their weddings, funerals, schooling, or taking civil service examinations.[77] But the majority of the rules limit the loans to non-clan members only.[78] Both principal and interest should be returned to the clan at the end of each year; and embezzlement or misappropriation should be punished.[79] When the surplus together with interest reaches a substantial amount such as several hundred silver dollars, it should be reinvested in land.[80]

Reinvestment in land should be made carefully. The rules advise against buying land which has been mortgaged, land with other complications, over-valued land and land offered by unscrupulous members who wish to evade the tax burden.[81] With regard to the size and location of property, a clan should neither buy scattered strips nor attempt to consolidate its holdings into "a square and round block" for such an attempt often causes bad feelings in the comumnity.[82]

The rules have many detailed regulations on the protection of common property against misuse, theft, and trespass. The ancestral hall is a sacred place reserved for ancestral rites, clan meetings, and occasional scholarly gatherings. Only by permission may young members use its siderooms as studies.[83] The following misuses are forbid-

[76] 1924–g, "Articles for the Charitable Land," p. 2a; 1917–a, "Regulations for the Management of the Property of the Ancestral Hall," p. 1b; 1918–k, "Regulations for the School Land," p. 7; and 1922–c, "*Tsung* Restrictions," p. 5a.

[77] 1921–e, "Regulations for *Tsu* Affairs," pp. 12–13; and 1919–e, "Family Teachings," p. 8a.

[78] 1919–c, "Regulations of the Charitable Estate" (1859), p. 16a; 1927–a, "Record of the Charitable Estate," p. 15b; and 1930–a, "Regulations of the Ancestral Hall," p. 12.

[79] 1924–g, "Articles for the Charitable Land," p. 2a; 1929–f, "*Tsung* Regulations," p. 2b; and see Table 20 in the Appendix.

[80] 1917–a, "Regulations for the Management of the Property of the Ancestral Hall," p. 1b.

[81] 1918–c, "New Regulations of the Ancestral Hall" (1880), p. 2b; 1919–c, "Regulations of the Charitable Estate" (1859), p. 15a; and 1921–c, "Regulations of the Ancestral Hall," p. 2b.

[82] 1919–c, "Regulations of the Charitable Estate" (1859), p. 15a.

[83] 1913–c, *op. cit.*, p. 5a; 1914–b, "Regulations of the Ancestral Hall," p. 8a; and 1921–o, "Regulations of the Ancestral Hall" (1779), p. 9a.

den: using its rooms as living quarters, operating a private school in it, using the yard for cotton processing, using the hall for private banquet, storage, or workshop. Members who gather there to gamble should suffer the punishment of flogging for their utter lack of respect.[84] The same principle governs the furniture and utensils in the ancestral hall. Only by permission may members borrow them for a wedding or a funeral. Unauthorized use should be penalized by monetary fine, even when the borrower returns everything intact. One who steals things from the ancestral hall should be punished by castigation or sent to the government for legal sentence.[85]

The ancestral graveyard, which is equally sacred, permits no burial without clan authorization. One who violates this injunction should be punished by castigation or deprived of the privilege of entering the ancestral hall.[86] Grazing on its grounds is similarly forbidden.[87] Gathering wood there is the responsibility of the clan officers for the purpose of getting some extra income for the organization. Ordinary members who gather wood for themselves should be fined or penalized.[88] One rule has very detailed regulations:[89]

The woods at our ancestral graveyard used to be very beautiful. Recently bad members have felled the woods and cleared the space for farming. When the leaves fall in the autumn, men and women, young and old, go around the graveyard to gather them, thinking that no harm is done. They should know that picking chestnuts harms the branches and the trees will wither. Gathering wood hurts the surface soil and erosion will follow. Moreover, ignorant women carelessly walk on top of the graves and sit in front of the tombstones in

---

[84] 1919–h, "Articles of the Ancestral Hall," p. 7a; 1921–b, "Articles for the Affairs of the Ancestral Hall," p. 2a; 1921–h, "Regulations of the Ancestral Hall," p. 1b; and 1933–b, *op. cit.*, p. 3b. See also Table 21 in the Appendix.

[85] 1921–h, "Regulations of the Ancestral Hall," p. 1b; and 1922–g, "Tentative Regulations of the *Tsung*," p. 1b. See also Table 22 in the Appendix.

[86] 1921–c, "Articles for the Ancestral Hall," p. 2b; 1921–n, "*Tsung* Agreement," p. 47b. See also Table 23 in the Appendix.

[87] 1925–e, "Common Decisions of the *Tsu*," item 6 on protection of ancestral graveyard; 1930–a, "*Tsu* Standards," p. 21. See also Table 23 in the Appendix.

[88] 1918–c, "New Regulations of the Ancestral Hall" (1880), p. 1b. See also Table 24 in the Appendix.

[89] 1924–h, "Agreed Restrictions for the Ancestral Graveyard," p. 4a.

a disgusting manner . . . From now on, all dry wood and chestnuts should be allowed to fall and remain on the ground. One who gathers them in violation of this injunction should be punished. No clan officer should shield him out of partiality . . . One who trespasses and cultivates the ground of the ancestral graveyard, regardless of sex or generation status, should be dealt with severely.

The above stipulation discloses that the poor members are not even allowed to have dry leaves or wood from the ancestral graveyard.

The renting of common land, the management of surplus income, and the various detailed measures of protecting the common property are, after all, relatively minor matters. The main concern is to preserve the common property forever. Sometimes, the clan property was registered with the government in order to prevent unscrupulous members from selling or mortgaging it. A number of rules regard the selling and mortgaging of clan property as offensive as filial impiety. Such offense should be punished by deleting the offender's name from the genealogy or by excluding him from the ancestral hall.[90] However, other rules have no such stipulation at all, indicating a weakness in their organizational strength.

The loss of clan property is most commonly caused by lack of control over the managers. Under the rules, the managers are bound by the decisions of the clan meetings and under the supervision of the clan officers.[91] Neither senior members nor the descendants of the original donors of the common property should interfere with the management. The fact remains that in many clans the managers usurped power and the clan land assumed the appearance of their private property.[92] In this regard, the clan rules have not been effective enough either in provision or in enforcement.

C. ANCESTRAL RITES AND CLAN MEETINGS

Ancestral rites and clan meetings are the principal means of promoting clan cohesion.[93] Ancestral rites, as defined in a typical clan

[90] 1924–h, "Family Decisions" (1860), p. 2a; and 1933–b, *op. cit.*, p. 3b. See also Table 25 in the Appendix.
[91] 1917–b, "Existing Regulations of the Charitable Estate," p. 1a; and 1930–a, "Regulations of the Ancestral Hall," p. 21.
[92] 1924–g, "*Tsung* Agreement," p. 1b; cf. *MSSHK*, p. 4.
[93] Weber, *op. cit.*, p. 87.

rule, "are memorial services at which all members express their gratitude to the ancestors."[94] The rituals have religious, aesthetic, and educational meanings as well as a socialization function.[95] The members are reminded that "they all come from the common ancestry just as everything comes from Nature."[96] Kardiner, in his study of the Tanala culture, explains that ancestral god is an inflated parental image whose functions, like those of the father, are to see that no hostilities are directed against the individuals upon whom such hostilities would naturally fall.[97] This explanation is probably applicable to the ancestral veneration in the traditional Chinese culture. One rule states: "One should wait on the ancestral spirits as if they were alive."[98] The respect due to the ancestors whose spirits are capable of causing good fortune or misfortune to their descendants is akin to the deference one has to show to his parents.[99] The ancestral rites are thus important means of social control.

In the family, according to the clan rules, "sacrifices are offered on the birthdays and death anniversaries of the ancestors four or more generations ago, during the New Year holidays, on other appropriate festival days, and in some instances at the beginning and the middle of each month."[100] Poor and declining families often neglected the rituals or reduced them to a minimum; while wealthy and harmonious families built small ancestral halls in their homes.[101] Of far greater significance are the ancestral rites observed by the clan group which gives offering to the founder, the foremost ancestor of each branch, the ancestors whose descent lines have been unfortunately discontinued, and other worthy members whose posthumous tablets are placed along with those of the ancestors.

The practice was for a clan to meet at least once a year and normally twice during the spring and autumn to honor its ancestors.

---

[94] 1922–g, "Tentative Regulations of the *Tsung*," p. 3a; cf. Morohashi, *op. cit.*, p. 131.
[95] Levy, *op. cit.*, pp. 33–40 and Shimizu, *Kazoku*, pp. 362–365.
[96] 1934–a, "Family Regulations," p. 5a.
[97] Kardiner, *The Individual and His Society*, p. 313 ff.
[98] 1919–b, "Family Instructions," p. 11.
[99] Hsu, *Under the Ancestors' Shadow*, p. 31.
[100] 1919–b, *op. cit.*, p. 11.   [101] Hu, *op. cit.*, p. 32.

According to the ancient tradition, the autumn rites were devoted to the distant ancestors and the spring rites to the founding ancestor of the family. This was no longer the case after the Sung period. Many rules describe both occasions to be in pious memory of all the ancestors.[102] The spring rites are generally scheduled around the same time as the visitation to the ancestral graves. Some clans which have no ancestral hall should simply observe them before the ancestral graves.[103] As harvest time varies in different parts of China, not a few rules schedule the autumn rites actually in the winter.[104]

Some rules require, in addition, rites at New Year, the beginning and the middle of each lunar month.[105] These rites are neither found in the majority cases nor nearly as important as the spring and the autumn (or winter) rites, as the contents of the rules of 78 clans show:

	Number of Clans
Spring rites	69
Autumn rites	48
Winter rites, a variation of the above	27
New Year's rites	20
Rites at the beginning and the middle of each lunar month	17

The exact dates designated for the spring and the autumn or winter rites vary a great deal. Many rules put the date of the spring rites at *Ch'ing-ming* (清明), Festival of Clear-and-Bright, the customary time for "sweeping the ancestral graves," which falls around the first week of April.[106] A few rules move the date ahead to *Li-ch'un* (立春, Beginning of Spring), around the first week of February. Others set it back to *Hsia-chih* (夏至, Summer Solstice), around the third week of June.[107] In short, the date is either before or after the spring sowing. The dates for the autumn or winter rites vary even more. In some

---

[102] 1921–c, "Family Regulations," p. 2a; 1921–o, "New Regulations of the Ancestral Hall" (1899), p. 12b.
[103] 1928–b, "Family Instructions," p. 1a; cf. Morohashi, *op. cit.*. p. 16.
[104] 1934–f, "*Tsu* Regulations," p. 1b.
[105] 1921–j, "Regulations of the Ancestral Hall," p. 20a and 1927–a, "Regulations for Ancestral Sacrifices" (1837), p. 2a.
[106] Hu, *op. cit.*, p. 34.
[107] 1918–j, "Family Instructions," p. 26a; and 1919–h, *op. cit.*, p. 7a.

rules, it coincides with *Chung-yüan* (中元, Festival of the Middle Full Moon) in the seventh lunar month or around August, a time to offer sacrifices to the spirits in accordance with Buddhist practice.[108] Others schedule it at *Ch'iu-fen* (秋分, Autumn Equinox), around the third week of September, or on the first day of the tenth lunar month, which is usually in November.[109] Some rules have it as late as *Tung-chih* (冬至, Winter Solstice), which is toward the end of December.[110]

The activities prescribed by the rules for the spring and the autumn rites are generally the same. They begin with moral instructions:[111]

Before the sacrifices are offered to the ancestors, the meeting should begin by having a clan member of exemplary conduct read from the Imperial Injunctions on Moral Conduct or quote a few famous mottoes from the ancestors or ancient sages in order to remind the young members . . . All members, young and old, should listen carefully while remaining standing.

In some rules, the titular head or his assistant should give a lecture of a similar nature. The lecturer should enjoin the present generation to follow the illustrious examples of the ancestors.[112] The sacrifice then follows. The use of cooked meat, choice dishes, rice, bread, and wine reflects a food anxiety of the agricultural society.[113] After the sacrifice, the clan meeting should take up necessary business items: financial report, matters of clan concern, commendation of exemplary members and punishment of misbehaving members. No private dispute should be aired. Those who bring it up and get into an argument should be punished for their disrespect toward the ancestral spirits.[114]

No business meeting is held immediately after the New Year rites which should emphasize celebration and clan cohesion. One clan rule explains:[115]

[108] 1922–d, "Regulations of the *Tsung-tsu*," p. 19a.
[109] 1921–n, "*Tsung* Agreement," p. 47a and 1935–b, "Family Discipline Decided by *Tsu* Organization," p. 2b.
[110] 1930–c, "Regulations of the Ancestral Hall," p. 1a and 1933–g, "Articles by Common Decision" (1844), p. 4.
[111] 1921–o, "New Regulations of the Ancestral Hall" (1899), p. 12b.
[112] 1916–a, "Regulations for Controlling a Family," p. 1b; and cf. Martin C. Yang, *op. cit.*, p. 139.
[113] Cf. Kardiner, *The Individual and His Society*, p. 220.
[114] 1933–b, *op. cit.*, p. 1b.
[115] 1915–h, "Regulations for the Ancestral Hall and Graveyard," p. 73a.

THE CLAN RULES ON CLAN FUNCTIONS AND RELATIONSHIPS 119

When the clan members multiply into great numbers, they become more and more separated and they neglect to greet one another even at the time of mourning and celebration as required by the custom. They seem to forget their blood relationship and definitely lose the spirit of mutuality. The New Year's greetings, it is hoped, will bring them together again.

The ancestral rites on the first and the fifteenth day of each lunar month, required by only a few rules, are relatively simple. The clan officers should have the incense and candles ready. The members after paying their respect to the ancestral spirits should sign their names in the attendance record. The sacrifices consist of only tea and simple refreshments. The occasions may be used by the clan officers, if they wish, to make financial reports, to arbitrate disputes, to administer clan punishment, or to discuss urgent business.[116]

The rules consider the semi-annual rites and meetings to be the most important clan activities. The master of rites must be chosen carefully: he should be either the titular leader himself, the clan head accompanied by the titular leader, a scholar-official, a degree-holder, or the member with the highest official rank.[117] As the duty includes the reading of a memorial address in classical language dedicated to the ancestors, a scholar-official is naturally the most qualified.[118]

Attendance at the ancestral rites is both an obligation and a privilege of all male adults. Some rules allow the participation of boys as young as ten years old when led by their elders and for 'teen-age boys receiving formal education.[119] This is intended to promote education as well as to honor a potential scholar. The usual definition of an adult is over sixteen years of age; those who are younger "do not understand the rites and therefore need not attend."[120] Certain adult

---

[116] 1921–o, "New Regulations of the Ancestral Hall" (1899), p. 12b; 1929–b, "Ancestral Hall Agreement," p. 5a; and 1919–e, "Family Proprieties," p. 2a.

[117] 1913–b, "Family Regulations," p. 24b; 1915–i, "Regulations for Sacrifices," p. 1a; 1921–b, "Articles for the Affairs of the Ancestral Hall," p. 2b; 1926–b, "Regulations of the Literary Association," p. 3a; and 1925–c, "Regulations of the Ancestral Hall," p. 2b.

[118] Hu, op. cit., p. 23.

[119] 1935–f, "Regulations of the Ancestral Hall," item 4; and 1918–c, "New Agreement of the Tsung," p. 1b.

[120] 1913–c, op. cit., p. 3a.

members should be excluded. Generally speaking, exclusion is a clan punishment imposed upon misbehaving members. In a few rules, members who do not pay the required fees to the ancestral hall are also excluded. Some of these rules stipulate that a boy upon reaching sixteen years of age should pay 100 coins before he should be allowed to attend the ancestral rites.[121] One rule requires the following sum: one-tenth tael of silver from an adult married member and half the amount from an adult bachelor.[122] Poor members who cannot afford the amount are in effect deprived of their privilege to greet the ancestors. They tend to lose all interest in clan meetings.[123]

Most rules permit no women at the ancestral rites. A woman, if present, should be told to leave or punished by flogging her husband or son forty times.[124] Only a few rules grant the privilege of attendance to the ladies who prepare the sacrificial food and clean the ancestral hall.[125] However, if a female servant comes to help and stays around, her master should suffer a penalty and she herself should be flogged.[126]

The rules call upon their scholar-official members to set good examples by attending the rites regularly. Foul weather, an ordinary inconvenience, is no legitimate excuse for absence.[127] Only those ill or away from home are excused.[128] Some rules require the mild punishment of absence at semi-annual rites by reducing in half the sacrificial food ration normally distributed to each member family.[129] Others stipulate the fine of two-hundredths of a tael of silver.[130] But consecutive absences should be punished severely by flogging.[131] Even

---

[121] 1925–b, *op. cit.*, p. 6a.
[122] 1921–o, "Regulations of the Ancestral Hall" (1779), p. 10a.
[123] Martin C. Yang, *op. cit.*, p. 138.
[124] 1921–o, "New Regulations of the Ancestral Hall" (1899), p. 12b; 1934–f, "*Tsu* Regulations," p. 4b; and 1921–b, "Articles for the Affairs of the Ancestral Hall," p. 2a.
[125] 1916–c, "Additional Family Discipline," p. 2b.
[126] 1919–e, "Family Teachings," p. 2a.
[127] 1919–h, *op. cit.*, p. 7a.
[128] 1925–b, *op. cit.*, p. 6a.
[129] 1921–b, "Articles for the Affairs of the Ancestral Hall," p. 4a.
[130] 1928–d, "Family Instructions," p. 1a.
[131] 1922–f, "Regulations of the Ancestral Hall," p. 10b.

members who arrive late should be rebuked and sometimes excluded from the commensal meal after the ancestral rites.[132]

Both solemnity and the generation-age order should be stressed during ancestral rites.[133] The rules forbid conceited manners and arrogant language, which are obnoxious to other members and disrespectful to the ancestral spirits. Members who argue against the arrangement of the procession or who take their places out of order should be punished by rebuke or even with penalty.[134] One rule has a vivid description:[135]

Sacrifices in the ancestral hall require utmost respect and piety. Oftentimes, careless members make noises, enter and depart at will, sit or stand without proper manners. Some members even deliberately avoid the rites of kneeling and bowing before the ancestral tablets and yet shamelessly take part in eating and drinking at the ensuing commensal meal . . . The master of rites and his assistant should line up the members according to the generation-age order, lead them in procession to the ancestral tablets, usher them in turn to perform the rites with dignity and serenity.

Attending members are expected to dress properly; otherwise, they should be excluded from the ancestral rites. Members who come in short dresses should be told to leave; and poor members who cannot afford proper dress should at least wear a hat to show appropriate piety.[136]

After the ancestral rites and the clan meeting are over, certain qualified members have the privilege of attending a commensal meal, toasting sacrificial wine, and sharing sacrificial meat. The joyous occasion, though joyous, is bound by etiquette: no game should be permitted, not even the "fist game" popular at ordinary banquets.[137]

[132] 1918–c, "New Regulations of the Ancestral Hall" (1880), p. 1a.
[133] 1933–b, op. cit., p. 2a; 1929–f, "*Tsung* Regulations," p. 2a; 1916–b, "An Epitome of Family Regulations," p. 1a.
[134] 1915–i, "Regulations for Sacrifices," p. 1a; 1935–f, "Regulations of the Ancestral Hall," item 5.
[135] 1921–c, "Articles of the Ancestral Hall," p. 2a.
[136] 1915–a, "Family Regulations," p. 29b; 1916–c, "Additional Family Discipline," p. 2a; and 1919–h, op. cit., p. 7b.
[137] 1933–b, op. cit., p. 1b; 1935–f, "Regulations of the Ancestral Hall," item 5. In the fist game, the two opponents try to guess instantly the total of the fingers both of them are going to hold out.

Good table manners preclude excessive drinking and any one who becomes drunk, boisterous, quarrelsome, or abusive should be punished.[138] Nor should the members make fun in bad taste or use the occasion as an opportunity "to air one's private complaint against another and to dispute in an unbecoming manner." The offender, according to one rule, should be punished by the ritual penalty of kneeling before the ancestral tablets for the duration of one burning incense stick.[139]

The punishment for not observing proper manners at the ancestral rites and during the ensuing activities are, generally speaking, not severe.[140] The majority of the rules merely require "a penalty to be considered." The penalty, as befitting the occasion, is usually a ritualistic one.[141] A clan officer seems to deserve some consideration; when he commits such an offense, he gets a rather lenient punishment such as a monetary fine for buying candles to be used at future rites.[142] In any event, for the members and the officers alike, corporal punishment is seldom stipulated for punishing these minor offenses.[143]

Only a limited number of official and qualified members are designated by the rules to enjoy the privilege of toasting sacrificial wine and of attending commensal meal. The official members are the titular leader, the clan head, the branch heads, and the members who assist in the ancestral rites. The qualified members are those who have contributed to the social prestige of the clan, such as described in the following example:[144]

Commensal banquet is only for members over fifty years of age and the members with government degree and official ranks. Unqualified members who slip in should be ousted. An exception is made, however, for young members of no social distinction but who come from a

---

[138] 1916–b, "An Epitome of Family Regulations," p. 1a; 1919–a, "Family Teachings," p. 2a; 1922–f, "Regulations of the Ancestral Hall," p. 10b.
[139] 1921–c, "Articles of the Ancestral Hall," p. 2a.
[140] See Table 32 in the Appendix.
[141] 1919–e, "Family Teachings," p. 1; and 1921–c, "Articles of the Ancestral Hall," p. 2a.
[142] 1916–b, "An Epitome of Family Regulations," p. 2a.
[143] 1922–f, "Regulations of the Ancestral Hall," p. 10b.
[144] 1921–c, "Articles of the Ancestral Hall," p. 2a.

great distance in the company of their elders for the purpose of visiting the ancestral hall.

Aged members are qualified, for longevity is believed to be a symbol of prosperity.[145] Those with government degrees and official ranks are eligible, but those who have purchased official titles through financial contributions to the government are not included.[146] Members who come from a distance are given this special privilege, for they are the living evidence of clan cohesion. Not mentioned in the above quotation, but in some other rules, are pious sons who have received government commendation, members who have donated land to the clan, and others of whom the clan organization is proud.[147] The seating at commensal meal should be carefully arranged beforehand.[148]

After the rites, the sacrificial food, usually meat and bread, is sent to various members, though the ration system varies from one rule to another. Liberal rules provide the ration for all adult male members, while others limit it to those who have attended the rites and paid their fees to the ancestral hall.[149] For the sake of convenience, the ration is sometimes converted into cash payment as in the following case:[150]

When one reaches fifteen years of age, he is admitted to the ancestral hall and pays one-twentieth tael of silver. His name is put on the list of members to receive the sacrificial food ration. The ration, originally consisting of one catty of meat per member, has been converted into cash payment in the amount of thirty coins. However, the membership is now so large that the amount has to be reduced from now on to twenty coins.

A number of rules restrict the ration only to the clan officers, to the same members who are qualified to attend the commensal meal, and

---

[145] 1917–a, "Regulations for the Spring and Autumn Sacrifices," p. 1b; and 1921–b, "Articles for the Affairs of the Ancestral Hall," p. 3b.
[146] 1917–a, "Regulations for the Spring and Autumn Sacrifices," p. 1a.
[147] 1924–g, "*Tsung* Agreement," p. 1b; and 1933–b, *op. cit.*, p. 2.
[148] 1925–c, "Regulations for Annual Sacrifices," p. 2a; and 1933–b, *op. cit.*, p. 2a.
[149] 1924–h, "Family Decisions" (1860), p. 2a; and 1921–b, "Articles for the Affairs of the Ancestral Hall," p. 3a.
[150] 1921–b, "Articles for the Affairs of the Ancestral Hall," p. 3a. A catty is about the equivalent of 1.3 pound.

to the managers of the ancestral hall in recognition of their service.[151] Another variation is in the amount of the ration, depending on the qualification of the recipient. A scholar-official member receives several times the unit ration; the higher his rank is, the more he gets. A clan officer receives a double ration; a member over sixty-five years of age or a member who has donated land, one ration.[152] Some rules increase the ration for venerated, aged members and for members known for their virtuous conduct, filial piety, or unusual generosity. A scholar-official who has drafted and read the memorial address at the ancestral rites may receive an additional ration for his service.[153]

Ancestral rites involve numerous expenses. One rule reports in 1915 the annual cost of the spring and autumn rites to be 10,000 coins; another reports the same in 1924 to be 50,000 coins; and several others mention the amount as between twelve and fifteen dollars.[154] In view of the low standard of living in rural China, this is not a small sum. A detailed account of the miscellaneous expenses is given in one rule around the year 1860:[155]

One who helps carrying the hog shall be paid 75 coins; one who helps carrying the lamb and incense burner, 50 coins; one who plays the drum and carries the ceremonial umbrellas and banners, 30 coins. The musicians shall be paid the total sum of 1,100 coins and they are to take care of their own meals. The fire-cracker man shall receive one catty of sacrificial meat; the butcher, 300 coins; and the caretaker of the ancestral graveyard, also one catty of sacrificial meat in annual recognition of his service.

Clans with ritual land or other sizable common property can meet these expenses from their income, while other clans have to raise money by such means as registration fees of members coming of age,

---

[151] 1932–a, "Regulations of the Ancestral Hall," p. 9a; and 1917–a, "Regulations for the Spring and Autumn Sacrifices," p. 2.
[152] 1917–a, "Regulations for the Spring and Autumn Sacrifices," p. 1b.
[153] 1921–b, "Articles for the Affairs of the Ancestral Hall," p. 3a; and 1933–b, op. cit., p. 2.
[154] 1913–c, op. cit., p. 3a; 1915–d, "Record of the Charitable Land"; and 1924–g, "Articles for the Charitable Land," under the subject of prosperity, p. 6a.
[155] 1924–h, "Family Decisions" (1860), p. 3a.

contributions required of all the members eligible to attend the ancestral rites, or donations payable upon placing a posthumous tablet in the ancestral hall.[156] A large but not well endowed clan often assigns the duty of preparing the ancestral rites to its branches or leading families by annual rotation.[157] A few rules specifically provide punishment for the evasion of such an assignment.[158] In other cases, an irresponsible branch is to be given up by the clan as being hopeless and the members of that branch excluded from the ancestral hall.[159] Many clans must have found the expenses of the ancestral rites hard to meet. One rule laments that the group, owing to the lack of funds, has observed the ancestral rites only for a few times in many years and eventually discontinued them entirely.[160]

Clan cohesion is strengthened by the ancestral rites. Yet the ancestral rites in turn depend upon the clan's ability to defray the expenses. This is the reason why so many rules appeal to the scholar-official and wealthy members for support on the one hand and, on the other, give these members special privileges at the ancestral rites, at the commensal meal, and in other ways. The ordinary members have little ground to complain of the discrimination. They contribute only modest amounts and stand to gain many peripheral advantages in attending the ancestral rites, such as standing together with the socially prominent members, or by the generation-age order, even ahead of the latter. Only the poor members who cannot pay the required fees or cannot afford proper clothing are excluded. To be a clan member in good standing, one must have a minimum income. This explains why the rules stress the need of a gainful vocation and the virtue of industriousness and thrift, for these are important not only for the individual members themselves but also for the clan in order to carry on its essential function of ancestral rites.

---

[156] 1925–b, *op. cit.*, p. 6a; 1934–f, "*Tsu* Regulations," p. 10a.
[157] 1921–l, "Regulations for Annual Sacrifices," item 7.
[158] See Table 31 in the Appendix. 1925–c, "Regulations of the Genealogy," p. 1b.
[159] 1934–f, "*Tsu* Regulations," p. 3a.
[160] 1932–a, "Additional Regulations of the Ancestral Hall" (1843), item 1.

D. CLAN REWARD AND CLAN RELIEF

The clan customarily used their common fund also for clan reward and clan relief. Reward is for the purpose of promoting the collective clan prestige, of recognizing the worthy individuals, and of inducing other members to aspire to the same distinctions. Relief is for the members in need. Reward and relief are only general terms. These measures as provided in the rules of 75 clans may be classified into five categories: (1) celebration for worthy members (excluding scholars); (2) celebration for graduating scholars and degree-holders; (3) educational award and assistance for students and scholars; (4) occasional aids for members in need; and (5) regular relief rations. The following summary in itemized form presents a general pattern:

	Number of Clans
Celebration of worthy members:	
Application for government commendation of worthy members, mostly widows of distinguished chastity	13
Celebration of longevity for members reaching eighty years of age	2
Celebration for members receiving degrees from civil service examinations or in modern times graduating from schools	19
Educational award and assistance:	
For schooling	24
For taking civil service examinations	16
Occasional aids:	
Helping funerals and burials	15
Helping weddings	13
Helping newborn babies	2
Helping illness	1
Regular relief ration:	
For poor, unemployed members	33
For poor widows and orphans	31
For aged widows without family support	20
For disabled and invalid members	9

As may be seen from a comparison of the various amounts stipulated, reward connected with clan prestige is valued considerably higher than relief of members in need. One rule, for example, gives an eighty-year old member three taels of silver and a hundred-year old member

THE CLAN RULES ON CLAN FUNCTIONS AND RELATIONSHIPS   127

ten times the amount. Longevity is praised as a result of virtuous conduct and, more significantly, as a source of clan pride.[161] The use of clan funds to reward worthy members, mostly widows of distinguished chastity, is discussed in the following section rather than here; for the subject is closely connected with the control of exemplary conduct. It may be noted here, however, that the clan rules are in favor of gaining as much group prestige as possible through distinguished chaste widows.

The greatest emphasis is placed, however, upon the honoring of successful scholars and promising aspirants as well as assisting them in the consecutive stages of their career, as the public honors and prestige they gain are shared by the clan group. One rule states that when a member obtains a high degree, the clan should celebrate the event by staging plays in the ancestral hall for the enjoyment of both the ancestral spirits and all members.[162] Another rule stipulates that the clan should pay twelve taels of silver to a holder of high government degree to cover the cost of his ceremonial parasol, a privilege of official distinction.[163]

The traditional examination system had three successive degrees: the first to be earned at the prefectural examination; the second, at the provincial examination; and the third, at the national examination. Those who obtained their degrees at the national examination then took another palace examination to compete for the high honors and the highest honors. Nine rules, compiled in the period between 1847 and 1894, stipulate the clan awards in honor of these degree-holders in varying amounts either in coins or in taels of silver.[164] It is sufficient to summarize the range of these respective amounts:

[161] 1921–c, "Articles of the Ancestral Hall," p. 6a.
[162] 1933–g, "Articles by Common Decision" (1844), p. 1b.
[163] 1921–b, "Articles for the Affairs of the Ancestral Hall," p. 6b.
[164] 1918–c, "New Regulations of the Ancestral Hall" (1880), p. 3a; 1918–k, "Record of Combined Regulations for Award of the School and Ritual Land" (1891), pp. 23a–28b; 1919–c, "Regulations of the Charitable Estate" (1859), p. 18b; 1921–b, "Articles for the Affairs of the Ancestral Hall," p. 6b; 1921–c, "Articles of the Ancestral Hall," p. 6a; 1923–b, "Regulations of the Charitable Estate" (1876), p. 22; 1924–d, "Regulations of the Charitable Estate" (1847), p. 6b; 1924–g, "Articles for the Charitable Land," pp. 5–6; 1924–h, "Family Decisions," item 8.

	In Coins	In Taels of Silver
First degree	1,000–2,000	2–10
Second degree	10,000–40,000	12–20
Third degree	20,000–60,000	12–30
High honor at palace examination	40,000–60,000	40
Highest honor at palace examination	80,000	80

The amount of these awards depends on the financial resources of the clan. The rules of wealthy clans are quite liberal. One rule, among the nine, allots to the degree-holders of the various grades not only cash awards from the income of the ritual land but also awards in rice from the school land owned by the clan.[165]

Awarding the degree-holders is important, but educating promising students and helping them go to the civil service examinations are equally desirable. Most rules appeal to their members to help in this good cause. An old rule dated 1880 states: "Our clan has long remained undistinguished, since few members ever become officials or degree-holders. All of us should therefore give in order to help promising members study."[166] Another rule points out that helping the education of fellow members is helping them "bring glory and prestige to the whole clan."[167] Yet, generosity of individual members is not nearly as dependable as having some common property designated as the school or educational land. Even in the wealthy clans endowed with such common property, the opportunity for free education still tends to be limited. One clan which had its own school decided in 1901 to limit free schooling to sixteen boys and to give the priority to orphans and poor members.[168] Another clan which had 120 *mou* of school land with an annual income of 240,000 coins allotted half of it as the teacher's salary and the other half as scholarships. The scholarship fund, 120,000 coins, was to be granted evenly: one half

---

[165] 1918–k, "Record of Combined Regulations for Award of the School and Ritual Land," pp. 23a–28b.
[166] 1918–c, "New Regulations of the Ancestral Hall" (1880), p. 3a.
[167] 1919–a, "Family Regulations," p. 3a.
[168] 1921–o, "Record of the Reconstruction of the Ancestral Hall and the *Tsu* School" (1901), pp. 6a–7a.

for the financially poor members; and the other half for the descendants of the original donor of the school land.[169]

Many clans gave aids in various ways to their members who prepared for and took the government examination. In the traditional days, one clan kept a set of the thirteen classics, a set of the twenty-four dynastic histories, and other useful books at its charitable estate for the use of its studying members. When the government abolished the examination system in 1905 and began to promote modern education, this clan, as in a few other cases, founded a modern elementary school for the children in the clan.[170] Several rules suggest semi-monthly essay contests at the ancestral hall with meals provided by the clan organization in order to encourage their studying members to excel themselves.[171] A number of rules stipulate definite sums to help members pay traveling expenses while taking a government examination.[172] These figures vary within a narrow range as shown in the following:

Candidates of the first degree	700–5,000 coins
Candidates of the second degree	3,000–10,000 coins
Candidates of the third degree	8,000–30,000 coins

The aids given to the candidates are, by comparison, far less generous than the awards for the degree-holders. There are probably several reasons for this difference. The degree-holders give the clan great prestige; and they can be expected to give financial contributions to the clan later on. On the other hand, candidates do not necessarily succeed, their number tends to be larger by comparison and clan funds may be limited.

---

[169] 1924–g, "Articles for the Charitable Land," p. 1a.
[170] 1927–a, "Additional Regulations of the Ancestral Hall" (1885), p. 19a and p. 23a.
[171] 1917–a, "Miscellaneous Articles" (1847), pp. 1a–1b.
[172] 1914–i, "Additional Regulations of the Ancestral Hall" (1821), p. 2a; 1917–a, "Miscellaneous Articles" (1847), p. 1b; 1918–c, "New Regulations of the Ancestral Hall" (1880), p. 3a; 1919–c, "Regulations of the Charitable Estate" (1859), p. 18b; 1921–n, "Supplementary *Tsung* Agreement," p. 55b; 1923–b, "Regulations of the Charitable Estate" (1876), p. 22; 1924–d, "Regulations of the Charitable Estate" (1847); 1924–g, "Articles for the Charitable Land," pp. 1–2; and 1924–h, "Family Decisions" (1860), p. 3a.

Clan relief does not receive as much emphasis as do clan rewards. Most rules simply rely upon the kindness of individual members. According to one rule, the clan head has the authority as well as the duty to issue a circular to all members calling upon them to help a family which cannot pay for a wedding or a funeral, members who lack livelihood, or members who suffer from extraordinary calamity. To this appeal for mutual aid, the members are obliged to respond and wealthy members should contribute more than the average.[173] Many rules vaguely suggest that a clan meeting should be called to discuss the need of relief for such members.[174] It is doubtful, however, to what an extent such a circular or a meeting could achieve its purpose.

In the case of seven clans well endowed with charitable estates, their rules have concrete detailed provisions on the relief of poor members. One rule dated 1923 may serve as a typical example. Among its numerous provisions, the following are the major ones: for childbirth, three *yüan* or silver dollars; for wedding of a son, fifteen *yüan*; for marrying off a daughter, seven and a half *yüan*; for funeral of an adult, twenty-one *yüan*; for funeral of a child more than ten years old, ten and a half *yüan*; for burial of an adult, nine *yüan*; for the burial of a child more than ten years old, four and a half *yüan*; for a member who has signed up to be an apprentice, fifteen *yüan*; and for one who has finished his apprenticeship, six *yüan*.[175]

Seven clans which have rules on the management of their charitable estates provide regular relief.[176] The following points summarize the outstanding features of their detailed contents. First, the clan members eligible for relief are the aged, the widowers, the widows, the

---

[173] 1925–b, *op. cit.*, p. 7a.
[174] 1921–n, "*Tsung* Agreement," p. 47b.
[175] 1923–b, "Revised Regulations of the Charitable Estate" (1923), p. 28a. For an earlier version, see its "Regulations of the Charitable Estate" (1876), pp. 22a–23a.
[176] 1914–i, "Additional Regulations of the Ancestral Hall" (1914), pp. 1–2; 1917–b, "Existing Regulations of the Charitable Estate" (1917), pp. 1–3; 1919–c, "Regulations of the Charitable Estate" (1859), p. 17; 1922–d, "Old Regulations of the *Tsung-tsu*," p. 11a; 1923–b, "Regulations of the Charitable Estate" (1876), pp. 10b–20b; 1924–g, "Articles for the Charitable Land," Articles on relief, p. 3b; 1927–a, "Additional Regulations of the Charitable Estate" (1926), p. 24a.

orphans, the disabled, the extremely poor, the poor descendants of the original donor of the estate, and the unemployed. Second, these members eligible for relief are further differentiated according to age: the elderly members receive more than the young members. Third, there are special considerations. For instance, the poor descendants of the original donor receives a larger sum than others. A young widow under thirty years of age gets more because her widowhood is especially commendable. Those who have no family support whatsoever get more than those who may have a little. Fourth, the relief varies in form, in time, as well as in amount among these seven cases. If it is a monthly ration of rice, the amount varies between fifteen and forty *sheng*, a *sheng* being one-hundredth of a picul. If it is an annual ration of rice, the relief ranges from forty *sheng* to one picul and eighty *sheng*. If the relief in rice as originally stipulated has been converted into annual cash relief, the amount ranges from small fractions to about six *yüan*, or six taels of silver. Some charitable estates, among the seven, give in addition either winter clothing or additional amounts intended for clothing.

It is by no means easy either to establish and maintain a charitable estate or to administer the relief of poor members. The case history of one charitable estate is well worth citing.[177] It started in 1837 but, during the occupation by the T'ai-p'ing rebels, the land was left uncultivated. Fortunately, a capable member of the clan, apparently a prominent official, contributed his salary to clan relief in cash in 1863 toward the end of the rebellion. After the charitable estate resumed its normal function, the cash relief was continued as a subsidiary relief until 1890. Then, the charitable estate made a change in its regulations in 1900, converting the normal relief in rice into cash also. The members on relief welcomed the change. In 1926, it was found that the relief in cash could no longer buy the same amount of rice as originally intended. Consequently, the charitable estate decided to raise the amount of cash by about one-third. The fact that it could do so testifies to its successful management; on the other hand, this points out the need of adjustment from time to time to meet changing conditions.

[177] 1927–a, "Additional Regulations of the Charitable Estate" (1926), pp. 16–25.

Another well-managed charitable estate also raised the amount of its cash relief in 1923 because of inflation and price fluctuation. It was found that, during the period between harvest seasons, the food prices went up so high that the members could hardly buy enough food with their cash relief.

In retrospect, these charitable estates are the admirable examples of an outstanding and renowned feature of the clan institution in traditional China. Several of them, it should be added, extended their relief activities to married daughters who were not in the clan and even to non-clan persons such as poor scholars and other unfortunate people in the community by monthly relief, loans at a very low rate of interest, and philanthropic cemeteries.

From the viewpoint of social control, relief activities of the clan serve more than their apparent purpose. They not only take care of the minimum material need of the members in distress but also promote the collective moral well-being of the entire group. Unfortunately, many clans do not seem to have ample resources at their disposal for relief purposes. Even when they have, poor management and failure to adjust to changing conditions often result in the disruption of this function.

E. EXEMPLARY CONDUCT
AND INTRA-CLAN RELATIONSHIPS

Exemplary conduct and intra-clan relationships are frequently mentioned together in the clan rules. There is a close connection between the two: the former is the ideal norm which directly or indirectly helps to strengthen the clan's control of the latter. In discussing exemplary conduct, the clan rules place their emphasis upon positive encouragement, while in discussing intra-clan relationships, the emphasis is in negative restraint.

The rules of 35 clans contain definite measures to honor the specified exemplary conduct. The general pattern of these provisions is seen in the following itemization:

THE CLAN RULES ON CLAN FUNCTIONS AND RELATIONSHIPS 133

	Number of Clans
Distinguished chastity of a widow	24
Charity to clan organization or members	21
Exemplary filial piety and brotherly conduct	21
Unusually praiseworthy moral conduct	8
Distinguished service to the state or the society	4

Three emphases stand out clearly: First, chastity both as moral conduct and as a source of clan pride; second, the spirit of clan cohesion concretely expressed in charity; and third, the valued qualities which help family harmony.

There are a number of ways for the clan to recognize and reward its exemplary members. The first is ceremonial commendation with or without the award of a ritualistic gift.[178] The description of such a ceremony is given in the following quotation:[179]

After the ancestral rites, the clan officers shall begin the ceremony of commending the highly virtuous members. Those who are so honored shall kneel before the ancestral tablets while the commendation is read. Upon rising, they shall drink a cup of sacrificial wine.

Such an honor is often given to members of notable charity who have helped fellow members in distress, made liberal contributions to the clan organization, or given generous relief to the community.[180]

Second, commendable members may receive honorary titles in the clan. As mentioned in a previous section, one rule requires the designation of a charitable person as an "esteemed member" and a person of "high moral integrity who properly fulfills his roles without the slightest fault" as a "sagacious member," even though the economic status or generation-age status of that person may be quite humble.[181] Another rule mentions the title of "virtuous elder members," which should be given to those who are "over sixty years of age, with such virtues as honesty, integrity, filial piety, industriousness in vocation, and without disputes whatsoever with their fellow members throughout their lives."[182] They are the ones who have combined the prestige

[178] 1919–e, "Family Discipline," p. 11a.
[179] 1915–h, "Regulations of the Ancestral Hall and Graveyard," p. 71a.
[180] 1918–f, "New Family Regulations," p. 22a.
[181] 1918–c, "New Regulations of the Ancestral Hall" (1880), p. 1.
[182] 1914–d, "*Tsung* Agreement," p. 1b.

of old age with moral authority. However, this form of commendation is not found in most clan rules.

A third form of commendation provided in a few rules is connected with a routine record of both good and bad behavior of individual members, much like a grade book. At the end of a year, the members should receive commendation or rebuke at the clan meeting according to their cumulative merits and demerits. One rule stipulates that those who have earned the highest merits should have their names so entered in the next edition of the genealogy.[183]

Fourth, honorable mention in the genealogy is highly regarded. The scholar-official members are "assured of having their biographies" in the genealogy. But the same honor should be given to the members "who have exceptional virtue and noble conduct" and the members "who are extremely devoted to their parents and brothers."[184] This form of commendation is especially applicable to widows of distinguished chastity, to whom many rules give a great deal of attention. Some rules commend the widows who "resist temptation or violence" and those who "take care of the orphans and keep the family in good order."[185] Other rules honor those who begin their widowhood before the age of thirty and remain in chastity for the rest of their lives.[186] According to one rule, such a widow should receive mention in the genealogy, even though she dies before reaching old age.[187]

Fifth, commendation may take the form of granting the privilege of entering the posthumous tablet of an exemplary member into the ancestral hall, an honor in the ancestral cult. In the words of one rule:[188]

The honor is reserved for those who are well known for their extreme filial piety, brotherly conduct, honesty, and loyalty, for those who have given generous contribution to the ancestral hall, for those who have government degrees and official ranks, for those whose exemplary moral conduct is well known, and for those who have otherwise brought glory to the clan.

[183] 1919–e, "Family Teachings," p. 5a and 1925–b, *op. cit.*, p. 7a.
[184] 1928–b, "Rules of Genealogy," p. 117b.
[185] 1916–a, "General Rules," p. 23b; 1929–d, "Regulations of the Genealogy," p. 1b; and 1919–a, "Family Regulations," p. 2a.
[186] 1928–b, "Rules of Genealogy," p. 18a.
[187] 1916–d, "Additional Rules of the Genealogy," p. 2a.
[188] 1921–c, "Articles of the Ancestral Hall," p. 1a.

Another rule describes the detailed arrangement in the ancestral hall:[189]

The western ancestral hall . . . is divided into two sections: the general and the special. The general section is used for the tablets of all the ancestors, while the special section is for those who have the merits of filial piety, brotherly conduct, honesty, loyalty, contribution to the compilation of genealogy, contribution to the repairing of the ancestral hall, contribution of ritual land, and other merits which deserve the same honor.
The southern ancestral hall has its east room designated as the Gratitude Hall reserved for the tablets of the virtuous and the meritorious ancestors. Its west room is designated as the Chastity Hall reserved for the tablets of all chaste women in the clan. In former days, widows of distinguished chastity were honored by the government. Since the system has been abolished, the only honor a chaste woman can now get is to have her tablet placed in the Hall. These chaste women deserve sympathy and our members should not regard such commendation as an obsolete custom.

Ordinary members generally cannot have their posthumous tablets in the ancestral hall, though a few rules grant the privilege to members whose families have made a substantial contribution. This reflects an anxiety to increase the clan's income. One rule, for example, grants the privilege to its scholar-official members and members of exemplary conduct without charge, but to an ordinary member only upon receiving the donation of fifty taels of silver.[190] Another rule is very interesting. First, it requires a donation from its scholar-official members as well. Those with high ranks and degrees should contribute more according to an ascending scale. Second, the place which a tablet occupies in the ancestral hall is governed by a differentiated rate: 100,000 coin donation for a tablet to be placed in the main hall; 50,000 coin donation, in the eastern side-hall; and 30,000 coin donation, in the western side-hall.[191] Several other rules are interested more in land property than in cash donation. In one case, donation

[189] 1913–c, *op. cit.*, pp. 2a–2b.
[190] 1921–b, "Articles for the Affairs of the Ancestral Hall," p. 4b.
[191] 1933–g, "Articles by Common Decisions" (1844), pp. 5a–5b. The same principle is adopted by the more recent and revised rule of the clan, "Regulations of the Ancestral Hall throughout Kiangsi Province" (1933), p. 1b.

of five *mou* of land qualifies for the privilege. In another case, the amount required is exceedingly large: 100 *mou* of land or 1,000 taels of silver.[192]

The above cases are exceptional rather than typical. Most rules reserve this privilege to worthy members only. One who, without authorization, tries to put the posthumous tablet of a deceased member into the ancestral hall should be subject to the punishment of monetary fine.[193] Some rules refuse to consider a large donation as a justifiable basis of granting the privilege:[194]

To have a tablet in the ancestral hall is to enjoy sacrificial rites along with the ancestors. It is a sacred clan honor. A deceased member who does not qualify for this privilege should never get it through the use of pressure by his descendants. Otherwise, the ancestral spirits would resent it and the other clan members would protest. Generous donation of either cash or land should not be allowed to change this stipulation.

Finally the most honorable form of commendation coveted by both the individual and the clan is government citation. One rule states:[195]

The clan should send a gift to a member whose loyalty to the state, filial piety, chastity, or righteousness has been widely acclaimed and also pay the expenses of an application for government citation.

When a member receives government citation, the clan should make a *pien* (匾)—a votive tablet with a horizontal inscription—to be placed above the gateway of his family. One rule, among several others, mentions the sum of 4,000 coins for a votive tablet.[196] This honor is especially applicable in the case of distinguished chastity. The clan in applying government citation pays all the expenses.[197]

A distinguished widow who has received government citation may also be entitled to a commemorative arch, a monument of prestige

---

[192] 1915–d, "Record of the Charitable Land," p. 2; and 1927–a, "Regulations for Ancestral Sacrifices" (1837), p. 3b.
[193] 1918–e, "Regulations of the Ancestral Hall," item 3.
[194] 1921–c, "Articles of the Ancestral Hall, p. 1a.
[195] 1929–f, "*Tsung* Regulations," p. 3b.
[196] 1923–b, "Regulations of the Charitable Estate" (1876), p. 23b.
[197] 1914–d, "*Tsung* Agreement," p. 1b; and 1934–c, "Family Standards," p. 8a.

which the clan should be willing to build, if her family cannot afford it.[198] One rule shows great eagerness for this prestige in stipulating that when the clan does not have enough funds available, it should raise the necessary amount from the members, especially the wealthy ones.[199]

The commendation of exemplary conduct does not occupy, however, as much attention as the emphasis on a well-ordered group life through the observance of the generation-age order. To abide by the generation-age order in a clan seems to be more difficult than in a family. The reasons are several. First, the generation status does not always agree with the age status. "Members may be senior by generation but not by age. Elder members may actually belong to a junior generation and *vice versa*. Certain flexible adjustments in ritual propriety toward one another will be desirable in such cases." The principle upheld by the rule is for members to be mutually respectful: one should respect the other for his age and the latter should respect the former for his higher generation status.[200] Second, clan status often does not agree with socio-economic status. Sometimes a senior clan member may, in fact, work as a servant in the family of a wealthy member. The rules merely advise the master in this case to treat the unfortunate member with kindness, as his status is different from that of other servants.[201] Even under normal circumstances, class differentiation causes tension that is harmful to clan cohesion. One rule laments: "Wealthy members are often unkind, while poor members are frequently seeking petty advantages."[202] Third, it is inevitable in the close-knit clan life that some members will get into disputes. A common dispute is "for a member of a junior generation-age status to defy a senior member and for a senior member to take advantage of and humiliate a junior member."[203]

---

[198] 1912–a, "*Tsu* Regulations," p. 5a.
[199] 1928–a, "Family Regulations," p. 1b.
[200] 1922–e, "Family Instructions of Ancestor Tan-ya-kung," p. 60; and 1930–a, "*Tsu* Standards," p. 20.
[201] 1930–a, "*Tsu* Standards," p. 20.
[202] 1936–b, "Miscellaneous Statements of Family Instructions," p. 8b.
[203] 1916–d, "Additional Rules of the Genealogy," p. 2b.

The rules of 106 clans list one or more of the following kinds of misconduct as undesirable from the standpoint of clan cohesion and harmony:

	Number of Clans
Junior members being disrespectful toward or insulting senior members	83
Senior members humiliating junior members	38
Wealthy and powerful members being conceited and oppressing other members	64
Flagrant violation of the ethical relationship (such as incest)	26
Dispute of property and money between members	24
Other aggressive misconduct toward fellow members	24

The above summary shows that the generation-age order is the main concern. The rules urge members "to set good examples for their own descendants;" otherwise, when they become senior, they cannot expect respect from their junior members.[204] Respect of seniority in the clan consists of proper manner in general and proper addressing in particular.[205] "Members of junior status should greet their senior members according to the kinship order. Violations should be penalized."[206] One rule has a detailed stipulation:[207]

A junior member should stand up when a senior member approaches. In walking together, a junior member should always stay behind. In conversation, a junior member should never address a senior member by pronoun, but always by his personal name followed by the kinship term such as elder brother or uncle.

Since the generation-age order favors the senior members, punishment for them is more lenient than that for the junior members. According to one rule, for example, a junior member who used improper language toward a senior member should be punished by flogging. But a senior member who commits the same offense in

---

[204] 1928-c, "Ancestors' Mottoes," p. 1.
[205] 1922-c, "*Tsu* Agreement," p. 4a; see also Table 27 in the Appendix.
[206] 1921-n, "*Tsung* Agreement," p. 48a.
[207] 1931-b, "Ancestors' Instructions," item 2.

abusing a junior member is punishable only by oral censure.[208] This discrimination is well described in another rule:[209]

If a junior member insults or assaults a senior member, he should be flogged in front of the ancestral tablet at the home of the latter and be made to apologize by kneeling before the latter in person. In a reversed situation, the offending senior member should be punished by the penalty of providing a banquet with wine to make up to the offended junior member.

When rebuked by a senior member, one should listen respectfully and desist from arguing. However, the order in clan life should not be autocratic; the rules urge the senior members to treat the junior members "with kindness as if the latter were their own family youngsters."[210] No senior member "should take advantage of the status, threaten to beat a junior member, pull him up by his sleeves, make his humiliation intolerable by using abusive and profane language."[211] Nor should a senior member, "unsuccessful in his attempt to trample upon a junior member, falsely accuse the latter of being disrespectful. The clan has the responsibility to ascertain the actual circumstances."[212] "When a dispute arises between a senior and a junior member, it should be reported to the clan officers who shall settle the case impartially at a meeting of all members according to the consensus of opinion."[213]

A common cause of conflict is the disparity between social status and generation-age status. Members of families with high social standing are likely to look down upon ordinary members. The rules of 64 clans, in the hope of preserving clan cohesion against class differentiation, list many common faults of their powerful and wealthy members:

---

[208] 1923–a, "Family Instructions," p. 1b. See Table 29 in the Appendix.
[209] 1924–h, "Family Decisions" (1860), p. 2b.
[210] 1921–q, "Miscellaneous Instructions for Controlling a Family," p. 20b; and 1916–a, "Regulations for Controlling a Family," p. 6b.
[211] 1916–c, "Family Instructions," p. 1b.
[212] 1921–k, "Family Discipline," p. 3b.
[213] 1935–f, "Regulations of the Ancestral Hall," p. 6a.

	Number of Clans
Oppressing poor and weak members	58
Allowing one's servants to show disrespect to other members	10
Using influence to maneuver a majority against certain members in a minority	10
Relying on one's family influence to trample upon other members	8

The rules maintain the position that since the clan comes from the same root, "the members should not discriminate against one another because of wealth or poverty." The wealthy members "should not belittle the poor."[214] The members with government ranks should refrain from showing off their prestige but should continue to respect other members by their generation-age status.[215] It is unbecoming for "the powerful members to trample upon the weak ones, for members to flatter the wealthy ones or to humiliate the poor ones, for the influential members to use force against others just because the others dare not retaliate."[216] The worst case is for one to allow his servants to insult his poor kin.[217] The rules hold the belief that such disregard of ethical principle will lead to the downfall of his family.[218]

The rules also advise the powerful members not to manipulate clan or community matters to their own selfish advantage. "Scholar-officials who have high social status should not . . . conspire with government clerks in manipulating law suits."[219] What the clan rules do not mention, however, is the fact that a clan often expected its scholar-official members to use their influence to help the clan or other members.

The types of misconduct discussed so far are relatively minor, involving little more than a mere slight of the generation-age status. When the generation-age relationship suffers from a flagrant violation, such as marrying a widowed sister-in-law or adultery with

[214] 1914–g, "Family Instructions," p. 2a.
[215] 1914–j, "Family Regulations," p. 9a; and 1928–g, "Ancestors' Instructions," item on *tsu* discipline.
[216] 1916–a, "Regulations for Controlling a Family," p. 2b.
[217] 1917–d, "Family Regulations," p. 2a; 1921–i, "Family Instructions," p. 2b.
[218] 1922–e, *op. cit.*, p. 60.
[219] See Table 38 in the Appendix.

one's own kin, the offense is far more serious. Most rules require the severe punishment of such offenses by exclusion from the ancestral hall, expunction of his name from the genealogical record, formal expulsion from the clan, or sending him to the local government for punishment under the law.[220]

Aggression within the clan often stems from ulterior motives of getting property or money from another member, as seen in the rules of 24 clans:

	Number of Clans
Defrauding a fellow member	17
Conspiring with a non-clan person against a fellow member	7
Deliberately disputing over or trespassing on a fellow member's property	6
Using pressure to borrow money or goods from a fellow member	5

Both rich and poor might indulge in such misconduct, as one rule states:[221]

The clan officers should flog wealthy members who infringe upon the property of poor members, scholar-official members who threaten other members, members who conspire against a minority, and members who cheat good but meek members. If an offender by his family influence and prestige should defy the clan authority, the clan officers shall petition the government for legal punishment.

Members who have no moral integrity may use threats, fraud, or blackmail against others. Often, a poor member on the mere pretext that he is poor or old will demand aid from his fellow members. Upon refusal, such a person may even threaten to commit suicide in the house of his intended victim.[222] Scheming members resort to more subtle means:[223]

---

[220] 1916–a, "Regulations for Controlling a Family," p. 2a; and 1919–a, "Family Regulations," p. 7a. See Table 30 in the Appendix.
[221] 1914–h, "Family Instructions," p. 4a.
[222] 1918–k, "Regulations of the Genealogy," p. 22b; 1915–e, "Family Regulations," p. 6b; and 1913–b, "Officially Registered Regulations," p. 2b.
[223] 1914–h, "Family Instructions," p. 4b.

They will manipulate other members by their eloquence, incite litigation by sarcasm, slander others by distributing anonymous, indecent writings, wreak their vengeance upon others by maneuvering a third party to injure their victim, or receive bribery while pretending to be impartial. The clan officers shall punish these offenders by either oral censure or castigation. In fact, the clan officers should prevent these offenses by warning the clan members beforehand.

Disloyal members who conspire with non-clan persons to defraud a fellow clan member and secretly divide the spoils should be punished either by castigation or by the government.[224] The clan organization has the responsibility to protect the individual wealth of its members as well as its common property against any such illegal offense.[225]

The rules also forbid other minor misbehavior in the clan that neither involves status nor infringes upon property rights, such as cursing, slandering, inciting disputes, and anonymous writings of a libelous nature.[226] Moreover, in order to promote cordial relations among the clan members, congratulations and condolences on appropriate occasions are regarded as their mutual obligation; to neglect this obligation or to be indifferent is an offensive slight.[227] Sometimes, a clan rule puts this obligation on an organized basis: for important weddings, birthday celebrations, and funerals, the clan leaders should issue a notice to all members, decide on the amount each family should contribute to a group gift with the exception of the very poor families, gather the members at the ancestral hall and proceed together to the celebrating or bereaved family. Absence should be penalized by doubling the amount of contribution to the group gift.[228]

Misconduct of clan members occasionally involves other clans. The clan rules, though partial toward their own members, cannot condone misbehavior. Those who create trouble for another clan should be punished. "In a dispute with outsiders, if the clan member is right, the clan ought to help him settle it. If he errs, the clan should not

---

[224] 1914–d, "*Tsung* Restrictions," p. 3a.
[225] 1916–a, "General Rules," p. 24a; 1916–b, "An Epitome of Family Regulations," p. 1b; and 1919–a, "Officially Sanctioned Regulations," p. 1b.
[226] 1934–e, "*Tsung* Agreement," p. 22b.
[227] 1922–d, "*Tsu* Standards," p. 13b.
[228] 1925–b, *op. cit.*, p. 7a.

shield him, but punish him by flogging."[229] On the other hand, if outsiders trample upon a clan member or subject him to an injustice, through no fault of his own, other clan members should not stand aside without coming to his rescue.[230] Feuds between clans, especially notorious in southern China, are prohibited by the rules as a violation both of the law and of Confucian morality.

Generally speaking, the punishment of intra-clan misbehavior may be summarized in five points. First, flagrant violation of status in clan relationship, such as incest, is viewed with the utmost concern and punishable by such severe measures as exclusion from the ancestral hall, expurgation from the genealogy, expulsion from the clan, or appeal to the local government for punishment. Second, the punishment of disrespect toward senior members parallels the punishment of minor cases of filial impiety, namely, by castigation or flogging. Third, the punishment of senior members who abuse their junior members are at the lenient level of oral censure, monetary, ritualistic penalty, or at most castigation. Fourth, the punishment of aggression against fellow members, depending on the seriousness of the aggression, varies from oral censure to corporal punishment. Fifth and last, the rules generally do not advise appeal to the local government in any of these cases, unless the offender is incorrigible and the clan no longer has effective control over him.[231]

F. SUMMARY

The content of the rules on clan functions and intra-clan relationships dicloses that they have four major objectives: clan cohesion, clan prestige, internal order of the group, and welfare benefits for the individual members. Clan cohesion largely depends upon the performance of the ancestral rites. Clan prestige is principally the cumulative social honors which the individual members have earned such as government degrees, official rank, government citations, individual wealth, other forms of social prominence, and absence of disgraceful

---

[229] 1930–a, "*Tsu* Standards," p. 20.
[230] 1921–a, "*Tsung* Regulations," p. 10; and 1921–k, "Family Discipline," p. 4a.
[231] See Tables 26–30 inclusive in the Appendix.

misconduct. Internal order in the group is maintained by requiring the members to accord one another due respect according to the generation and the age status, to refrain from taking advantage of one's own social status, and from committing aggressive acts against other members. Nonetheless, class differentiation is difficult to overcome. The clan has only limited capability in controlling the misbehavior of powerful members and limited resources to help weak and poor members. Nor does the clan have any choice but to rely upon the powerful members for leadership. Under these circumstances, it is natural for the rules to resort to moral appeals, status-ethics, and ritual-ethics.

CHAPTER V

THE CLAN RULES ON SOCIAL RELATIONSHIPS AND INDIVIDUAL BEHAVIOR

THE CLAN RULES are so oriented toward the family and the clan that the relationships and behavior other than such are generally considered matters of secondary importance which are, furthermore, always governed by family interest and clan considerations. The term, social relationships, is used here in a specific sense in the context of the life in traditional China, referring to one's relationships with persons or organizations outside of the clan such as relatives by marriage, friends, family tutors, neighbors, people in the community, the local government, and religious groups. Similarly, the term, individual behavior, is used here in the specific sense denoting one's strictly individual activities, conduct, and misconduct which have no primary bearing upon either the family or the clan relationships.

A. RELATIONSHIPS WITH NON-CLAN INDIVIDUALS

The non-clan individuals discussed in this section are limited to those who are socially connected with the family in one way or another such as relatives by marriage, friends, and family tutors. The clan rules generally advise cordiality as the guiding principle to govern one's relationships with the relatives on his mother's side, on his wife's side, and on his sister's side.[1] The rules of 19 clans contain the following:

	Number of Clans
The relationship should be cordial (no specification)	16
Maintaining cordiality even when the relatives are poor	9
Assisting and helping the relatives in need	8
Visiting and greeting the relatives whose family has celebration or mourning	5
No extortion of the related family when a daughter or a sister married into that family has died an unnatural death	4

[1] Cf. Hsü Ch'ao-yang, *Ch'in-shu fa*, p. 11.

Cordiality means more than ordinary good will. One should greet his relatives by marriage on appropriate occasions and exchange gifts with them. "Gifts, while necessary, need not be luxurious. The purpose is to express regard, not to show off."[2] Nor does cordiality mean partiality. For example, a common fault is for one to side with the relatives on his wife's side. From the viewpoint of the clan, this is undesirable.[3]

Class differentiation is the main hindrance of cordiality. The rules, always emphasizing status, advise that one should not disregard his relatives by marriage even though they may be poor and socially inferior.[4] It is necessary to address them properly in keeping with their kinship status.[5] One rule commends a wealthy family that "remains cordial with its poor relatives for this is a sign of loyalty and kindness."[6] Another rule points out realistically: "One should not draw away from poor relatives . . . who may be poor and socially inferior at present, but there is no telling that they may become prominent and wealthy in the future."[7] On the other hand, poor people really cannot afford the expenses of retaining the normal social relations with their relatives. With fewer opportunities of visiting and lesser ability of exchanging gifts, they gradually lose touch with their kinship circle.[8]

Confucianism believes that friendship is one of the five cardinal relationships. A few rules lament the fact that the righteous meaning of friendship unfortunately has become much obscured by neglect.[9] Nevertheless, many rules take a negative attitude on the question of friends. They reflect the fear of well-to-do families lest their members should fall into bad company.[10] Hence, they choose caution as the watchword of selecting and making friends. One rule defends its

[2] 1914–g, "Family Instructions," p. 5b.
[3] 1921–i, "Mottoes of the Former Scholar Lu Ch'in-hsien," p. 2b.
[4] 1933–e, "Ancestors' Instructions," p. 4b.
[5] 1914–g, *op. cit.*, p. 14a.
[6] 1930–c, "Family Instructions," p. 10b.
[7] 1914–g, *op. cit.*, p. 2b.
[8] Lang, *op. cit.*, pp. 166–167.
[9] 1916–c, "Family Instructions," p. 2b.
[10] 1914–h, "Family Instructions," p. 5a.

departure from Confucianism: "Though friendship is one of the five ethical relationships and should not be disregarded, yet one must be very careful about it."[11] A usual advice is that one should have neither friends of all sorts nor many friends. To have many friends is unnecessarily expensive; and to the few chosen friends, one should be "loyal and helpful."[12] Another rule tells its members how to distinguish people: "Be careful in making friends. Look for such qualities as earnestness, kindness, loyalty, and honesty. Befriend those who will point out your faults to you. Keep away from those who are flattering, flippant, arrogant, or slack, for they lead you into evil."[13] The advice on the selection of friends in the rules of 72 clans may be presented as follows:

	Number of Clans
General principles:	
Carefulness in selecting friends	69
Not to have many friends indiscriminately	7
Qualities of desirable friends:	
Virtue and integrity	37
Talent and learning	9
Superior knowledge	6
Qualities of undesirable and prohibited friends:	
Unorthodoxy or rebelliousness	27
Power or wealth	10
Unscrupulousness	9
Treacherousness	3
Foolhardiness	3
Sharpness in making profit	3
Being a member of a secret society	3
Litigiousness	2
Dissoluteness	1

Though many rules require members to select their friends with care, only a few provide punishment for those who have befriended undesirable elements.[14] The severity of punishment varies. Minor cases are punishable by castigation and corporal punishment. One who persists in keeping bad company and disregards the warning of

[11] 1924–a, "Family Instructions," p. 27a.
[12] 1914–d, "Family Regulations," p. 4a–6b.
[13] 1921–j, "Mottoes," words of Chu Hsi, p. 10b.
[14] See Table 33 in the Appendix.

clan officers should be excluded from the ancestral hall or even from the genealogy. From then on, the clan disclaims the responsibility for his wrong doings. In serious cases, a clan may even ask the government to punish a member who keeps dangerous company.[15]

The clan rules frown upon superficial friendship.[16] Another commonplace fault is to befriend people in power but discard them as soon as their prestige declines. Even acceptable friendship is, however, a rather limited relationship.[17] One rule expressly warns that one should not confide his secrets to his friends, for some day, if friendship disappears, they may use the secrets against him.[18] A person should also remain aloof "when two of his friends dispute with each another."[19] Proper and improper attitude and behavior toward friends is described in the rules of 40 clans in the following manner:

	Number of Clans
Proper relationship with friends:	
To remonstrate friend's mistakes	21
To be loyal and righteous with friends	15
To be cautious in speech with friends	12
To help friends in trouble	6
To maintain proper etiquette with friends	2
Improper relationship with friends:	
To indulge in feast, wine, or recreation	10
To be intimate and disrespectful	3
To be boastful and conceited	3
To joke, to talk nonsense	1
To demand or reprove excessively	1

The rules do not always agree with the common Confucian saying that friends have the righteous obligation to help each other financially. To help is a virtue, but help should be given to family and clan members first rather than extended indiscriminately to friends.

---

[15] 1919–a, "Officially Sanctioned Regulations," p. 1b; and 1924–i, "*Tsung* Regulations," p. 1b.
[16] 1914–d, "Family Regulations," p. 4a.
[17] *Ibid.*, p. 4b.
[18] 1921–j, "Mottoes," p. 11b.
[19] 1914–f, "Family Instructions," p. 4a.

The classical Chinese literature frequently mentions teachers and friends together, for both are expected to exert moral influence. In the context of the clan rules, teachers generally refer to the family tutors. A family tutor is important for he usually stays with the family at a time when his students are of an impressionable age. In addition to the selection of a good teacher, the rules of 39 clans stress the need of respecting him:

	Number of Clans
Qualities of a good teacher:	
Virtuous conduct	29
Superior scholarship	23
Sternness and conscientiousness in teaching	17
Ability to arouse interest in students	1
Proper respect for teacher:	
Respect according to etiquette	12
Generous accommodation and attentiveness	10
Adequate salary	3
Ban on improper attitude toward teacher:	
Not to treat a teacher rudely and stingily	7
Not to find fault with a teacher	3
Not to criticize a teacher behind his back	1

The rules suggest that one should engage a teacher of strong moral character who is able "to use stern discipline to mould the character of his pupils."[20] However, one who accepts a teaching position is by no means a successful scholar or a wealthy person. The family who hires him often fails to accord him due courtesy.[21] He can hardly assert his moral authority in the face of the class differentiation between him and his pupils, especially when the family is only interested in the success of the pupils in government examination.[22]

B. NEIGHBORHOOD AND COMMUNITY RELATIONSHIPS

When the Sung scholars revived the clan institution, they made a parallel, though not nearly so successful an, effort to promote com-

---

[20] 1917-d, "Family Regulations," p. 2a; and 1921-c, "Family Regulations," p. 3b.
[21] 1935-e, "Family Regulations," p. 17a.
[22] 1930-c, "Family Instructions," pp. 8–9; 1921-i, "Mottoes of the Former Scholar Lu Ch'ing-hsien," p. 3a.

munity solidarity. This background has influenced the clan rules in looking upon neighborhood and community relationships as deserving due attention. Practical experience has also taught the same. Most villages are not clan villages but communities consisting of a number of clans.[23] Mutual help and absence of friction would be desirable. Many rules quote the common saying: "Close neighbors are more valuable than remote relatives."[24] Of 50 clans, 49 rules stress harmony as the governing principle of neighborhood and community relationships, while 29 rules advise that assistance should be extended to the poor and unfortunate people in the community.

Some rules urge that neighbors should join efforts in maintaining night watch and vigilance against robbery and theft. They should help one another in emergencies such as flood, fire, illness, and death.[25] As noted earlier, the charitable activities of a few wealthy clans did take care of the village poor. One clan, for example, designated 3.5 *mou* of its land as the charitable cemetery for the poor people in the community.[26] This was not motivated by altruism alone, but also by a desire to cultivate goodwill for the poor people were often jealous and resentful of a wealthy clan.[27]

The key of community peace is deference. One clan explains that deference toward other people basically stems from the same spirit as loyalty to the emperor and filial piety toward parents; in other words, a recognition of other people's status.[28] The way to achieve harmony among family members is being projected to achieve community harmony. "One should tolerate his neighbors, rather than expect or demand that they should tolerate him."[29] Neighborhood argument being rather commonplace, "one cannot always insist on arguing who is right and who is wrong."[30] One should also be tactful.

---

[23] Lang, *op. cit.*, pp. 111–118.
[24] 1914–b, "The Six Items of the Village Agreement," p. 2a.
[25] 1921–b, "*Tsu* Regulations," p. 2a; 1935–d, "Family Standards," p. 2b.
[26] 1919–c, "Regulations of the Charitable Estate" (1859), p. 14b.
[27] 1936–b, "Miscellaneous Statements of Family Instructions," p. 12a.
[28] 1916–c, "Family Instructions," p. 2b; see also 1924–f, "Proclaimed *Tsu* Regulations," p. 3a.
[29] 1916–b, "An Epitome of Family Regulations," p. 2b.
[30] 1921–i, "Family Instructions," p. 2a.

THE CLAN RULES ON SOCIAL RELATIONSHIPS

It is better to give a neighbor who asks for help a gift rather than a loan.[31] To expect the return of a loan often results in unpleasantness. Nor should one get involved in financial transactions by serving as a guarantor or witness.[32] What the rules advocate is politeness, deference, but no involvement. They hardly suggest active efforts to promote community solidarity.

Tension between clans hurts community solidarity. It has been observed that clans often vied with one another for prestige and power as well as competed in ritual and ceremonial showings, the size of their ancestral graveyards and ancestral halls, and the quality of their genealogies.[33] These competitions are no more than petty jealousy. What really divides a community is the aggression by the members of a powerful and influential clan against the members of other clans. The rules prohibit such undesirable misconduct, though most of them provide no punishment and a few of them only lenient measures. In most cases, the prohibition is only in the form of a warning.[34] For example, one rule warns: "He who is prominent and wealthy today may become socially inferior and poor in the future." Therefore, he should be considerate and conciliatory toward people in the community.[35] Power and prestige are no reasons to become conceited:[36]

Those who rise from poverty into wealth and from obscurity into prominence, and even those who are nationally known, should not make themselves an object of hatred in the community. As to others who, through no effort of their own, enjoy the wealth which their parents have earned, live a comfortable life with everything provided for them, and consequently find it easy to advance themselves into prominence, they are really not distinguished in their own rights or superior to other people. For them to be proud and self-important is shameful.

The rules indicate that community relations should be improved indirectly by restraining the misconduct of their individual members,

[31] 1920–c, "Standards for Succeeding Generations," pp. 15a–16a.
[32] 1914–g, *op. cit.*, p. 15b.
[33] Hsu, *Under the Ancestors' Shadow*, pp. 125–126.
[34] See Table 34 in the Appendix.
[35] 1921–i, "Family Instructions," p. 2b.
[36] 1930–a, "Family Instructions," p. 15.

especially those who are scholar-officials. It is wrong for scholar-officials to use their corruptive influence with the local government, to profit themselves by intervening in tax matters, or to use bribery to turn the government against other people in the community.[37] Other rules point out that aggression against community people often brings retaliation and the initial offender loses in the end. When a misbehaving person is punished by the government, "he disgraces not only himself but also his ancestors."[38] A clan should always watch its reputation by preventing its members from harming outsiders and by refusing its offenders clan protection.[39] Punishment of a member who misbehaves against a non-clan member in the community is usually oral censure. The punishment for siding with outsiders in an aggression against fellow clan members is, however, much more severe: for minor cases, it is castigation or flogging; and for grave offenses, appeal to the local government for legal sentence.[40] The group interest is placed far higher than community solidarity.

C. RELATIONSHIP WITH THE GOVERNMENT

Under the traditional Chinese system of government, the clans took care of minor matters within their groups. At the same time, people wished to avoid dealings with the government as much as possible. The advice given by the clan rules is simple: pay taxes to the government and settle disputes within the clan without resorting to litigation.

The rules urge their members to pay taxes honestly and promptly without evasion by bribery, falsified reports, or resort to any other devious means. It is unwise to rely upon the clerks and tax collectors to transmit one's tax or to bribe them in order to cheat the government. In the end, whatever one gains by evasion is not worth the

---

[37] 1921–h, "Regulations of the Ancestral Hall," p. 1b; 1914–h, *op. cit.*, p. 5a; and 1921–a, "*Tsung* Regulations," p. 3.

[38] 1930–a, "Family Instructions," p. 15; 1914–g, *op. cit.*, p. 3a; and 1921–i, "Mottoes of the Former Scholar Lu Ch'ing-hsien," p. 3b.

[39] Martin C. Yang, p. 142; 1921–f, "Additional *Tsu* Regulations," p. 4b; and 1921–k, "Family Discipline," p. 3b.

[40] See Table 35 in the Appendix.

trouble he will get into.[41] Some rules warn their members not to listen to people who boast of their influence with the local government offices and offer to settle their tax cases for them. These people will flee when the misdeed is discovered, leaving the taxpayers to take the unhappy consequences.[42]

Both positive and negative reasons in favor of prompt tax payment appear in the rules of 33 clans:

	Number of Clans
Positive reasons:	
Duty of citizen	5
Loyalty to the emperor	3
Gratitude for government protection	3
Negative reasons:	
To avoid trouble from tax collectors	13
To avoid extra expenses in connection with tax arrears	12
To avoid implicating the clan	8
To avoid torture in court when punished for tax arrears	7
To avoid anxiety	2

The positive reasons are commonplace. Taxation is a matter of course. "Whenever there is property, there is taxation."[43] A good citizen should be loyal and grateful to the ruler and willing to pay the taxes. One pays taxes and in return gets protection from the government.[44] In the traditional days, land taxes were collected semi-annually, during the fourth and the tenth lunar month. A clan head should remind the members by a circular notice for them to pay promptly.[45]

When it comes to the negative reasons why one should not fail to pay taxes on time, the language in the clan rules becomes very emphatic. First of all, peaceful family life depends on having no

---

[41] 1914–d, "Family Regulations," p. 1b; and 1921–i, "Family Instructions," item on tax.
[42] 1929–a, "The Twelve Injunctions," p. 3a.
[43] 1928–a, "The Ten Regulations," p. 7a.
[44] 1913–b, "Officially Registered Regulations," p. 1a; 1924–b, "Family Instructions," p. 14b; and 1929–c, "Family Instructions," p. 4a.
[45] 1921–f, "Officially Sanctioned Regulations," p. 1a.

trouble with the government or the tax collectors.[46] Tax arrears often cause trouble to one's descendants, the branch head, and other clan officers. If a clan manager fails to pay the taxes on the common property, the clan organization will have difficulties.[47] Any member who deliberately delays tax payment should therefore be penalized or punished at the ancestral hall.[48]

Some rules portray a dark picture of tax collection. Bad tax collectors use abusive language, make threats to extort bribery, and force the victim family to entertain them with food and wine.[49] One clan rule describes the danger of default in tax payment by these words:[50]

A defaulting family knows no peace. Before it can pay the tax arrears, it has to spend money to appease and entertain government runners. Should it fail to do so, its members will be arrested and sent to the court where they inevitably suffer corporal punishment and thus disgrace their ancestors.

As a result, the family loses more money than what it has originally owed the government.[51] But the rules do not mean to be hard on their members who honestly do not have enough to pay the taxes; punishment is meant only for those who cheat and even then the punishment is not severe.[52]

Besides the sad commentary on tax collection, the rules reflect a lack of faith in legal justice. They agree with a common saying that the gates of government offices are wide open, but one who has no money need not enter.[53] The usual corruptive practice was to entertain government clerks who were able to influence the outcome of legal cases. The rules look upon the clerks as persons of low social

---

[46] 1916–a, "Regulations for Controlling a Family," p. 8a; 1920–d, "Additional Family Regulations," p. 8a; Lang, *op. cit.*, pp. 17–18; and Shimizu, *Kazoku*, pp. 510–520.
[47] 1913–c, "Regulations of the Ancestral Hall," p. 2b.
[48] 1919–e, "Family Discipline," p. 8a.
[49] 1928–a, "The Ten Regulations," p. 7a.
[50] 1914–f, "Family Instructions," p. 7b.
[51] 1914–j, "Family Regulations," p. 7a.
[52] See Table 37 in the Appendix.
[53] 1924–i, "*Tsung* Instructions," p. 4a.

status and generally lacking in moral scruples. Some rules describe them as "tigers and wolves."[54] Nor do the rules trust the officials. Some magistrates may not look into a case carefully but follow "their own unpredictable emotions."[55] Under good magistrates who have wisdom and integrity, justice prevails. Under corrupt and cruel magistrates, "one has no assurance of getting justice at all."[56]

Justice ought to be expeditious. Unfortunately, according to numerous rules, the contrary is often true. When a case goes on for years, even if one wins, it is hardly worth the expenses.[57] One clan rule warns its members in no uncertain terms:[58]

Many people do not seem to realize that litigation is dangerous. Thinking that they would gain advantages by it, they will bring a small dispute into court. Yet trials consume not months, but years. Some bad elements will offer to sell their influence with the government as if it were a rare commodity. They are the people who encourage others to engage in litigation by claiming that they can manipulate it. Their own motive is to seek profit for themselves . . . The outcome of litigation is so unpredictable. Some lose their lives and others, their family property, causing the discontinuation of the family descent line.

Besides the costs and often the humiliation which come with litigation, people are left with little time to attend to their own vocation. "Whenever one enters the government office, petty clerks will push him around and extort money from him. Day and night, he has to stay there to wait on their pleasure."[59]

The rules have reasons to be pessimistic. Nine out of ten families who resorted to law, according to a community study, had to sell a large part of their property. Countless stories and proverbs also point

---

[54] 1914–e, "Regulations for Controlling a Family," p. 9a; 1914–b, "The Six Items of the Village Agreement," p. 4a; and 1928–a, "Family Instructions," p. 4b.

[55] 1922–c, "Family Instructions," p. 4a.

[56] 1930–c, "Family Instructions," p. 1; 1915–g, "Ancestors' Instructions," p. 6b.

[57] 1914–b, "The Six Items of the Village Agreement," p. 6b; and 1924–i, "*Tsung* Instructions," p. 4a.

[58] 1929–a, "The Twelve Injunctions," p. 4.

[59] 1915–g, "Ancestors' Instructions," p. 5b.

toward the costliness of trials. This is the realistic reason, besides Confucian ethics, which has made private mediation the quasi-legal mechanism to settle disputes. Social justice has played a far more important role than the formal legal system.[60] The rules of 46 clans give one or more of the following reasons against litigation:

	Number of Clans
On the government side:	
Extortion of clerks, runners, and government servants	14
Officials are unpredictable and unreliable	8
Officials are corrupt	3
From the individual's standpoint:	
Litigation is costly or bankrupting	39
Litigation causes enmity with community people or fellow clan members	14
Litigation is time consuming	11
Litigation entails torture or punishment in court	10
Gains from litigation are less than its cost	2

The rules suggest that the clan officers should dissuade members from litigation. If it is a dispute within the clan, arbitration is required.[61] As one rule states: "Patience is the best counsel. It is far more gratifying to settle a dispute than to resort to litigation. One should realize this, especially when he has some difference with a fellow clan member."[62] Many rules stipulate the procedure of clan arbitration. When a case is brought to their attention, the clan officers should notify the members of all branches to meet at the ancestral hall. No clan officer should be partial, play favoritism, or refuse to take up a case. The fact that a party has senior generation-age status or close blood relationship with a leading clan officer should in no way influence the decision.[63] Once a just decision has been reached, the parties at dispute should abide by it with no further argument. If a member by-passes clan arbitration and directly resorts to litigation, he should be punished by the clan, regardless of the merits of his legal

[60] Martin C. Yang, op. cit., pp. 166–167; and 1914–e, op. cit., p. 9a.
[61] 1918–f, "New Family Regulations," p. 22b.
[62] 1921–n, "*Tsung* Agreement," p. 46b.
[63] 1914–j, "Family Regulations," p. 8a; and 1916–a, "Regulations for Controlling a Family," p. 8b.

case. One may appeal to the court only when the clan arbitration has been unjust.[64] The following rule regulates the clan arbitration in great detail:[65]

If unfortunately criminal offenses of a grave nature arise within the clan, litigation is naturally unavoidable. If it is only dispute over small property or controversy over minor matters, the clan should be able to mediate between the parties and neither party should directly go to the government. A disputing party should first submit his argument to the clan organization in oral or written form. Branch heads in the presence of the clan members shall summon both sides and arbitrate the case before the ancestral tablets. The one who is in the wrong shall be penalized immediately or even flogged. He should be told to repent and to correct himself. If he should ignore the decision, the clan organization shall publicly condemn him and send him to the government for due punishment. If his offense is serious, he should be henceforth excluded from the ancestral hall and his name deleted from the genealogy. The clan officers should not shield any such offender out of private sympathy or partiality. One who takes the case into court without submitting it to the clan organization, even if justice is on his side, should also be penalized for having forgotten that the other party who has wronged him is a fellow clan member and a descendant from the same origin.

Similar regulations are found in the rules of 57 clans:

	Number of Clans
Clan arbitration is required	57
Prohibition of litigation without going through clan arbitration	27
Prohibition of disobeying the decision of clan arbitration	14
Litigation permitted when clan arbitration is unsatisfactory	10

It is the responsibility of the clan officers also to dissuade members from going into court against non-clan members. "Whether one is right or wrong can be readily ascertained by the public opinion in the neighborhood and the community."[66] If a clan member has been

---

[64] 1919–e, "Family Discipline," p. 10a.
[65] 1918–c, "New Regulations of the Ancestral Hall" (1880), p. 3b.
[66] 1921–f, "Officially Sanctioned Regulations," p. 3a.

wronged, the clan should help him reach a satisfactory settlement by negotiating with the other clan. In the opinion of all the clan rules, litigation is the last resort and unfortunately the least desirable.

The passive attitude of the clan rules toward the relationship with the government is revealed in another manner. Only a few rules seek to control the official conduct of their members in government service. These few rules remind their scholar-official members not to be avaricious, not to play favoritism, and not to put their private interests before public duties. Members who are notorious in their public careers are subject to such clan punishment as exclusion from the ancestral hall and elimination from the genealogy.[67] The lack of similar provisions in most rules indicates that scholar-officials with a much higher social position than ordinary clan members are presumably under other forms of social, government, and legal control, rather than clan control.

D. VOCATIONS AND ECONOMIC BEHAVIOR

Family prosperity requires both earning and saving. Numerous clan rules repeatedly stress the twin values of thrift and industriousness in vocation. The ideal is to keep spending within means and to be economically independent "without asking for help from any one."[68] What ruins a family are such things as loafing, luxurious indulgence, expensive housing, and litigations.

Many specific ways of saving appear in the clan rules. Entertaining guests, while a social obligation, need not be lavish. Exception to this is permissible only for the banquets on special occasions such as celebration, wedding, and events in honor of government superiors. It is wrong, however, for people to use such occasions to display their wealth or to entertain lavishly.[69] The rules find it deplorable that the rich people have made the ceremonies more and more expensive while the poor people blindly try hard to imitate. A funeral is somewhat an ambiguous case. The ancestral cult and filial piety forbid one

---

[67] See Table 32 in the Appendix.
[68] 1930–c, "Family Instructions," pp. 1a and 3b.
[69] 1919–e, "Family Proprieties," p. 3a; and 1921–n, "*Tsung* Agreement," p. 48b.

to be miserly over his parent's funeral.[70] He should not save on what is meant for the deceased such as the coffin and the burial. On the other hand, he certainly should not over-spend on entertaining the guests who come to offer condolence at the service. Nor should guests expect a good meal on such occasions.[71] One rule finds many prevailing customs to be wrong. Relatives often came to a funeral with some small gift and then had all their meals with the family for several days in succession on the pretext that they were there to render help. This rule specifically suggests that a funeral banquet should be by invitation only; those who render actual service should be provided with lunch but not with breakfast or supper. Guests who call to offer condolences should be entertained simply with tea. On the other hand, having received no invitation to a funeral banquet cannot be used as an excuse for not calling on the bereaved family.[72]

The following items summarize the advice on funeral expenditure given in the rules of 19 clans:

	Number of Clans
Funerals should be up to the standard corresponding to family wealth but not overly expensive	13
One should not be miserly over funerals	5
Funerals should not be wasteful in entertaining guests	1

The general principle on funeral expenditure is to do one's best within one's means; be neither too niggardly nor too elaborate.

The ideal of industriousness and thrift is well grounded in the experience of countless generations. According to research on the field, the widely upheld qualities of carefulness, rationality, thrift, industriousness, and sincerity are correlated to the rising prosperity of a family, whereas the undesirable qualities of vanity, impulsiveness, extravagance, neglect, and arrogance are either the symptoms or the causes of many declining families.[73] This is why one rule says: "Wealth is accumulated with difficulty but squandered easily. Therefore, what is laboriously earned by the grandfather and the father should be saved as carefully by the son and the grandson."[74]

[70] 1935–d, "Family Standards," p. 3a.   [71] 1919–e, "Family Proprieties," p. 3a.
[72] 1923–c, "Regulations and Instructions," p. 6a.
[73] Hsu, Under the Ancestors' Shadow, p. 7.
[74] 1921–g, "Family Restrictions," p. 4b.

With regard to earning, the rules emphasize mainly industriousness in vocation rather than skill. This is primarily due to the static nature of the traditional society, with a relative lack of social mobility. Under these circumstances, the essential thing was to find for all productive family members, sometimes including female members, gainful employment.[75] Once a member had a vocation, continuous application of efforts was far more important than changing vocation or acquiring new skill.[76]

Vocation also involves status as determined by the social structure and the value system. The social structure of traditional China consisted mainly of four classes: the scholar-officials, the farmers, the artisans, and the merchants in the order of social status. The rules of as many as 130 clans urge the choice of a good vocation and generally show their preference in the same order, though not without some ramifications. The essential substance of the contents in these rules may be summarized as follows:

		Number of Clans
Studying being the preference		12
Studying mentioned alone	11	
Studying, followed by medicine or fortune-telling	1	
Studying and farming being the preference		100
Studying and farming mentioned only	21	
Studying and farming, followed by trade and craft	67	
Studying and farming, followed by trade, craft, medicine, fortune-telling, astrology, and geomancy	9	
Studying and farming, followed by trade, craft, and military service	3	
Studying, trade and craft being the preference		14
Studying, trade, and craft mentioned only	8	
Studying, trade, and craft followed by farming	6	
Farming being the only preference		3
Farming mentioned alone	1	
Farming, followed by trade, craft, and studying	2	
Trade and craft being the preference		1

[75] Herbert D. Lamson, "The Chinese Laborer and His Family," *Sociology and Social Research*, Vol. IX (1932), pp. 203–212.
[76] Cf. Kardiner, *The Individual and His Society*, pp. 297-298.

The summary shows an overwhelming preference for studying and farming, though trade and craft are also desirable as the next preference. However, more detailed analysis is in order, for some vocations are merely mentioned, while others are emphasized and highly praised. This qualitative differentiation produces the following results in which the first column of figures indicates the number of clans which mention a vocation in their rules and the second column of figures indicates the number of clans which emphasize a vocation in their rules:

Studying	128	70
Farming	111	51
Trade	91	11
Craft	89	10
Medicine, fortune-telling, bookkeeping, astrology, geomancy, or painting	16	–
Military service	4	–
Domestic servant	3	–
Pasturage and fishery	2	2
Porter	1	–
Government clerk	1	–
Boxer and pugilist	1	–

It is evident that trade, craft, and other productive vocations, are not really emphasized by the clan rules.

The rules also take realistic factors into consideration. In the first place, not many scholars would succeed in getting degrees and becoming government officials. Unsuccessful ones have to find other employment such as teaching. A tutor, as mentioned in a previous section, is not likely to receive much remuneration or respect from the host family who hires him. He may even find it hard to maintain his dignity and make ends meet.[77] Many frustrated scholars would prefer to be medical doctors, fortune-tellers, astrologists, geomancers, artists, or the like; at least to be their own masters. A number of rules object to these vocations, however, as being neither respectable nor productive. What a frustrated scholar definitely should not do is to

[77] 1930–c, "Family Instructions," p. 9a; 1935–e, "Family Regulations," p. 17a; 1921–i, "Mottoes of the Former Scholar Lu Ch'ing-hsien," p. 4a; 1928–d, "Family Instructions," p. 8a.

engage in irregular activities such as making contact and negotiating with government offices on behalf of other people.[78]

Many rules urge their members to study regardless of the outcome. One rule argues:[79]

Studying is for the purpose of attaining a degree. However, the chances of getting a degree are less than one in ten ... Even so, those who have studied benefit themselves by knowing the proper rituals and manners. At least, they can write and do the bookkeeping for themselves.

Other rules identify education with moral training. "Education reforms one's disposition after the examples of the sages. It does not matter much if one fails to become a prominent and wealthy official."[80] Knowledge of the Confucian classics has a kind of "impractical usefulness" because of its intrinsic moral values.

Next to studying, farming is the preferred vocation in many rules. It is believed to be the most reliable means of livelihood. One rule thus compares farming with other regular vocations:[81]

Artisans have a low social status because they render service for other people. Merchants have little assurance of earning enough profit. It is more desirable either to study or to farm. But the chance for a scholar to become a high official is one in ten. On the other hand, the chance for a farmer to earn a decent living is ten to one.

No doubt, a successful farmer is often better off than a frustrated scholar. Another rule takes an equally realistic point of view:[82]

Studying, farming, craft, and trade are all regular vocations. Though studying leads as the first, success in becoming a scholar-official is decided by fate. If one does not succeed, what he then gets is but enfeebled limbs and exhausted family wealth. It is, therefore, better to take farming or craft as vocation, especially farming, which is the basic means of livelihood.

---

[78] 1915–b, "Instructions of Ancestor Mien-wu-kung," pp. 1b–2b; 1914–j, "Family Regulations," p. 4b; and 1921–i, "Mottoes of the Former Scholar Lu Ch'ing-hsien," p. 3b.
[79] 1915–b, *op. cit.*, p. 1b.
[80] 1915–i, "Instructions of Ancestor Mi-yen-kung," p. 1.
[81] 1915–b, *op. cit.*, p. 2b.
[82] 1926–a, "Instructions of Ancestor Ch'ing-yin-kung," p. 13a.

Farming is generally sufficient to provide food, clothing, and the essential necessities of life. According to research on the field, farmers who work on their own land do enjoy social respect.[83] On the other hand, some rules admit that farming is no easy work.[84] When the rules discuss farming, they hardly mean tenancy but essentially the vocation of land-owning farmers or "gentlemen farmers." It is the property right which gives a farmer social prestige and respectable status.[85]

The Confucian scholars who compiled the rules have expressed their physiocratic prejudice against trade and craft. Some rules cast the suspicion that people in trade and craft tend to seek large profits at the expense of moral scruples such as using tricks and dishonest means.[86] This generalization has to be qualified, however, for wealth is regarded quite highly. The status of a merchant in part depends on the size of his trade: for example, wholesale traders have more prestige than small retailers. Some rules make a clear distinction between "traders" and "storekeepers," the former being superior to the latter.[87] A fairly large number of rules agree that "merchants have a legitimate way of earning profit."[88] A few rules even encourage the wealthy members to engage in trade and build up their family fortune.[89]

The clan rules, on the negative side, forbid idleness as well as impermissible vocations. Wealthy families are warned not to allow their members to loaf. Indulgence in hobbies such as raising hawks and hunting dogs, though not particularly harmful, are considered wasteful.[90] Indulgence in gambling, drinking, and visiting prostitutes is condemned as being disgraceful and even dangerous. These indulgences, in the opinion of the rules, all stem from the lack of a regular

[83] Martin C. Yang, *op. cit.*, pp. 50–53.
[84] 1915–c, "Family Regulations," p. 17.
[85] Levy, *op. cit.*, pp. 42–44.
[86] 1933–f, "Family Regulations," item on vocation.
[87] 1924–a, "Family Instructions," p. 2.
[88] 1920–a, "*Tsung* Discipline," p. 11b; and 1913–e, "Regulations of the Ancestral Hall and Family Instructions," item on vocation.
[89] 1916–a, "Regulations for Controlling a Family," p. 5a; and 1917–a, "Regulations for the Sharing of Sacrificial Meat by Successful Members," p. 2a.
[90] 1921–q, "Miscellaneous Instructions for Controlling a Family," p. 22a.

vocation. Poor families have different faults. They often give up the children to a religious order, Buddhist or Taoist. The rules regard such abandonment of children as contrary to the wishes of ancestors. Members who have joined a religious order have no place in the ancestral hall.[91]

Impermissible vocations are those which have an extremely low social status and those which involve activities contrary to the Confucian morality. Servants, lictors, butchers, buglers, sedan-chair carriers, and the like, who are required to render humble personal service to other people in private families or government offices are frowned upon by the rules. Members should retain their self-respect rather than go into such lowly vocations.[92] If they so degrade themselves, their names should be deleted from the genealogy forever, even if their descendants who become prominent later on offer to donate land in redemption of their disgrace.[93] Some rules are realistic enough to suggest that the clan should arrange for its poor members to work in the families of wealthy members, raise money to set free those who have made themselves indentured servants elsewhere, and out of sympathy readmit to the clan the descendants of indentured servants who have emancipated themselves.[94] The rules consider that soldiers, boxers, and pugilists do not have a regular vocation, and regard their activities as another form of loafing. Such members should be excluded from the ancestral hall.[95] The lowest vocations are those of prostitutes and entertainers. The injunction against prostitutes is perfectly understandable, while the injunction against entertainers requires some explanation. From the viewpoint of the rules, most songs, stage shows, and plays are of an immoral, suggestive, and licentious nature. To be a musician, actor, player, or singer is to propagate immoral influence. Even amateur acting in which young members of wealthy families sometimes indulge should be forbidden.[96]

[91] 1917–a, "Regulations for Placing Tablets in the Ancestral Hall," p. 1b.
[92] 1913–e, *op. cit.*, p. 6; 1917–a, "Regulations for Placing Tablets in the Ancestral Hall," p. 1b; and 1924–f, "Proclaimed *Tsu* Regulations," p. 4b.
[93] 1922–e, "Family Instructions of Ancestor Tan-ya-kung," p. 60.
[94] 1916–c, "Additional Family Discipline," p. 1a; and 1919–g, "*Tsung* Regulations," p. 3b.
[95] 1930–e, "*Tsu* Agreement," pp. 4–5; and 1919–i, "Family Regulations," p. 9a.
[96] 1928–a, "Family Regulations," p. 1b; 1913–e, *op. cit.*, p. 6; and 1921–k, "Family Discipline," p. 3a.

Many rules also forbid their members to be clerks in local government offices. The traditional Chinese made a clear distinction between officials who were appointed by the imperial government and clerks who were locally hired by the officials to serve under them. Though the clerks had some education and handled written documents, their vocation was beneath the dignity of an educated person. One rule states:[97]

Officials are socially prominent, but clerks in the government offices belong to an inferior class. Since the clerks are literate, people often address them as sir. However, they have to crook their knees before the officials and wait upon the pleasure of the latter. It is a very humble vocation.

Another reason for this injunction is the fear that many corruptive practices going on in local government office may cause one to lose his moral integrity.[98]

Various punishments are provided in the rules to deal with members who engage in these impermissible vocations.[99] The first step is usually castigation or corporal punishment in the hope of making the offender repent and take up instead an acceptable profession. If he does not, the clan should then punish him by exclusion from the ancestral hall, deletion of his name from the genealogy, or expulsion from the group. The principle behind these severe measures is the safeguarding of status. An offender who engages in a socially disgraceful or a morally wrong vocation has compromised his own status. The clan has no choice but to protect itself by refusing to recognize him as a member in good standing.

Not many rules impose monetary fines on members in an impermissible vocation. Presumably, these members have been poor. Still fewer rules stipulate punishment for members who have become government clerks. Perhaps, it is because the government clerks, though socially humble, are not without some influence. This discrepancy between the injunction and the lack of punishment indicates that clan control in this area is rather weak or ineffective.

[97] 1924–i, "*Tsung* Instructions," p. 4a.
[98] 1928–a, "The Ten Regulations," p. 9a.
[99] See Table 40 in the Appendix.

E. RELIGIONS AND BELIEFS

Religion in China presents an exceedingly complex picture. No particular religion dominated the country and religious beliefs were often overshadowed by moral values. Among the religions, Buddhism was perhaps the strongest, but Taoism also had considerable influence. Besides these two leading religions, there appeared from time to time in different regions a number of minor religions which were really little more than variant sects of syncretic beliefs. The majority of Chinese were accustomed to the simultaneous existence of several religions side by side; and relatively few were completely devoted to one religion to the exclusion of the rest.

Nor were the religious beliefs of the Chinese confined to the organized religions. The ancestral cult and many folk religious beliefs intermingled with those of the organized religions. Numerous examples are at hand. Some clans placed Buddhist idols next to the ancestral tablets and many clans invited Buddhist or Taoist monks to reside in and take care of their ancestral halls.[100] A few rules openly profess certain beliefs in Buddhism, Taoism, or folk religion, without in any way abandoning their faith in the ancestral cult.[101]

What dominated the Chinese mind are not these religious beliefs, but the moral values of Confucianism. Whether Confucianism is a religion, a state cult, or merely a body of moral tenets is a difficult question on which contemporary scholars are still in disagreement. The answer depends on how one defines religion. It is generally agreed, however, that the Chinese held the moral values of Confucianism to be more important than the religious beliefs and that the former should be used as criteria to judge the latter.

The clan rules, from their Confucian standpoint, raise at least four major objections against certain aspects of the religions. First, a distinction is made between good, morally helpful, and law-abiding religions on the one hand, and improper religions on the other. The good religions, according to the rules, should give people beneficial

[100] Morohashi, *op. cit.*, pp. 133–136; and *MSSHK*, p. 338.
[101] 1919–c, "Regulations of the Charitable Estate" (1859), p. 21b; and 1918–k, "Thirty-three Items of Family Discipline," p. 72a.

teachings that "will help their moral well-being."[102] The improper religions often lead people astray in violation of the moral principles. The beliefs in alleged gods and demons, in promised good fortunes, and in threatened misfortunes frequently make people disregard their social roles. Some of the improper religions even cause their converts to violate the law and to rebel against the government. Such religions should be strictly prohibited.[103]

Second, the clan rules permit no religion to subvert the family institution. It is forbidden for men and women to leave their families and join religious orders, for they should remember that "they are not reared by their parents to become monks and nuns."[104] Nor is it proper to follow the widespread custom of inviting Buddhists and Taoists to pray for the ancestral spirits in the mistaken belief of cleansing their sins. To imply that one's ancestors have sinned is an offense of filial impiety.[105] Many rules advise that priests should not be hired to take part in funeral services. The funeral rituals, prescribed by the ancient tradition, allow no such deviation.[106]

Third, the clan rules are very critical of religious services in mixed company for "it is revolting to have men and women sitting together indiscriminately."[107] As discussed earlier in connection with sex segregation, many rules do not permit their female members to visit temples precisely because of this objection.

Finally, the rules express a mild skepticism of the magic powers which various religions claim to have. Some rules argue that to pray and give offerings to deities for the sake of pleasing them and asking good fortune seems like a form of bribery, and the deities would probably be offended rather than pleased.[108] But interestingly this argument is never raised against the ancestral cult in which the

[102] 1930–a, "Family Instructions," p. 17.
[103] 1914–f, "Family Instructions," p. 6b; and 1921–a, "*Tsung* Regulations," item on religious sects.
[104] 1914–f, "Family Instructions," p. 6a.
[105] 1928–g, "A Collection of Family Instructions," p. 15b.
[106] 1916–d, "*Tsung* Regulations," p. 4b; and 1935–d, "Family Standards," p. 3a.
[107] 1914–a, "*Tsung* Regulations," p. 3b.
[108] 1924–f, "*Tsung* Agreement," p. 10b; and 1915–b, *op. cit.*, p. 5a.

ancestral spirits are believed to be capable of protecting or punishing their descendants. What the rules really aim at is to do away with the superstitions which are incompatible with the ancestral cult. Besides this principle, rationality is generally preferred. In sickness, for example, "one should go to a good doctor rather than to pray before spirits and deities."[109]

On account of these objections, numerous rules advise their members to keep away, to remain aloof from, or not to believe in either Buddhism or Taoism. Such stipulations in most cases are not followed by provisions of punishment. The mildness of the language and the lack of punishment confirm the point that the clan rules do not oppose the religions as such, but only some of their beliefs and practices. When the clan rules do provide punishment for certain religious practices, it is because these practices conflict with the moral values cherished by the social convention, especially by the family and the clan institutions.[110]

Some superstitious beliefs, intermingled with the ancestral cult, pose a somewhat difficult question for the rules. An outstanding example is geomancy or the belief in "wind and water" which holds that the burial site of an ancestor because of its geographical location and geological composition may have some mysterious latent effects on the good fortune or misfortune of the descendants in the future. Since geomancy was widely accepted, wealthy people would hire professional geomancers to prospect desirable sites. The prospecting sometimes took a long while and kept the burial in waiting. The rules do not have a unanimous opinion on geomancy. A few of them in strict accordance with Confucianism reject it. They advise their members to place no belief in this superstition but to select burial sites purely from a practical viewpoint, such as the sites that are free from flood and ants.[111] Many clan rules take an ambiguous position by sidestepping the main issue of belief or disbelief in geomancy but raise instead some attendant issues. Some rules suggest that it is possible but

---

[109] 1915–b, *op. cit.*, p. 5a; and 1914–d, "*Tsung* Restrictions," p. 3b.
[110] See Table 39 in the Appendix.
[111] 1913–a, "*Tsung* Instructions," p. 4a; and 1914–j, "Family Regulations," p. 6b.

difficult to find burial sites that are good from the viewpoint of geomancy.[112] Other rules permit the belief in geomancy provided that it does not conflict with the ritual-ethics. The search for a good site should not, for example, cause the burial to wait for an excessively long period. If a burial has been delayed too long, the clan officers should intervene.[113] Once buried, a coffin should not be removed to another site geomantically believed to be more desirable.[114] The following summary shows how the rules of 30 clans differ in their opinions:

	Number of Clans
Positive attitude:	
Geomancy is a valid belief	4
Geomantic site may be located unexpectedly but not necessarily by search	3
Negative attitude:	
Geomancy is a superstition	6
Search for a good site, but not to believe in its effects on fortune or misfortune	6
Ambiguous attitude:	
The burial of the dead should not be delayed because of waiting for a good geomantic site	16
The remains of the dead should not be removed because of geomantic reason	4

The Chinese also believed in fate or destiny. Some clan rules confirm that prominence and wealth, poverty and humble status are predetermined by one's fate.[115] The general attitude in the clan rules is to entrust everything to the way of Heaven. However, Heaven is believed to be a moral force which will bless the people of good moral conduct, especially those who have unostentatious virtues or virtues not generally known to others. One should not resign oneself to a fate in a negative way but should strive positively to improve upon his destiny by kind deeds.[116] These beliefs expressed in the rules of 49 clans may be summarized here:

[112] 1916–c, "Family Instructions," p. 4a.
[113] 1914–d, "*Tsung* Restrictions," p. 2b; and 1918–g, "Family Instructions," p. 6b.
[114] 1924–b, "Family Regulations," p. 20.
[115] 1930–a, "Family Instructions," p. 12.
[116] 1917–c, "Mottoes for Self-cultivation by Ancestor Wen-kung," p. 13a.

	Number of Clans
Unostentatious virtue will bring blessings	34
One's fate is predetermined by Heaven	19
Heaven will bless good people and punish bad people	4
Good conduct brings good fortune and bad conduct brings bad fortune	3

The strong faith in the reward of unostentatious virtue is an ethico-religious belief which integrates the religious beliefs and the moral values. Unostentatious virtue means the kind acts done to others without the knowledge of the others or of the public.[117] It is believed that such would be amply rewarded by Heaven in some unfathomable way and the reward would be bestowed on the kind person himself or his family and his descendants in the future. This belief had a long and involved origin. It began with the ancient belief in ordeal by divine power and in ultimate supernatural justice.[118] With the rise of moral philosophies, especially Confucianism, the belief in Heaven and divine power came to rest upon moral grounds. Ultimate justice administered by Heaven was believed to be based upon one's conduct or misconduct.[119] This ethico-religious belief is in perfect harmony with an ethico-social concept of *pao* (報) or "reciprocity," that one gets for himself and his family by what he has done to others.[120] It also agrees with the Buddhist belief that one's merits and demerits in this life would determine the next incarnation, except that the Chinese have substituted the next incarnation in this belief by the life of one's family members, or of his descendants.[121] Thus, the primitive belief in divine power, the moral tenets of Confucianism, the influence of Buddhism, and the values of the family institution are all integrated in the belief of unostentatious virtue.

Unostentatious virtue means both to do good to others and not to harm others.[122] To do good in the hope of gaining advantages in

---

[117] 1923–c, *op. cit.*, p. 15a.   [118] Ch'ü, *op. cit.*, pp. 197–201.
[119] Hsü Ch'ao-yang, *Chung-kuo hsing-fa su-yüan* [*The Origin of Chinese Criminal Law*], pp. 37–38.
[120] Yang Lien-sheng, "The Concept of 'Pao' as a Basis for Social Relations in China," in John K. Fairbank (ed.), *Chinese Thought and Institutions*, pp. 291–309.   [121] Ch'ü, *op. cit.*, pp. 205–206.
[122] 1917–c, "Mottoes for Self-cultivation by Ancestor Wen-kung," p. 13a.

return or of advancing one's own reputation is regarded as selfish.[123] "One should remember [the good deeds] others have done for him, but should forget [the good deeds] he has done for others."[124] The true Confucian should feel happy in doing the good act itself; while the average person takes comfort in the belief that his good deeds, though not known to others, will bring him good children and bless them with both prominence and wealth.[125]

There are good reasons why noble deeds should remain unpublicized. Kardiner in his study of the Tanala culture points out that in a society without much mobility, restraint is the desired quality for people to live harmoniously in group life. The value of restraint agrees with the ego structure which has such traits as deification-lineage cult, the belief in the futility of strife, and yet being jealous of others. The value of restraint also agrees with the social institution of the belief in fate.[126] This analysis is to a large extent applicable to the case here of traditional China. Restraint means unostentation; while publicity is not conducive to group harmony and even disadvantageous to one's self.

The value of restraint is implied not only in the belief of unostentatious virtue but also in many other moral values. The clan rules repeatedly uphold the virtues of cautiousness of speech, courtesy and modesty, forbearance and conciliation, forgiveness and patience, and many similar qualities. One should be reserved or restrained in speech, for careless conversation often antagonizes people without being meant to. Courtesy and modesty attract people, whereas complacency and pride offend people.[127] These desired qualities are well summarized in the following quotation:[128]

One who has influence should refrain from using all of it. One who has wealth should refrain from spending all of it. One who has good fortune should refrain from enjoying all of it. And one who has something to say should refrain from expressing all of it.

[123] 1914–f, "Mottoes," p. 13a; and 1921–g, "Family Restrictions," pp. 4b–5a.
[124] 1923–c, *op. cit.*, p. 13a.
[125] 1914–f, "Mottoes," p. 15a; and 1923–c, *op. cit.*, p. 15a.
[126] Kardiner, *The Individual and His Society*, pp. 326–327.
[127] 1933–e, *op. cit.*, pp. 4b, 5a and 10a; and 1915–j, "Ancestors' Instructions," p. 3.
[128] 1929–c, "Family Instructions," p. 4a.

In other words, one should always consider others with kindness and tact. When conflicts arise, one should abide by other moral values. For example, "the virtue of conciliation causes the people in dispute to think twice, the people aroused by anger to resolve it, and the people who complain to feel gratified."[129] Forbearance, forgiveness, and patience are the best medicines to cure all disputes. All these moral values can be stated in one phrase: harmony through mutuality and self-restraint.

The traditional Chinese believed in a definite connection between belief in unostentatious virtue and these moral values. One rule quotes an experienced observer:[130]

To lose something is to gain in blessing. The way of Heaven always works without failure to bless the virtuous and to punish the misbehaved. People who take advantage of others hardly have good fortune coming to them. I have seen in many villages and towns, large and small, people who are aggressive, people who scheme against others, people who swindle others. These people make everyone in the community afraid of them. Yet in the end, their families suffer from rapid decline. I have also seen many decent people who are admittedly so weak as to allow others to take advantage of them. Yet eventually, their families enjoy good fortune.

When one follows the teachings in these rules, he is likely to have the ideal type of an introspective personality, contented with an inner satisfaction as well as his firm conviction that his virtues will bring good fortune either to himself or his family members and future descendants. However, it also suggests that the traditional Chinese society has not had sufficient direct and immediate reward for the good deeds of the virtuous people.

F. VICES AND CRIMINAL OFFENSES

The clan rules mention a large number of vices and criminal offenses which may be classified into four categories: individual indulgence and self-debasement, misbehavior that gives rise to notoriety, misdemeanors that are not serious legal offenses, and criminal offenses

[129] 1921–j, "Mottoes," p. 17.
[130] 1914–d, "Family Regulations," p. 5a.

THE CLAN RULES ON SOCIAL RELATIONSHIPS   173

that are punishable by penal sentence. The rules on the whole are not too concerned with the last category, for serious crimes did not occur frequently and if they did, the government would deal with them. What the clan itself should deal with are the first three categories. These include, among others, such undesirable conduct as gambling, being drunk and disorderly, visiting prostitutes, other sex misbehavior, opium smoking, theft, and the like.[131]

The largest number of injunctions in the rules are against gambling, a seemingly commonplace indulgence that leads to many others. Gambling begins as a diversion and an emotional outlet for many individuals in a society heavily laden with convention and completely surrounded by the requirements of group life.[132] Unfortunately, it corrupts moral character and wastes family fortune.[133] As one rule puts it:[134]

A thousand coins disappear at a single dice-throwing amidst wild shouting. People who indulge in it do not seem to realize its foolishness. When no more property is left, a gambler will resort to theft and crime.

Habitual gambling almost knows no end. A person who has lost everything in gambling may take such disastrous steps as to sell his children into indentured servitude. He may even join the unlawful persons in committing criminal offenses.[135] Another rule lists no less than ten evils which come from gambling:[136]

Gambling corrupts morality, compromises good behavior, hurts health, disgraces one's ancestors, betrays family instruction, squanders family property, breeds untoward incidents, separates family members, leads to violations of the law, and incurs the wrath of Heaven.

Punishments stipulated for gambling are generally within the range of oral censure and flogging. For serious cases and incorrigible gam-

[131] See Table 4 in the Appendix.
[132] Hsu, *Under the Ancestors' Shadow*, p. 26.
[133] 1930–a, "Family Instructions," p. 15; and 1921–c, "Regulations of the Ancestral Hall," p. 5b.
[134] 1929–a, "The Twelve Injunctions," p. 4a.
[135] 1921–b, "*Tsu* Regulations," p. 1a; and 1936–b, "Miscellaneous Statements of Family Instructions," pp. 31b–32a.
[136] 1914–b, "The Twelve Injunctions," p. 11a.

blers, the clan should send them to the local government for severe punishment.[137]

Excessive drinking is another vice frequently prohibited by the clan rules with punishment.[138] Drunkards disturb both family life and good order in the community. Nor can they be depended upon to assume their normal social roles. Intoxication which leads to fights and causes serious bodily injuries to other people is punishable under the law. If it is a minor case, the clan should flog the offender.[139]

The self-debasing indulgence of smoking opium receives far less attention than gambling. Only a small number of the rules compiled in relatively recent years mention it and provide prohibition. They point out that opium smoking is bad not only for the individual addicts but for their families as well. The addicts waste family property almost as rapidly as the gamblers. But these rules stipulate no definite punishment for this vice.[140]

Visiting prostitutes is a vice frequently mentioned by the rules along with gambling and excessive drinking.[141] Though prostitution itself was not necessarily illegal, no self-respecting clan should allow members to visit prostitutes.[142] The vice is wasteful, disease-contracting, and the forerunner of licentious activities and adultery. Adultery sometimes drives the involved persons in desperation into committing murder.[143] Illegal sex behavior is often connected with criminal offenses such as decoying or kidnapping women, selling them into servitude, and forcing them into prostitution. All these offenses should be punished by the clan by flogging, by expulsion from the clan, or by handing the offender over to the local government for punishment.[144]

[137] See Table 41 in the Appendix.
[138] See Table 42 in the Appendix.
[139] 1929-a, "The Twelve Injunctions," p. 3b; 1921-k, "Family Discipline," p. 3b; see also Table 43 in the Appendix.
[140] See Table 44 in the Appendix.
[141] 1921-k, "Family Discipline," p. 3a; and 1933-a, "The Ten Omissions from the Genealogy," item 6.
[142] See Table 45 in the Appendix.
[143] 1916-a, "Regulations for Controlling a Family," p. 9b; and 1936-b, "Miscellaneous Statements of Family Instructions," p. 31a.
[144] See Table 46 in the Appendix.

When vices cause people to lose money and self-respect, they begin to commit other criminal offenses, especially when they fall under the influence of the unlawful persons often found in a gambling den.[145] Some of these offenses may be classified as illegal profiteering: selling opium, operating an opium den, selling gambling instruments, operating a gambling den, forgery, counterfeiting money, swindling, defrauding others, and the like. Some others may be classified as offenses against private property: arson, theft, and robbery. Repeated offenders or serious cases should be turned over to the government for punishment according to the law. The punishment which the clan should administer itself is more lenient than that under the law.[146] The purpose is not so much to punish the offenders but to prevent the offenses from happening again and, above all, to correct the misbehaving members before they get into the hands of the government. Sometimes, a clan member may become so involved with the unlawful non-clan persons that he shelters them in his house. This threatens the safety of the entire clan.[147] According to one rule, the clan officers should exclude such misbehaving member from the ancestral hall, delete his name in the genealogy, or send him to the government for punishment.[148] Other rules stipulate similar punishment for members who befriend persons of unknown origin, of suspicious background, affiliated with a secret society, or suspected of rebellious activities against the state and the law.[149] These measures are necessary to absolve the collective responsibility of the clan group before the law discovers the connection between the members and the criminal elements.[150]

---

[145] 1934–e, "*Tsung* Agreement," p, 22; 1919–e, "Family Teachings," p. 5a; 1919–a, "Officially Sanctioned Regulations," p. 1b; and 1921–f, "Officially Sanctioned Regulations," p. 2b.
[146] See Tables 47 and 48 in the Appendix.
[147] 1921–f, "Additional *Tsu* Regulations," p. 4a.
[148] 1921–a, "*Tsung* Regulations," item on harbouring criminals.
[149] 1933–d, "Regulations of the Second Edition of the Genealogy," p. 1a; 1924–f, "*Tsung* Agreement," p. 10a; see also Tables 49 and 50 in the Appendix.
[150] 1922–f, "Regulations of the Ancestral Hall," p. 10a; and 1924–i, "*Tsung* Regulations," p. 1b.

G. SUMMARY

The social control exerted by the clan rules tends to confine the individuals to the family and the clan group without developing in them an active interest in the society at large. A person who follows a rule strictly remains cordial with his relatives by marriage, chooses his friends very carefully, concentrates on his own vocation in order to build up his family fortune, and lives at peace with the community people. Though the rules uphold community solidarity, they have very little to say about positive steps. They raise many pointed criticisms of and complaints of corruption in local government administration, but they advise no protest. They condemn the town gangs, the gamblers, the opium dens, and the houses of prostitution, but the only instruction they give is for their own members to stay away. According to the Confucian doctrine, one should extend the moral influence of the family and the clan to the community and the society at large. But the clan rules' over-emphasis on the family, the clan, and the introspective personality does not seem to substantiate this Confucian ideal.

CHAPTER VI

THE CLAN RULES AND MODERNIZATION

WITH THE SPREAD OF MODERNIZATION in the present century, the clan institution in China rapidly declined to such an extent that most of the modern educated Chinese broke away from it. Only a few old conservatives, diminishing in influence, held on to the tradition of compiling clan genealogies. The majority of the clan rules found in the genealogies printed during 1912–1936 are mere reprints of the earlier editions without touching upon the question of social change. Only the rules of forty clans, most of them dated after 1927, the year when the Nationalist Revolution succeeded, acknowledge the need of adjusting to modern conditions and make certain limited modifications in their contents. From these modified clan rules, two questions emerge: (1) In what ways and to what extent do they respond to the modern conditions ? and (2) Do they reveal some evidence which may explain in part the decline of the clan institution, especially the weakening of the clan's control over the conduct of its members ?

A. LIMITED ADJUSTMENTS AND THEIR DIFFICULTIES

The modified clan rules uphold the same ideals as the old editions, namely, the promotion of harmony in the family, mutual respect in the clan, clan cohesion, and clan prestige.[1] Their response to modernization is limited to the deletion of certain obsolete stipulations and the adding of a few modern features that are compatible with the old ideals.[2] Some modified rules seek to guard against radical changes in the future by stipulating that should further changes become necessary, these changes must be made with the advice of learned members who are well versed in the traditional ritual-ethics and status-ethics.[3]

[1] 1923–b, "Revised Regulations of the Charitable Estate" (1923), p. 27a.
[2] 1918–a, "Family Instructions," p. 7a.
[3] 1934–f, "*Tsu* Regulations," p. 1a.

Ideology is the most sensitive area of adjustment. The modified rules face a two-front struggle: to prohibit undesirable modern ideas which threaten the clan institution and to make use of certain compatible modern ideas in order to justify the clan institution. One rule laments that young people can no longer distinguish between what is right and what is wrong. It is up to the clan to give them proper moral guidance.[4] The idea of freedom, for example, should be placed within the limits of traditional moral values. Such radical ideas as "family revolution" are considered to be the negation of all morality.[5]

The modified rules insist that without teaching the young people to respect their family superiors and their clan seniors the society will be thrown into complete chaos.[6] One rule is particularly vehement in its criticism of social Darwinism:[7]

The theory of the survival of the fittest through continuous struggle has become fashionable in our time. People abandon the traditional moral values of courtesy and deference. Some even consider these moral values to be the very reasons why China is weak. It is of course necessary for a nation to struggle hard in order to survive among other nations. Yet the last two decades have witnessed many civil wars within the nation causing much disruption of trade and decline in the living standard. Are these civil wars not traceable to the mistaken emphasis upon struggle? The moral values of courtesy and deference, in actuality, are never meant for military defense and diplomacy. The existence of a nation is an entirely different matter. Courtesy and deference are the values for social order and harmony within the nation.

To justify the clan institution, the modified rules mainly draw upon modern political theories, especially nationalism. Several rules argue that the clan group is the logical basis of democracy. Only after people have been trained to govern themselves in the clan, are they qualified to organize local self-government. One rule admits that the clan institution may have had the fault of over-emphasizing the particular group interest to the detriment of national interest and the

[4] 1929–b, "Family Regulations," p. 8b.
[5] 1928–a, "Family Instructions," p. 8a; and 1935–b, "Preface of Genealogy," pp. 13–14.
[6] 1935–e, "Family Regulations," p. 15a.
[7] 1930–a, "*Tsu* Standards," p. 18.

fault of a conservative outlook which hinders progress. However, with proper renovation the clan institution can still help national progress.[8]

A number of modified rules attempt to introduce democratic features such as a constitution of the clan with by-laws, a two-thirds majority for resolutions, the division of power between a legislative committee, a supervisory committee, and an executive committee in the clan's governing body.[9] In some cases, the traditional life tenure of the clan head is reduced to either three or five year terms for at most two or three consecutive terms.[10] Election of all officers should use modern balloting and the financial matters should be governed by a budget.[11]

The ideal of developing clan democracy has many difficulties. Democracy presupposes the equal status of constituent members, but the modified rules do not wish to abandon either the generation-age order and hierarchy. When the democratic features are introduced, they tend to weaken the traditional authority and its function of social control.

Nationalism is a popular idea among these modified rules. One of them, in citing Dr. Sun Yat-sen, the republican leader, attempts to integrate Confucianism with both nationalism and anti-imperialism:[12]

Since the end of the Empire and the establishment of the Republic, many people mistakenly believe that the change in the political system renders loyalty useless . . . Confucius emphasized loyalty to friends as an ethical requirement of proper friendship. Tseng Tzu, his disciple, pointed out that one should be loyal to his own moral principles in daily self-examination. Sun Yat-sen, in advocating the revolution and in establishing the Republic, continued to urge fellow countrymen to abide by the virtues of loyalty, filial piety, compassion, love, honesty, justice, and peace. It is evident that the family and the

---

[8] 1935–b, "Preface of the Genealogy," pp. 13–14.
[9] 1915–d, "Regulations for *Tsu* Meeting," 1919–f, "*Tsu* Regulations," p. 2a; 1924–g, "Abridged Constitution of *Tsu* Self-governing Association;" 1931–a, "Family Regulations," p. 2b; and 1933–g, "Regulations of the Ancestral Halls throughout Kiangsi Province,"
[10] 1919–f, *op. cit.*, p. 2a; 1931–a, *op. cit.*, item 6; 1934–b, "*Tsung* Regulations," item 4; and 1933–h, "*Tsu* Organization," the concluding statement.
[11] 1935–b, "Family Discipline Decided by *Tsu* Organization", p. 2; and 1934–b, "*Tsung* Regulations," item 3.
[12] 1934–c, "Family Standards," p. 2a.

clan must cultivate these virtues. Among them, loyalty is especially important. The imperialistic foreign powers surround China like threatening tigers ready to devour a weak victim. If the people are not loyal to the nation, China can hardly escape the tragic fate of partition. It is earnestly hoped that our clan members shall through the study of Confucian classics become loyal citizens. When they become government officials, they should love the nation as much as they love their own family and love the people as much as they love their own children.

Another rule stresses cultural nationalism. It regrets the coming of Christianity to China through the use of military force. The Western missionaries have been by treaties placed beyond Chinese jurisdiction. As a diplomatic expediency, the Chinese government has found it necessary to adopt tolerance under such humiliating terms. While Christianity has many good teachings, this rule continues, many shameless Chinese become Christians merely for the sake of borrowing the prestige of the Western missionaries in order to trespass upon their fellow countrymen. This rule reminds clan members that they have enough to learn from the ancient sages and no need to abandon their own national culture in favor of a Western religion. The important task is to reinforce the traditional ethics.[13]

Nationalism is a crucial, if not decisive, change in the value system. It pushes the family and the clan institutions into a secondary place. Furthermore, it is in favor of centralization and state control, rather than tolerating clan control. The modified rules in upholding nationalism to justify the clan institution are actually defeating their own purpose.

The weakening of clan control under modern conditions is especially noticeable in the area of clan punishment. The modern government neither imposes collective responsibility on the clan, nor gives the clan the quasi-judiciary power of punishing its own members. At the same time, with the weakening of the status-ethics and the ritual-ethics, such punishment as oral censure and ritual penalties have become outmoded and ineffective. Left in the modified rules are mainly two forms of clan punishment: monetary fines and denial of clan privileges. Though a few modified rules still insist that the clan

[13] 1914–e, "Regulations for Controlling a Family," p. 10.

head empowered by the common decision of the members may use corporal punishment to discipline the young members under sixteen years of age, the clans generally speaking have no more punitive control than an ordinary social organization.[14]

Another important area of adjustment is the equality of women and the modern idea of marriage. The modified rules generally agree to emancipate the women from seclusion, to give them property rights and educational opportunities. These do not mean, however, the complete removal of sex segregation. One clan rule advises a compromise between the old mores and the new ideas:[15]

Women's independence has been commonly accepted. The old custom of sex segregation can no longer be enforced as it was before. However, women who are truly learned should conduct themselves carefully by exercising self-restraint and confining themselves within proper limits. When they are in mixed company, they should especially be respectable and correct . . . The old rituals seem antiquated and no longer applicable. But their original purpose remains valid, namely, to respect women's integrity and to prevent improper intentions between the sexes. People influenced by the modern vogue dismiss the old rituals without really understanding the purpose behind them. In discarding the old rituals, they commit the mistake of swinging over to the other extreme. Some even advocate freedom to the point of having no restraint whatsoever. Under the pretext of being broad-minded, these modern people fail to take due care of chastity and purity. The discipline of women in modern times calls for a happy medium.

The essence of the stipulation is perfectly clear: social changes, no matter how radical they are, should not negate ethical values, social control, and individual self-restraint.

Most modified rules agree with the modern law that women should have equal property rights. One rule points out that there is no difference in blood relationship between a son and a daughter. Offspring of both sexes should have equal rights of inheritance. The same applies to a matrilocal marriage in which the family property belongs to the daughter rather than to her husband, though he has joined her family.[16]

[14] 1921–e, "*Tsu* Regulations," p. 8a.   [15] 1930–b, "Regulations," p. 7b.
[16] 1914–e, *op. cit.*, p. 8.

The education of women receives considerable attention, though the predominant emphasis is still placed upon the education of males. The same rule which suggests a compromise formula for sex segregation cited above argues that women should have modern education, but not to the exclusion of traditional training. These are its words:[17]

Since the Republic has superseded the Empire, the country is rapidly changing into new ways. As individual rights and obligations continue to expand, individual ability should correspondingly increase. Women should have education so that they can acquire a fair amount of knowledge and no longer remain inferior in their ability to deal with matters outside the family. The old theory believed that women were by nature dependent upon their husbands and did not need any ability other than cooking and weaving. This is an obsolete belief. Our clan members should depart from the tradition so far as women's education is concerned. Depending on the family's financial condition and the intelligence of the girls themselves, girls should try to attain knowledge and skill at the level of the sixth grade or junior high school. However, their education should also include ancient Chinese classics, specifically the traditional virtues of women such as filial piety to parents-in-law, respect of husband, harmony with sisters-in-law as well as the traditional skills of cooking, mending, weaving, pickling, and husbandry. These are all necessary for women after marriage to manage the home economy, to supplement family income, and to be active in the society.

In suggesting a compromise, the rule carries the hope that women with modern education will somehow remain loyal to the family institution. But the half-way measure can hardly stop the tide which has largely disrupted the traditional type of joint family and moved toward the modern type of conjugal family.

Several modified rules criticize the custom of betrothal in childhood and concubinage. "The bad custom of betrothal in childhood and that of concubinage interfere with family life. Both are against humanity and have long been prohibited in the civilized countries. Our clan should also prohibit them."[18] Marriage, as one rule stipulates, should take place when the young people have the ability to make a living by themselves.[19] Another rule regulates: "Marriage of a girl

---

[17] 1930–b, "Regulations," p. 7b.   [18] *Ibid.*, p. 8b.
[19] 1927–b, "Family Mottoes," item 18.

should take place around the age of twenty, and of a boy, around twenty-four, so as not to interfere with their education, working ability, and health."[20] Other rules disapprove of the wasteful custom of elaborate wedding ceremonies on two grounds: it agrees neither with the traditional virtue of thrift nor with the modern concept of economy. A wedding should be a solemn ceremony and need not have lanterns, banners, and other decorations all over the house, expensive banquets for several days in succession, or shows to entertain the guests.[21]

These renovations are minor issues. The essential conflict between the traditional ways and the modern ways is the question of who has the authority to decide on a marriage proposal. In the traditional way, the parent had the authority; and the modified rules cannot accept the modern concept of marriage as an individual matter in which the right to decide belongs to the individuals. They merely concede that the wishes of the individuals concerned should be considered. As one rule stipulates:[22]

Betrothal from now on should be arranged after the young people are over seventeen years of age when they have enough common sense. Although the parents or the family head should take charge of the arrangements, individual consent is necessary. The parents or the family head should not force the young people to agree to it.

Another rule permits courtship between young men and young women but insists that marriage should meet with the approval of the respective parents as a necessary check upon the young people.[23] These two rules are in a minority; most modified clan rules will not even go that far. To the latter group, courtship is suspect of immorality and may lead to elopement.[24] The individuals' right to decide upon their own marriage is also seriously questioned by one rule:[25]

Young people neglect to find out from each other the family background and the moral training. They want to marry only because of

[20] 1930–b, "Regulations," p. 8b.
[21] 1914–e, *op. cit.*, p. 6b.
[22] 1930–b, "Regulations," p. 8b.
[23] 1914–e, *op. cit.*, p. 6b.
[24] 1928–a, "Family Instructions," p. 8a.
[25] 1929–b, "Family Regulations," p. 8b.

their affection. Should they be given the freedom to do so, they would disregard important considerations such as ritual propriety and righteousness.

The basic reason why the modified rules refuse to relinquish parental authority on the marriage of their children is the insistence on family continuity. When individuals marry on their own, most likely they will set up a new, separate family unit. The modified rules are caught in a dilemma: If they persist in the traditional ways, the modern educated young people will rebel; if they yield to the modern ideas, the decline of the traditional family system will be inevitable.

Limited and half-way adjustments cannot stabilize the traditional family and clan institution. Whenever the modified rules adopt or accept modern concepts in the hope of using them to help the survival of the traditional family and clan institution, the result will be the very opposite. No way has been found to reconcile the inherent divergence between the old culture and the modern ways.

The same observation applies to the minor areas of adjustment such as etiquette and ritual. Kneeling of junior members in greeting senior members at the time of ancestral rites and kneeling of all members before ancestral tablets are replaced by bowing in a few modified rules.[26] According to one rule, the form and the content of the memorial address to be read on the occasion should also be changed to fit modern conditions.[27] Such revisions, likewise, tend to weaken the ritual solemnity and thereby the effectiveness of the traditional ritualistic control.

On vocation and economic behavior, several modified rules stress national economy and the desirability of commerce and industry. One of them, quoting Adam Smith, criticizes the traditional ruling class of scholar-officials for not being economically productive.[28] Another rule regards business as the most desirable vocation and expresses the hope that wealthy merchant members will help the

---

[26] 1917-a, "Regulations for Spring and Autumn Sacrifices," p. 1a; 1936-b, "Regulations of the Ancestral Hall," p. 1a.

[27] 1936-b, "Regulations of the Ancestral Hall," p. 1a.

[28] 1917-a, "Regulations for the Sharing of Sacrificial Meat by Successful Members," p. 2a.

clan.[29] Several rules require the common fund of the clan to be deposited at modern banks or in postal savings accounts for such deposits are safe from embezzlement.[30] However, the clan institution largely has its roots in rural areas. Members who go into modern business and industries invariably move into cities and relatively few will remain loyal to their clan organization or contribute large sums of money to it. Their descendants who grow up in the cities will have little clan affiliation at all.

Only in the area of public health, no conflict emerges between the traditional ideals and the modern ways. One clan rule, for example, supports modern hygienics in reminding its members not to buy cheap food from open stalls in market places because such food is likely to be unhealthful and full of germs.[31] Another rule opposes the modern habits of smoking tobacco and eating candies for they are not healthy either.[32] Many modified rules emphasize the prohibition of opium smoking. Opium smoking during social gatherings may turn people into addicts inadvertently before they realise it, and addicts soon become paupers, thieves, and robbers.[33] One rule says that it impoverishes the nation and impairs national health.[34] Several rules, in deploring the failure of the government to enforce the ban, forbid their members to use the absence of legal force as an excuse.[35] When the National Government outlawed opium smoking, several rules urged their members to abide by the law and advised the members who have become addicts to get themselves cured.[36]

---

[29] 1920–a, "*Tsung* Discipline," p. 11b.
[30] 1934–b, "*Tsung* Regulations," p. 3b; and 1933–g, "Regulations of the Ancestral Halls throughout Kiangsi Province," Article 26.
[31] 1927–b, *op. cit.*, p. 1a.
[32] 1924–f, "*Tsung* Agreement," p. 8a.
[33] 1921–a, "*Tsung* Regulations," item 11; 1936–b, "Miscellaneous Statements of Family Instructions," p. 30; and 1930–e, "Contemporary Acupuncture," p. 1b.
[34] 1930–a, "Family Instructions," p. 15.
[35] 1929–a, "The Twelve Injunctions," p. 5b.
[36] 1930–a, "Family Instructions," p. 15 and 1934–f, "*Tsu* Regulations," p. 3b.

B. CLAN CONTRIBUTION TO MODERN EDUCATION

It is difficult for the traditional clan institution to make even limited adjustments to the modern conditions; but it will be a mistake to regard the clan institution as having played no part in modernization. The clan rules disclose that the change from the classical education to modern education has been not only accepted but given enthusiastic and substantial support.

The modified clan rules generally equate those who have received modern education with the scholars of the old days. One rule has a conversion scale: a graduate from elementary school, elementary normal school, or trade school has the equivalent of the first degree under the imperial examination system; a graduate from high school, technical school, or secondary normal school, the equivalent of the second degree; a graduate from college, technical institute, or teacher's college, the equivalent of the third degree; and one who has a post-graduate degree, the equivalent of high honor at palace examination. The clan should give them the traditional congratulatory gifts upon their graduations in the respective amount of eight, sixteen, thirty-two, or sixty-four silver dollars. These members are also entitled to the ration of sacrificial meat in the respective amount of one, two, four, or eight catties.[37]

Several rules provide for the honoring at the ancestral rites of the members who have received modern education.[38] One rule suggests that a graduate from a modern school who has become a government official should be asked to serve as the master of rites every time he gets a promotion. The purpose is to encourage other clan members to follow his example.[39] Another rule provides exceptionally liberal aids to their members who study in modern schools. Members who enroll in the elementary school maintained by the clan pay neither tuition nor board. When they go on for further education, the clan shall give them annual grants according to the following scale:[40]

[37] 1917–a, "Regulations for Awards of Educational Achievement," pp. 2a–3b.
[38] 1927–a, "Additional Regulations of the Charitable Estate" (1926), p. 25a; and 1926–b, "Regulations of the Literary Association," p. 3a.
[39] 1925–c, "Regulations of the Ancestral Hall", p. 2b.
[40] 1917–b, "Existing Regulations of the Charitable Estate," p. 2a.

High School	150 silver dollars
College	250 silver dollars
Studying in Japan	400 silver dollars
Studying in Europe or America	500 silver dollars

It may be noted that modern education is far more expensive than the classical education and usually beyond the ability of a clan organization to support.

All the modified clan rules favor the modern ideal of free and compulsory education.[41] But only a few well-organized clans with charitable estates and educational lands have been able to realize this ideal to a significant extent. They concentrated their efforts on primary education either by modernizing their clan schools or by converting them into community educational institutions. Since 1905 when the Manchu government introduced modern schools to replace the old, a number of clans have done so.[42]

Among these clans, three outstanding examples are noteworthy. A clan in Shanghai named Wang raised no less than 5,000 silver dollars in the early years of the present century to build seven modern rooms to house two elementary classes, two classes of classical Chinese, and two classes of Western learning. Unfortunately, no qualified teacher was available for the last group, as the few persons who read Western languages were employed by commercial firms at high salaries. Moreover, these persons had only a superficial knowledge of Western languages and knew next to nothing about Western civilization.[43]

A Chang clan near the port city of Ningpo in Chekiang province, about 200 miles south of Shanghai, distinguished itself in its continuous adaptation to changing conditions. Its clan school started in 1879 with only a few rooms and inadequate facilities. The son of the original donor in following his father's wish built a new school building in 1899. Then the clan applied to the government in 1906, the next year after the official abolition of the traditional education system, for permission to reorganize the clan school by modern standards. The clan's common fund originally intended for civil

---

[41] 1934–a, "Family Regulations," p. 7b; and 1922–d, "*Tsu* Standards," p. 14b.
[42] 1927–a, "Additional Regulations of the Charitable Estate" (1926), p. 23a.
[43] 1924–d, "On Charitable School," pp. 19–20.

service examination candidates was made available for those who wished to study abroad: as no one went, the money went to the clan school and made it possible to admit non-clan pupils. When China became a republic, the clan continued to raise funds from the members to expand the school into a regular private school with kindergarten and six grades, dedicated by the clan members to the following purposes: "To support the government policy of education, to meet the needs of society, and to train the youths who are spiritually sound, physically healthy, and mentally full of revolutionary spirits."[44]

The third and last case is the Chu clan, also in the Ningpo area. Its educational promotion is more involved as well as more interesting. Originally, a community school was supported by the clan with 300 *mou* of endowed land. Toward the end of the Manchu Empire, the school was reorganized into a private modern school, with the addition of an athletic field, something quite inconceivable in the minds of old fashioned scholars. Under the Republic, unfortunately, the responsible leaders in the clan one after another left the community. Not only was the school disrupted but the property rights of the endowed land were in dispute after 1924. Meanwhile, the clan leased the school building to the local government to house the Institute of Adult Education. Efforts were finally made to revive the school in 1935. A campaign in the clan succeeded in raising the necessary money to repair the school building. The old tenants on the endowed land who had defaulted in their rent were evicted by government order; and the new tenants were required to pay their rent directly to the school.[45]

These three outstanding cases show how a few well organized clans have made significant contributions to the promotion of modern education. There must have been some similar cases elsewhere. To help modernization is by no means an easy task. The rule of the Chu clan last mentioned includes a lengthy discussion on four major difficulties of a welfare project. First, worthy members who have contributed to it easily become disillusioned when their merits are forgotten and the task turns out to be a failure. Second, unworthy

[44] 1934–f, "Common Welfare," p. 11a.
[45] 1936–c, "On Village School."

members often seek to monopolize it with ulterior motives of encroachment and embezzlement. Third, most clan members will come forward to claim its benefits but will not give it their moral support. Fourth, ignorance is a hindrance to modern progress. The Chu clan succeeded in reviving its private school. In another instance of modernization, failure occurred. Two members donated an engine pump in 1933 to the neighborhood fire association who had previously used water tanks and bamboo pipe lines. But no one knew how to operate the engine pump properly and it soon fell into disuse, leaving the ignorant clan members with complaint and criticism and the donors with disillusionment and chagrin.[46]

It is a tragedy that the traditional clan institution has disintegrated. In spite of minority efforts toward modernization, as evidenced in these clan rules, it cannot be successfully transformed into a modern agency of social welfare to promote moral education, to engage in philanthropic activities, to aid social progress, and to exercise social control. However, the content of these modified rules serve to remind those who study the clan institution how well it must have functioned in the old days.

[46] 1936-c, "Common Welfare," p. 4a.

CHAPTER VII

CONCLUSION

THE CLAN RULES describe the optimum social control exercised by the family and the clan in traditional China. This social control rests upon authority as determined by the group organization as well as the emphases of the value system.

The father's authority is the highest in the family but not an absolute one. The father has to consider the individual status of the other family members and their collective interest. His authority does not stem entirely from the actual power he possesses but depends to a significant extent upon the moral prestige that his personality commands. The value system qualifies his authority by such desirable traits as mutuality, patience, and self-restraint. The same traits should be shared by the other family members in order that they may cooperate with one another and achieve family harmony. The social control becomes most effective when such traits are accepted by each individual and become a matter of self-control.

Once the father's authority breaks down or disappears, the family organization faces danger of collapsing. Family continuity, though greatly cherished in the value system, is not readily attainable. The custom of giving each son an equal share of inheritance is the main organizational cause underlying family instability. Brothers after the death of their father often abandon the joint family system of common consumption and common income by setting up new family units of their own.

The clan's authority is not nearly as effective as that of the father in at least three respects. First, the clan officers who exercise the collective authority of the group do not have frequent face-to-face contact with many clan members, whereas a father can deal with his children and their dependants far more directly. Second, the clan is not primarily an economic group. It does not have ample common financial resources at its disposal to reward good conduct, in direct contrast with what a father can do in the family. The clan's ability to mete out punishment is limited for the same reason. Third, the clan organization is controlled by leaders who have achieved power in one way or another. Being powerful, these leaders sometimes use their influence and pressure in an abusive manner, contrary to the ideals of the clan institution. They may fail to enforce the kind of social control they should.

On the other hand, the clan's authority, when properly exercised, is greater than the father's authority for four reasons. First, in traditional days, the clan was armed with quasi-legal judiciary power recognized by the law. Second, the clan's authority is held to be higher than that of the father according to the status-ethics and the ritual-ethics. Third, the clan's authority is supported by the ancestral cult. The group or its officers can act in the name of the ancestors. Fourth, group pressure is quite effective in a closely knit life. Even lenient punishment such as oral censure means considerable loss of prestige to an offender.

The clan authority exercises the same kind of social control as the father does in his family. It relies more on moral principles than on the actual amount of power the group organization has. It resorts to persuasion and restraint far more often than to punitive measures. The best hope lies in the self-control of the members themselves. Punishment becomes necessary only when an offense deviates critically from the established norms of conduct, disrupts family order, damages clan reputation, or becomes intolerable to most clan members. The ideal is to achieve clan cohesion, a projection of family harmony. Consequently, the authority of the clan, like that of the father should be qualified by such attributes as mutuality, conciliation, and deference.

The emphasis on morality in the individual, in the family life, and in the clan group is in agreement with the Confucian value system. Several secondary institutions reinforce the value of morality. Moral conduct commands social prestige. It is also identified in social realities as the rational behavior that most probably contributes to individual success, family happiness, and family prosperity. The ethico-religious belief in the reward of unostentatious virtue promises blessings to a righteous individual, his family, and his descendants.

Morality is thus thoroughly integrated with both self-interest and religious tenets.

The clan rules as an instrument of social control may be further analyzed with respect to their functions of rewarding, normative orientation, and punishment. On the whole, the rules do not devote too much attention to the rewarding of exemplary conduct. Ample reward is already implied in the social realities other than clan action. Furthermore, the clan, limited in fund, cannot afford to give many substantial rewards. The rewards that the clan does provide mainly consist of ritualistic honors such as commendation at the ancestral rites, placing posthumous tablets in the ancestral hall, and recording exemplary behavior in the genealogy. When the clan rewards a distinguished member by applying for government citation in his or her behalf, the major objective is really the enhancement of the clan prestige.

Normative orientation is by far the most important function of the clan rules which contain concrete specifications and detailed description of what is desirable and undesirable conduct. The norms of conduct are in strict accordance with the status and roles in group life and further reinforced by the proper performance of rituals. The primary objective of these norms is to have proper kinship relations as determined by the kinship organizational structure. This objective, when realized, assures both the family and the clan of optimum order and well-being. This is the reason why the traditional Chinese felt so deeply about what they called status-ethics and ritual-ethics.

The majority of the rules do not contain stipulations on clan punishment of misconduct. This indicates that neither does the value system emphasize punishment, nor is the clan necessarily well organized enough to mete out punishment. Even in the rules which do provide punishment, the severe measures generally speaking are intended only for serious offenses. When clan punishment proves to be inadequate to bring a misbehaving member under control, the clan organization has to choose between two unhappy alternatives: the first, to make it known that he is no longer a member in good standing or that he ceases to be a member altogether; or the second, to ask the local government to punish him under the law. Both alternatives imply that the social control of the clan has exhausted its means.

The clan rules generally follow the Confucian doctrine. Several qualifications, however, should be added. First, the roles of the ruling class elements are open to serious question. The Confucian doctrine requires the scholar-officials to set the examples by their own moral conduct, to lead the other clan members, as well as to help them. These ideals, no doubt, have been realized in a countless number of cases. But the content of the clan rules also suggests that the opposite may well be equally true in numerous other instances. Second, the Confucian doctrine upholds the status hierarchy and role differentiation, but its cardinal value of humaneness is against excessive class inequality. The very purpose of the clan institution is to consolidate the entire group, irrespective of class. The clan rules disclose, however, that the scholar-official and the wealthy members on whom the clan organization depends for support are very much favored, whereas the financially poor and socially humble members tend to be left out from many clan activities. Only in a small number of cases have the unfortunate ones received the benefits of clan charity. Third, the Confucian doctrine assumes that the well-ordered family and clan, in moulding moral character, will produce individuals who are capable of leading the community and putting the nation in good order. But the rules in over-emphasizing the family and the clan interest tend to produce persons uninterested in matters outside these two kinship groups.

The discrepancies between the Confucian ideals and the clan rules are not serious faults of the latter. Given the clan authority as defined and given a limited amount of clan power, as the actual case may be, the clan rules have achieved the optimum social control they could to stabilize the relationships within the kinship groups.

BIBLIOGRAPHY

A. Data

This section lists the 151 genealogies printed in China during the period 1912 to 1936 which are in the collection of the East Asiatic Library, Columbia University. For the sake of brevity in the notes following, each genealogy is assigned a number, representing the year of printing, followed by a letter to distinguish it from others printed in the same year. The sequence of letters follows the order in which the genealogies appear in the library catalogue.

The titles of the genealogies are given in transliteration. Each title usually consists of the name of the place where the clan lived, the surname of the clan, and an expression meaning genealogy. To translate these titles would be superfluous. However, the titles of the clan rules in the genealogies, which are the data of the present study, have significant variations in meaning as analyzed in Chapter II. For the convenience of interested readers, English translations of these titles are felt to be more meaningful than transliterations. The same form is followed in the notes.

1912-a *Chiang-yin Li shih chih p'u* 江陰李氏支譜, "*Tsu* Regulations," "The Ten Instructions for the Youth," and "Admonitions for Women," Vol. IV, ch. 16.

1912-b *P'i-ling Yin-hsüeh Li shih tsung-p'u* 毘陵殷薛李氏宗譜, "Ancestors' Instructions" and "Family Instructions," Vol. I, ch. 1.

1913-a *Tan-t'u T'ao-i Li shih tsu-p'u* 丹徒陶裔李氏族譜, "*Tsung* Instructions," Vol. I, ch. 1.

1913-b *Wan Mu-shih-ch'iao Huang shih tsung-p'u* 皖木獅橋黃氏宗譜 "Family Regulations," "Family Instructions of Shih-chü-kung," and "Officially Registered Regulations," Vol. II, Preface.

1913-c *Chin-ling Ch'ü shih tsung-p'u* 晉陵瞿氏宗譜, "Regulations of the Ancestral Hall," Vol. IX, ch. 15.

1913-d *Ch'ang-chou Ma shih tsu-p'u* 常州馬氏族譜, "The Seven Instructions of Yung-huai-kung," Vol. I, Preface.

1913-e *Jun-chou Nan-chu Ch'ien shih tsu-p'u* 潤州南朱錢氏族譜, "Regulations of the Ancestral Hall and Family Instructions," Vol. I, ch. 1.

1914-a *P'i-ling Ting-yen Chang shih tsung-p'u* 毘陵丁堰張氏宗譜, "*Tsung* Regulations" and "Family Instructions," Vol. I, ch. 1.

1914-b *P'i-ling Ch'ien-fen-tang Chang shih tsung-p'u* 毘陵前墳蕩張氏宗譜, "Regulations of the Ancestral Hall," "The Six Items of the Village Agreement," "The Ten Essential Points for Controlling a Family," "Mottoes," and "The Twelve Injunctions," Vol. I, ch. 1.

1914-c *Wu-ti Chang shih chia-ch'eng* 無棣張氏家乘, "Family Agreement," Vol. IV, ch. 12.

1914-d *Hsi-shan Feng shih tsung-p'u* 錫山馮氏宗譜, "*Tsung* Agreement," "*Tsung* Restrictions," and "Family Regulations," Vol. I, ch. 1.

1914-e *Hsi-hsien ch'ien Su P'an shih chia-p'u* 歙縣遷蘇潘氏家譜, "Regulations for Controlling a Family," ch. 7.
1914-f *Chiang-yin Ke shih tsung-p'u* 江陰葛氏宗譜, "Family Instructions" and "Mottoes," Vol. XXIII, ch. 26.
1914-g *Yü-yao Po-shan Hu shih tsung-p'u* 餘姚柏山胡氏宗譜, "Family Instructions," Vol. I, Preface.
1914-h *Ching-ch'uan Hsiao-ling Ts'ao shih tsung-p'u* 涇川小領曹氏宗譜, "Family Instructions," Vol. II, ch. 2.
1914-i *Ch'ang-shu Tz'u-ts'un Chin shih chia-p'u* 常熟慈村金氏家譜, "Regulations of the Ancestral Hall" (1750), "Additional Regulations of the Ancestral Hall" (1821), and "Additional Regulations of the Ancestral Hall" (1914), Vol. I, ch. 1.
1914-j *Heng-yang Wei shih tsung-p'u* 衡陽魏氏宗譜, "Family Regulations" and "Record of Charitable School," Vol. II, Preface.
1915-a *Chiang-wan-ch'iao Chou shih tsung-p'u* 蔣灣橋周氏宗譜, "Family Instructions" and "Family Regulations," Vol. I, ch. 1.
1915-b *Chin-ling Kao shih shih-p'u* 晉陵高氏世譜, "Instructions of Ancestor Mien-wu-kung," Vol. I, ch. 1.
1915-c *P'i-ling Kao shih tsung-p'u* 毘陵高氏宗譜, "Family Regulations" and "Family Instructions," Vol. I, ch. 1.
1915-d *Ho-p'u Lien-hsi Huang shih tsung-p'u* 合浦練西黃氏宗譜, "*Tsu* Regulations," "Regulations for *Tsu* Meetings," and "Shih-chin-kung on Family Protection," Vol. III, ch. 7; "Record of the Charitable Land," Vol. III, ch. 13.
1915-e *Lo-i Yang shih tsu-p'u* 羅邑楊氏族譜, "Family Instructions" and "Family Regulations," Vol. I, Preface.
1915-f *P'u-yang Chao shih chia-ch'eng* 浦陽趙氏家乘, "Family Instructions," Vol. I, ch. 1.
1915-g *Yü-hang Hsien-lin Sheng shih tsung-p'u* 餘杭閑林盛氏宗譜, "Ancestors' Instructions" and "Family Discipline," Vol. I, ch. 1.
1915-h *P'i-ling Shih shih tsu-p'u* 毘陵是氏族譜, "Mottoes of *Tsung* Instructions," "Family Instructions," and "Regulations of the Ancestral Hall and Graveyards," Vol. I, ch. 1.
1915-i *Chin-ling Sheng-tung Liu shih tsung-p'u* 晉陵昇東劉氏宗譜, "Regulations of the Ancestral Hall," "Instructions of Mi-yen-kung," "Instructions of Ancestor Li-tseng-kung," and "Regulations for Sacrifices," Vol. I, ch. 1.
1915-j *P'i-ling Ch'en shih tsung-p'u* 毘陵陳氏宗譜, "Ancestors' Instructions," Vol. I, Preface.
1916-a *Lu-chou Li shih tsung-p'u* 廬州李氏宗譜, "General Rules," "The Six Omissions from the Genealogy," Vol. I, ch. 1; "Regulations for Controlling a Family" and "Family Admonitions," Vol. II, ch. 2.
1916-b *Fu-feng Cheng shih tsung-p'u* 扶風鄭氏宗譜, "Mottoes," "Management of the Ancestral Hall," "Regulations of the Ancestral Hall," "An Epitome of the Family Regulations," and "Restrictions of the Ancestral Hall," Vol. I, ch. 1.

1916-c *Shan-yin Hua-she Chao shih tsung-p'u* 山陰華舍趙氏宗譜, "Family Instructions," "The Sixteen Items of the Imperial Edict," "Family Regulations," and "Additional Family Discipline," Vol. I, ch. 1; "Regulations for Rotating Duties of Ancestral Sacrifices" and "Restrictions of the Ancestral Hall," Vol. II, ch. 2.

1916-d *P'i-ling Hsiao-nan-men Ch'en shih tsung-p'u* 毘陵小南門陳氏宗譜, "*Tsung* Regulations," "Ten Mottoes for Controlling a Family," "Twenty-one Rules of the Genealogy," and "Additional Rules of the Genealogy," Vol. II, ch. 2.

1917-a *Hsiao-shan Ch'e-li-chuang Wang shih chia-p'u* 蕭山車裏莊王氏家譜, "Regulations for Spring and Autumn Sacrifices," "Regulations for the Sharing of Sacrificial Meat by the Successful Members," "Miscellaneous Articles" (1847), "Regulations for Placing Tablets in the Ancestral Hall," "Regulations for the Management of the Property of the Ancestral Hall," and "Regulations for Awards of Educational Achievement," Vol. I, ch. 1.

1917-b *Ch'ing-ho Chang shih chih p'u* 清河張氏支譜, "Regulations for the Establishment of the Charitable Estate" and "Existing Regulations of the Charitable Estate," Vol. II.

1917-c *Shang-yü Ta-miao-hsiang Chu shih chia-p'u* 上虞大廟衖朱氏家譜, "Mottoes for Self-cultivation by Ancestor Wen-kung," "Family Instructions of Ancestor San-feng-kung," and "*Tsung* Standards," Vol. IV, ch. 8.

1917-d *Ch'ang-shou Li shih tsung-p'u* 長壽李氏宗譜, "Family Regulations," Vol. I, Preface.

1918-a *Chiang-tu Wang shih tsu-p'u* 江都王氏族譜, "Family Instructions," Vol. II, ch. 1.

1918-b *Ch'i-sha Hsia shih tsu-p'u* 祈沙夏氏族譜, "Family Instructions," Vol. I, ch. 1.

1918-c *Ch'ang-chou Chang shih tsung-p'u* 常州張氏宗譜, "New Regulations of the Ancestral Hall" (1880), "*Tsung* Restrictions," and "New Agreement of the *Tsung*" (1880), Vol. I, Preface.

1918-d *Hsiao-i K'ung shih tsung-p'u* 蕭邑孔氏宗譜, "Family Regulations," Vol. I, ch. 1.

1918-e *Hsiao-i Hsü shih tsung-p'u* 蕭邑徐氏宗譜, "Instructions for Succeeding Generations" and "Regulations of the Ancestral Hall," Vol. I.

1918-f *T'ung-shan Chiang shih tsung-p'u* 銅山江氏宗譜, "Family Instructions" and "New Family Regulations," Vol. III, ch. 2.

1918-g *Ku-su Tung-t'ing Feng shih tsung-p'u* 姑蘇洞庭鳳氏宗譜, "Family Instructions," Vol. II.

1918-h *Chen-chiang Tan-t'u-hsien Chiang shih tsu-p'u* 鎮江丹徒縣蔣氏族譜, "Family Instructions," Vol. I, ch. 1.

1918-i *P'i-ling Hu shih shih-p'u* 毘陵胡氏世譜, "Family Instructions," "Record of the Charitable School," and "Regulations for the Ancestral Sacrifices in the Ancestral Hall," Vol. II, ch. 3.

1918-j *Shanghai San-lin-t'ang Chao shih chia-ch'eng* 上海三林塘趙氏家乘, "Family Instructions," Vol. I, ch. 1.
1918-k *Ch'u Huang Sung-shan Ch'en shih hsü-pien pen-tsung p'u* 楚黃松山陳氏續編本宗譜, "The Thirty-three Items of the Family Discipline," Vol. I, Preface; "Regulations of the Genealogy," "Record of Combined Regulations for Award of the School and Ritual Lands" (1891), and "Regulations of the Residential Hostel for Examination Candidates," Vol. II, Preface; "Regulations for the School Land," Vol. III, Preface.
1919-a *Yeh shih tsung-p'u* 葉氏宗譜, "Family Regulations" and "Officially Sanctioned Regulations," Vol. I, ch. 1.
1919-b *Jun-chou Ch'en shih tsung-p'u* 潤州陳氏宗譜, "Family Instructions," Vol. I, ch. 1.
1919-c *T'ai-yüan Wang shih chia-ch'eng* 太原王氏家乘, "Regulations of the Charitable Estate" (1859) and "Additional Regulations of the Charitable Estate" (1915), Vol. VII, ch. 7.
1919-d *Chang shih tsung-p'u* 張氏宗譜, "The Ten Instructions," "The Ten Admonitions," and "Regulations for Family Rituals," Vol. 1, Preface.
1919-e *Shan-yin Chou-shan Wu shih tsu-p'u* 山陰州山吳氏族譜, "Family Proprieties" (1687), "Family Teachings," and "Family Discipline" (1687), Vol. III, ch. 3.
1919-f *Hsiao-kan Shen shih tsung-p'u* 孝感沈氏宗譜, "*Tsu* Regulations," Vol. I, Preface.
1919-g *P'i-ling T'ang shih tsung-p'u* 毘陵湯氏宗譜, "*Tsung* Regulations" and "Family Standards," Vol. I, ch. 1.
1919-h *Ch'uang-ch'i Fa-hua Li shih tsung-p'u* 潨溪法華李氏宗譜, "Articles of the Ancestral Hall," Vol. I, ch. 1.
1919-i *Tan-yang Chiang shih chih p'u* 丹暘蔣氏支譜, "Family Regulations," Vol. I, ch. 2.
1920-a *Tung-lu Tuan-mu shih hsiao-tsung chia-p'u* 東魯端木氏小宗家譜, "*Tsung* Discipline" and "Property for Sacrificial Rites," Vol. II, ch. 4.
1920-b *Kuan-t'ao Wang shih tsung-p'u* 舘陶王氏宗譜 "Family Regulations," Vol. II, ch. 2.
1920-c *Wu-men Yüan shih chia-p'u* 吳門袁氏家譜, "Standards for Succeeding Generations," Vol. VIII, ch. 8.
1920-d *Yen-ling Shen-p'u Huang shih tsung-p'u* 延陵申浦黃氏宗譜, "Additional Family Regulations" and "Instructions of Ancestor Shan-ku-kung," Vol. IV, ch. 4.
1921-a *Hu-pei Chin-k'ou-hsiang Ch'en shih tsung-p'u* 湖北金口鄉陳氏宗譜, "*Tsung* Regulations" and "Instructions and Injunctions," Vol. I, ch. 1.
1921-b *Nan-feng T'an shih hsü-hsiu tsu-p'u* 南豐譚氏續修族譜, "Articles for the Affairs of the Ancestral Hall" and "*Tsu* Regulations," Vol. I, Preface.

1921-c *P'i-ling Hsieh shih tsung-p'u* 毘陵謝氏宗譜, "Family Regulations," "Regulations of the Ancestral Hall" (1765), "Regulations of the Genealogy," and "Articles of the Ancestral Hall," Vol. I, Preface.

1921-d *Yü shih chia-p'u* 于氏家譜, "An Epitome of Family Instructions," Vol. III, ch. 2.

1921-e *Kuei-lin Chang shih chia-ch'eng* 桂林張氏家乘, "*Tsu* Regulations" and "Regulations for *Tsu* Affairs," Vol. VII, ch. 7.

1921-f *Mien-ch'eng Meng shih tsung-p'u* 沔城孟氏宗譜, "Family Regulations," "Officially Sanctioned Regulations," "Additional *Tsu* Regulations," and "Abridged Statements from the Law of Adoption," Vol. II, ch. 2.

1921-g *Jun-chou K'ai-sha Lu shih tsung-p'u* 潤州開沙盧氏宗譜, "Family Restrictions," "Regulations of the Ancestral Hall," "Record of the Charitable Land," and "Contributions to the Charitable Land," Vol. I, ch.1.

1921-h *Lu-chiang-chün Ho shih ta-t'ung tsung-p'u* 廬江郡何氏大同宗譜, "Regulations of the Ancestral Hall," "*Tsung* Instructions," and "Advice for *Tsu* Members," Vol. XX, ch. 13.

1921-i *Wu-hsi Liang-ch'i Jen shih tsung-p'u* 無錫梁溪任氏宗譜, "Family Instructions" and "Mottoes of the Former Scholar Lu Ch'ing-hsien," Vol. I, ch. 1.

1921-j *Hsia-p'u Hsü shih tsung-p'u* 夏浦徐氏宗譜, "Mottoes," Vol. II, ch. 2; "Regulations of the Ancestral Hall," Vol. XXV, ch. 24.

1921-k *T'ung-ch'eng Ma-ch'i Yao shih tsung-p'u* 桐城麻溪姚氏宗譜, "Restrictions by Common Decision" (1657) and "Family Discipline," Vol. I, ch. 1.

1921-l *Tan-t'u Hu shih chih p'u* 丹徒胡氏支譜, "Family Instructions," "Family Advice," "Regulations of the Ancestral Hall," "Regulations for Annual Sacrifices," and "*Tsung* Agreement," Vol. 11, ch. 2.

1921-m *Wu-hsi Tou-men Ch'in shih tsung-p'u* 無錫陡門秦氏宗譜, "Family Instructions," "Family Regulations," and "Proprieties for Ancestral Sacrifices," Vol. XXIII, ch. 2.

1921-n *Tan-yang Hsi shih tsu-p'u* 丹陽眭氏族譜 "*Tsung* Agreement" (1773), "Family Instructions," "Supplementary *Tsung* Agreement," "Regulations of the Ancestral Hall," and "Restrictions of Genealogy by Ancestor Hsiu-nien-kung," Vol. VIII, ch. 5.

1921-o *Ching-k'ou Meng-ch'i Yen shih tsung-p'u* 京口夢溪嚴氏宗譜, "*Tsung* Agreement" and "Family Standards," Vol. I, ch. 1; "Record of the Reconstruction of the Ancestral Hall and the Clan School" (1901), "Regulations of the Ancestral Hall" (1779), "New Regulations of the Ancestral Hall" (1899), "Additional Regulations of the Ancestral Hall" (1903), and "Family Proprieties for Ancestral Sacrifices," Vol. XVIII, ch. 10.

1921-p *Wu-hsi Chou-ch'i Liu shih tsung-p'u* 無錫鄒祁劉氏宗譜, "A Collection of Family Instructions," Vol. I, ch. 1.

1921-q *T'ung-shan Cheng shih chia-p'u* 通山鄭氏家譜, "Family Regulations," "Family Instructions," "The Four Items of Family Regulations," "Regulations for Married Women," and "Miscellaneous Instructions for Controlling a Family," Vol. I, ch. 2.

1922-a *Ch'ang-chou Ting-yen Chang shih tsu-p'u* 常州丁堰張氏族譜, "Family Instructions," Vol. I, ch. 1.

1922-b *Hsi-shan Chang shih tsu-p'u* 錫山張氏族譜, "Family Regulations" (1901), "Family Instructions" (1901), and "Miscellany of Family Proprieties" (1901), Vol. I. ch. 1.

1922-c *Yun-yang T'uan-chou Shen shih tsu-p'u* 雲陽團州沈氏族譜, "Family Instructions," "Righteous Obligations of *Tsu* Members," "*Tsu* Injunctions," "*Tsu* Agreement," and "*Tsung* Restrictions," Vol. I, ch. 1.

1922-d *Huang-chou Ch'i shih tsu-p'u* 黃州祁氏族譜, "Old Regulations of the *Tsung-tsu*," "*Tsu* Standards," "The Ten Injunctions of the *Tsung*," and "Regulations of the *Tsung-tsu*" (1922), Vol. I, ch. 1.

1922-e *Wu-yüan Tung-hsiang Huang shih chia-ch'eng ch'uan* 武緣東鄉黃氏家乘纂, "Family Instructions of Ancestor Tan-ya-kung," Vol. 1.

1922-f *Chou-p'u Chung-ch'eng Chao shih chih p'u* 周浦忠誠趙氏支譜, "Family Instructions" (1865), "Injunctions" (1865), and "Regulations of the Ancestral Hall," Vol. I, ch. 1.

1922-g *Hsüan-chuang Chou shih tsung-p'u* 宣莊周氏宗譜, "Tentative Regulations of the *Tsung*" and "Ancestors' Instructions," Vol. I, ch. 1.

1923-a *Tan-t'u Hsü shih chih p'u* 丹徒徐氏支譜, "Family Instructions," Vol. I, ch. 1.

1923-b *Wu-men P'eng shih tsung-p'u* 吳門彭氏宗譜, "Regulations of the Charitable Estate" (1876) and "Revised Regulations of the Charitable Estate" (1923), Vol. X, ch. 12.

1923-c *Hsiao-shan Hsi-ho Shan shih chia-p'u* 蕭山西何單氏家譜, "Regulations and Instructions," Vol. XII, ch. 12.

1924-a *Tz'u-ch'i Lin shih tsung-p'u* 慈谿林氏宗譜, "Family Instructions," Vol. I, ch. 1.

1924-b *Huai-ning Ma-tsui-ling Hu shih tsung-p'u* 懷甯馬嘴嶺胡氏宗譜 "Family Instructions" and "Family Regulations," Vol. I, Preface·

1924-c *Ch'u-nan Shao-ch'en Liao shih tsung-p'u* 楚南邵辰廖氏宗譜, "The Eight Instructions" and "The Eight Injunctions," Vol. I, p. 16.

1924-d *Shanghai Wang shih chia-p'u* 上海王氏家譜, "Regulations of the Charitable Estate" (1847) and "On Charitable School" (1897), Vol. IV, ch. 5.

1924-e *Hsi-li Hsia shih tsung-p'u* 習禮夏氏宗譜, "Family Mottoes," Vol. II, ch. 1.

1924–f *Han-ch'uan Chang shih tsung-p'u* 漢川張氏宗譜, "Proclaimed *Tsu* Regulations" (1867), "The Eight Instructions of Ancestor Chih-ssu-kung," "Additional Regulations" (1924), and "*Tsung* Agreement," Vol. XVI, ch. 16.

1924–g *Shao-hsing Sun shih tsung-p'u* 紹興孫氏宗譜, "*Tsung* Agreement," "Regulations of the Ancestral Hall," "Articles for *Tsu* Sacrifices," "Articles for the Charitable Land," and "Abridged Constitution of *Tsu* Self-governing Association," Vol. I, ch. 2.

1924–h *T'ai-hu-hsien Li shih tsu-p'u* 太湖縣李氏族譜, "Family Regulations," "A Written Agreement," "Family Decisions"(1860), and "Agreed Restrictions for the Ancestral Graveyard," Vol. I, Preface.

1924–i *P'i-ling Shu-tsun Chiang shih tsung-p'u* 毘陵墅村蔣氏宗譜, "*Tsung* Instructions" and "*Tsung* Regulations," Vol. II, ch. 2.

1925–a *P'o-nan Chang shih tsung-p'u* 陂南章氏宗譜, "Family Regulations" (1894), "Family Regulations" (1908), Vol. II, ch. 2.

1925–b *Chin-ling Hsü shih tsung-p'u* 金陵徐氏宗譜, "*Tsung* Regulations," Vol. I, ch. 1.

1925–c *Tan-t'u K'ai-sha Li shih tsung-p'u* 丹徒開沙李氏宗譜, "Family Instructions," "Regulations of the Ancestral Hall," "Regulations for the Annual Sacrifices," and "Regulations of Genealogy," Vol. III, ch. 2 (A).

1925–d *P'ing-chiang Yen shih tsu-p'u* 平江嚴氏族譜, "Family Instructions of Tzu-ling-kung" and "Family Regulations," Vol. I, ch. 1.

1925–e *Hua-t'ang Liu shih tsung-p'u* 花塘劉氏宗譜, "*Tsu* Agreement" (1894), "Family Instructions," and "Common Decisions of the *Tsu*," Vol. I, ch. 1.

1926–a *Han-ch'ü Chao shih tsung-p'u* 韓區趙氏宗譜, "A Collection of Family Instructions," "Instructions of Ancestor Ch'ing-yin-kung," "Family Instructions of Ancestor Yün-ch'ing-kung," "Family Regulations," and "Brief Rules for Sacrifices," Vol. I, ch. 1.

1926–b *Tz'u-ch'i Ch'in shih tsung-p'u* 慈谿秦氏宗譜, "Regulations of the Literary Association," "*Tsung* Instructions of Ancestor Ch'eng-kung," "*Tsu* Discipline of Ancestor Fan-hsiang-kung," and "Additional *Tsu* Agreement," Vol. II, ch. 2.

1927–a *Ta-fu P'an shih chih p'u* 大阜潘氏支譜, "Record of the Charitable Estate," Vol. XIV, Appendix 1; "Regulations of the Charitable Estate" (1837), "Regulations for Ancestral Sacrifices" (1837), "Additional Regulations of the Charitable Estate" (1885), "Additional Regulations of the Charitable Estate" (1906), and "Additional Regulations of the Charitable Estate" (1926), Vol. XIV, Appendix 2.

1927–b *Yü-hsien Chu shih chia-p'u* 禺縣朱氏家譜, "Family Mottoes," Vol. I.

1928–a *Kuo shih tsung-p'u* 郭氏宗譜, "Family Regulations," "The Ten Regulations," and "Family Instructions," Vol. II, ch. 1.

1928-b *P'i-ling Meng shih tsung-p'u* 毘陵孟氏宗譜, "Rules of Genealogy" and "Family Instructions," Vol. I, ch. 1.
1928-c *P'i-ling Hsi-chuang Ku shih tsung-p'u* 毘陵西莊顧氏宗譜, "Family Regulations," "Ancestors' Instructions," "Ancestors' Mottoes," "Family Standards," and *"Tsung* Agreement," Vol. I, ch. 1.
1928-d *T'ung-ch'eng Mu-shan P'an shih tsung-p'u* 桐城木山潘氏宗譜, "Family Instructions" and "Officially Registered Restrictions for the Ancestral Graveyard" (1914), Vol. II, ch. 1 (B).
1928-e *Shih-ch'iao Li shih ch'ung-hsiu tsung-p'u,* 石橋李氏重修宗譜, "Family Instructions," Vol. I, ch. 1.
1928-f *Shanghai Ke shih chia-p'u* 上海葛氏家譜, "A Collection of Family Instructions," Vol. II, ch. 2.
1928-g *Yüeh-tung Chien shih ta-t'ung p'u* 粵東簡氏大同譜, "A Collection of Family Instructions" and "Ancestors' Instructions," Vol. X, ch. 8.
1929-a *Huang-t'ien Chang shih Chien-fang ch'u-hsiu chih p'u* 黃田章氏間房初修支譜, "The Twelve Injunctions," "The Ten Items of Advice," and "Family Instructions" (1845), Vol. I, Preface.
1929-b *Jun-chou Chia shih chia-ch'eng* 潤州賈氏家乘, "Ancestral Hall Agreement" and "Family Regulations," Vol. I, ch. 2.
1929-c *Chi-yang Chang shih hui p'u* 暨陽張氏會譜, "Family Instructions" and "Family Regulations," Vol. I, ch. 1.
1929-d *Fu-ch'un Sun shih Yün-yang Pen-tuan chih p'u* 富春孫氏雲陽本端支譜, "Regulations of the Genealogy," Vol. II, ch. 2.
1929-e *P'i-ling Wu shih tsung-p'u* 毘陵伍氏宗譜, "Family Instructions," "Ancestors' Instructions," and *"Tsung* Regulations," Vol. II, ch. 2.
1929-f *Chin-ling Yu-t'ang Chi shih tsung-p'u* 晉陵游塘籍氏宗譜, *"Tsung* Regulations" and "Family Instructions," Vol. III, ch. 3.
1930-a *Yün-yang T'u shih tsu-p'u* 雲陽涂氏族譜, "Family Instructions," and *"Tsu* Standards," Vol. VI, ch. 11; "Regulations of the Ancestral Hall," Vol. VI, ch. 12.
1930-b *Hsiang-ch'eng Wei shih tsu-p'u* 項城魏氏族譜, "Regulations" (1912), pp. 4-9; "Regulations for the Ritual Land" (1919), pp. 10-11.
1930-c *P'i-ling Yüan shih tsung-p'u* 毘陵袁氏宗譜, "Regulations of the Ancestral Hall," "Additional *Tsu* Regulations" (1930), and "Family Instructions," Vol. I, ch. 1.
1930-d *Shao-hsing Yü-lin Chin shih tsung-p'u* 紹興漁臨金氏宗譜, *"Tsu* Regulations" and "Family Injunctions" (1930), Vol. I, ch. 1.
1930-e *T'an-ts'un Chin shih tsung-p'u* 鄭村金氏宗譜, *"Tsu* Agreement," *"Tsu* Standards," *"Tsu* Regulations," "Re-enacted Regulations," "Contemporary Acupuncture," and "Personal Advice of Chih-yüan-kung," Vol. II, ch. 2.
1931-a *Fu-kou-hsien Chang shih tsu-p'u* 扶溝縣張氏族譜, "Family Regulations," pp. 1-3.

1931–b *Hsiao-shan I-ch'iao Han shih chia-p'u* 蕭山義橋韓氏家譜, "Family Instructions" (1837), "*Tsung* Regulations" (1895), "Record of Examination Hostel" (1821), and "Ancestors' Instructions," Vol. I, Preface.

1931–c *T'ung-ch'eng Lien-hsi Chou shih tsung-p'u* 桐城練西周氏宗譜, "Instructions and Regulations," Vol. I, ch. 1.

1931–d *Tz'u-tung Ch'ing-lin Chiang shih tsung-p'u* 慈東青林姜氏宗譜, "*Tsung* Regulations," Vol. I, Preface.

1932–a *Huang-ke-ho Chu shih chia-p'u* 黃閣河朱氏家譜, "Regulations of the Ancestral Hall" and "Additional Regulations of the Ancestral Hall" (1843), Vol. I, ch. 1.

1933–a *Ning-ling Chang shih tsu-p'u* 甯陵張氏族譜, "Ancestors' Instructions and Injunctions," "The Four Injunctions," "The Four Items of Advice," and "The Ten Omissions from the Genealogy," Vol. I.

1933–b *Hsiao-shan Ting shih chia-p'u* 蕭山丁氏家譜, "Regulations of the Ancestral Hall," Vol. VI, ch. 12.

1933–c *Hsiang-hsiang Chin shih san-hsiu tsu-p'u* 湘鄉金氏三修族譜, "Record of Family School" (1886), Vol. I, Preface; "Family Regulations" and "Family Instructions," Vol. II, Preface.

1933–d *Hsüeh-shu Wu shih tsu-p'u* 薛墅吳氏族譜, "Family Instructions," "Regulations of the Second Edition of the Genealogy," and "Regulations of the Eleventh Edition of the Genealogy," Vol. II, ch. 2.

1933–e *Tai-chou Feng shih tsu-p'u* 代州馮氏族譜, "Ancestors' Instructions," Vol. II, ch. 2.

1933–f *P'i-ling Wang-ch'uan-li Li shih tsung-p'u* 毘陵輞川里李氏宗譜, "Family Regulations," Vol. I, ch. 1.

1933–g *Chiang-hsi Huang shih tsung-tz'u wu-hsiu chu p'u* 江西黃氏宗祠五修主譜, "Articles by Common Decision" (1844), "Regulations of the Ancestral Hall" (1898), and "Regulations of the Ancestral Halls throughout Kiangsi Province" (1933), Vol. I.

1933–h *Shanghai Yü shih chia-ch'eng* 上海郁氏家乘, "*Tsu* Organization," "Injunctions and Punishment," and "Common Property of the *Tsu*," Vol. I.

1933–i *Fu-ning Ch'en shih tsung-p'u* 阜甯陳氏宗譜, "Family Instructions,' Vol. I, Preface.

1934–a *Hu-pei Wu-ch'ang Chang shih tsung-p'u* 湖北武昌張氏宗譜, "General Rules of the Genealogy" and "Family Regulations," Vol. I, Preface.

1934–b *Lo-yang Chu shih chia-p'u* 羅陽朱氏家譜, "Family Instructions of Wen-kung" and "*Tsung* Regulations," Vol. I, ch. 1.

1934–c *Huang-kang Hsü shih tsung-p'u* 黃岡徐氏宗譜, "Family Standards," Vol. I, Preface.

1934–d *Ch'ang-shu Tou-men Shen shih tsung-p'u* 常熟陡門沈氏宗譜, "*Tsung* Regulations," "Instructions," and "Family Mottoes," Vol. I, ch. 1.

1934-e *P'ing-chiang Yeh shih tsu-p'u* 平江葉氏族譜, "Essay on *Tsu* Harmony," "Family Instructions," and "*Tsung* Agreement," Vol. I, ch. 1.
1934-f *Ssu-ming Ts'ang-chi Ch'en shih chia-p'u* 四明倉基陳氏家譜, "Family Instructions," Vol. V, ch. 14; "The Ten Injunctions of Ancestor Tao-li-kung," "*Tsu* Regulations—*Tsu* Restrictions and Appended Articles for Placing the Tablets in the Ancestral Hall," Vol. V, ch. 15; "Common Welfare," Vol. VI, ch. 21.
1935-a *Chi-yang Kao shih tsung-p'u* 暨陽高氏宗譜, "*Tsung* Instructions and Family Regulations," Vol. I, ch. 1.
1935-b *Hsiu-wu Hou-ma-tso Wang shih tsu-p'u* 修武後馬作王氏族譜, "Family Discipline Decided by *Tsu* Organization" (1922) and "Preface of the Genealogy" (1931), Vol. IV, Appendix.
1935-c *Chi-ch'i Miao-tzu-shan Wang shih p'u* 績溪廟子山王氏譜, "Proverbs," Vol. III, ch. 11.
1935-d *Ching-chiang Wang shih tsung-p'u* 京江王氏宗譜, "Family Standards," Vol. I, ch. 1.
1935-e *Shang-i Ho shih tsung-p'u* 商邑何氏宗譜, "Family Regulations," Vol. I, ch. 1.
1935-f *Shanghai P'an shih chia-p'u* 上海潘氏家譜, "Regulations of the Ancestral Hall" and "Family Instructions," Vol. I, ch. 1.
1936-a *Hsiang-ch'eng Chang shih tsu-p'u* 項城張氏族譜, "Disciplinary Codes by Common Decision" (1935), Vol. I, ch. 1.
1936-b *Chiang-yin T'ai-ning Hsing shih chih p'u* 江陰太甯邢氏支譜, "Regulations of the Ancestral Hall," "Miscellaneous Statements of Family Instructions," and "Mottoes of the Early Sages," Vol. XII, ch. 24.
1936-c *Ssu-ming Chu shih chih p'u* 四明朱氏支譜, "On Village School," Vol. II, ch. 15; "Common Welfare," Vol. II, ch. 19.

B. References

Abel, T. M. and Francis L. K. Hsu, "Some Aspects of Personality of Chinese as Revealed by the Rorschach Test," *Rorschach Research Exchange and Journal of Projective Techniques*, XIII (1949), 285–301.
Ayscough, Florence, *Chinese Women, Yesterday and Today* (Boston, 1937).
Becker, Howard, *Through Values to Social Interpretation* (Durham, 1950).
Bossard, James H. S. and Eleanor S. Boll, *Ritual in Family Living* (University of Pennsylvania Press, Philadelphia, 1950).
Chao Fung-chiai, *Chung-kuo fu-nü tsai fa-lü shang chih ti-wei* (Shanghai, 1934).
趙鳳喈　　中國婦女在法律上之地位
Ch'en Han-sheng, *Landlord and Peasants in China* (New York, 1936).
Ch'en Hung-mou, *Yang-cheng i-kuei* (*Ssu-pu pei-yao* ed., Shanghai, 1927).
陳宏謀　　養正遺規
Ch'en Ku-yüan, *Chung-kuo hun-yin shih* (Shanghai, 1936).
陳顧遠　　中國婚姻史

Chen, T. S. and J. K. Shryock, "Chinese Relationship Terms," *American Anthropologist*, n.s. XXXIV (1932), 623–629.
Ch'en Tung-yüan, *Chung-kuo fu-nü sheng-huo shih* (Shanghai, 1928).
陳東原　　中國婦女生活史
Cheng Ch'eng-k'un, "Characteristic Traits of the Chinese People," *Social Forces*, XXV (1946), 146–155.
—, "The Chinese Large Family System and Its Disorganization," *Social Forces*, XVII (1939), 538–539.
Chia Yüan-i, *Chung-kuo chia-t'ing chung ch'in tzu kuan-hsi chih yen-chiu* (Nanking, 1937).
賈元羮　　中國家庭中親子關係之硏究
Ch'iu Han-p'ing, *Li-tai hsing fa chih* (Changsha, 1938).
邱漢平　　歷代刑法志
Chu Ch'eng-hsün, *Ch'in-shu fa lun* (Shanghai, 1939).
朱承勛　　親屬法論
Ch'ü T'ung-tsu, *Chung-kuo fa-lü yü Chung-kuo she-hui* (Shanghai, 1947).
瞿同祖　　中國法律與中國社會
Dai, Bingham, "Personality Problems in Chinese Culture," *American Sociological Review*, VI (1941), 688–696.
Diamond, Arthur Sigismund, *Primitive Law* (London, 1936).
Elmer, Manuel Conrad, *The Sociology of the Family* (New York, 1945).
Fei Hsiao-t'ung, "Peasant and Gentry: An Interpretation of Chinese Social Structure and Its Changes," *American Journal of Sociology*, LII (1946), 1–17.
—, *Peasant Life in China, A Field Study of Country Life in the Yangtze Valley* (London, 1939).
— and Chang Chih-i, *Earthbound China* (Chicago, 1945).
Feng Han-yi, *The Chinese Kinship System* (Cambridge, Mass., 1948).
Fried, Morton H., "Community Studies in China," *Far Eastern Quarterly*, XIV (1954), 11–36.
—, *Fabric of Chinese Society: A Study of the Social Life of a Chinese County Seat* (New York, 1954).
—, *Kin and Non-kin in Chinese Society* (Ann Arbor, University Microfilms, 1951).
Gamble, Sidney David, *How Chinese Families Live in Peiping* (New York, 1934).
—, *Ting Hsien, a North China Rural Community* (New York, 1954).
— and J. S. Burgess, *Peking, A Social Survey* (New York, 1921).
Gurvitch, Georges, *Sociology of Law* (New York, 1942).
Hobhouse, Leonard Trelawney, *Morals in Evolution; A Study in Comparative Ethics* (London, 1951).
Hoebel, Edward Adamson, *The Political Organization and Law-ways of the Comanche Indians*, memoirs of the American Anthropological Association, no. 54 (Menasha, Wis., 1940).
Hsü Ch'ao-yang, *Chung-kuo ch'in-shu fa su-yüan* (Shanghai, 1926).
徐朝陽　　中國親屬法溯源

Hsü Ch'ao-yang, *Chung-kuo hsing fa su-yüan* (Shanghai, 1933).
中國刑法溯源
Hsu, Francis L. K., *American and Chinese—Two Ways of Life* (New York, 1953).
—, "The Differential Functions of Relationship Terms," *American Anthropologist*, n.s. XLIV (1942), 248–256.
—, "Guild and Kinship among the Butchers in West Town," *American Sociological Review*, X (1945), 357–364.
—, "The Myth of Chinese Family Size," *American Journal of Sociology*, XLVIII (1943), 555–562.
—, "Observations on Cross-cousin Marriage in China," *American Anthropologist*, n.s. XLVII (1945), 83–103.
—, "The Problem of Incest Tabu in a North China Village," *American Anthropologist*, n.s. XLII (1940), 122–135.
—, *Under the Ancestors' Shadow* (New York, 1948).
Hu Hsien-chin, "The Chinese Concept of 'Face'," *American Anthropologist*, n.s. XLVI (1944), 45–65.
—, *The Common Descent Group in China and Its Functions* (New York, 1948).
Kadō Jōken, *Shina kodai kazoku seido kenkyū* (Tokyo, 1941).
加藤常賢　支那古代家族制度研究
Kao Ta-kuan, *Chung-kuo chia-tsu she-hui chih yen-pien* (Chungking, 1944).
高達觀　中國家族社會之演變
Kardiner, Abram, *The Individual and His Society, the Psycho-dynamics of Primitive Social Organization* (New York, 1939).
—, *The Psychological Frontiers of Society* (New York, 1945).
KCTSCC: *Ku chin t'u-shu chi-ch'eng, Chia-fan tien* (Shanghai, 1888).
古今圖書集成　家範典
Kroeber, A. L., *The Nature of Culture* (Chicago, 1952).
—, "Process in the Chinese Kinship System," *American Anthropologist*, n.s. XXXV (1933), 151–157.
Kulp, Daniel Harrison, *Country Life in South China: The Sociology of Familism* (New York, 1925).
Lamson, Herbert Day, "The Chinese Laborer and His Family," *Sociology and Social Research*, XVI (1932), 203–212 and 326–335.
—, *Social Pathology in China* (Shanghai, 1935).
Lang, Olga, *Chinese Family and Society* (New Haven and London, 1946).
La Piere, Richard T., *A Theory of Social Control* (New York, 1954).
Lee, Rose Hum, "Researches on the Chinese Family," *American Journal of Sociology*, LIV (1949), 497–504.
Lee, Shu-ching, "China's Traditional Family: Its Characteristics and Disintegration," *American Sociological Review*, XVIII (1953), 272–280.
Leong, Y. K. and L. K. Tao, *Village and Town Life in China* (New York, 1915).
Levy, Marion J. Jr., *Family Revolution in Modern China* (Cambridge, Mass., 1949).
Lin Yüeh-hua, *The Golden Wing* (New York, 1944).

Lin Yüeh-hua, "Ts'ung jen-lei-hsüeh ti kuan-tien k'ao-ch'a Chung-kuo tsung-tsu hsiang-ts'un," *She-hui-hsüeh-chieh* (Peiping), IX (136), 1925–142.
林耀華　從人類學的觀點考察中國宗族鄉村　社會學界
Linton, Ralph, *The Cultural Background of Personality* (London, 1947).
Lo Tun-wei, *Chung-kuo chih hun-yin wen-t'i* (Shanghai, 1931).
羅敦偉　中國之婚姻問題
Lowie, Robert Harry, *An Introduction to Cultural Anthropology* (New York, 1934).
—, *Primitive Religion* (London, 1925).
Makino Tatsumi, *Kinsei Chūgoku shūzoku kenkyū* (Tokyo, 1949).
牧野巽　近世中國宗族研究
—, "Mei Shin zokufu kenkyū josetsu," *Tōhō gakuhō* (Tokyo), VI (1936), 261–288.
　　明清族譜研究序說　　東方學報
—, "Peiping Toshu-kan zo Mei-dai zenhon zokufu," *Tōhō gakuhō* (Tokyo), VI, extra number (1936), 169–202.
　　北平圖書舘藏明代善本族譜　　東方學報
—, *Shina kazoku kenkyū* (Tokyo, 1944).
　　支那家族研究
—, *Shina ni okeru kazoku seido* (Tokyo, 1935).
　　支那に於ける家族制度
—, "Shūshi to so no hattatsu," *Tōkō gakuhō* (Tokyo), IX (1939), 173–250.
　　宗祠と其の發達　　東方學報
Malinowski, Bronislaw, *Crime and Custom in Savage Society* (New York, 1926).
—, *The Father in Primitive Psychology* (New York, 1927).
—, *The Foundation of Faith and Morals* (London, 1936).
—, *Magic, Science and Religion and Other Essays* (Glencoe, Ill., 1948).
Manchukuo, Ministry of Justice, *Manshū kazoku seido shūkan* (Hsinking, 1944).
滿州家族制度習慣
Mano Senryū, "Mei-dai no kaki ni tsuite," *Tōhō gaku* (Tokyo), n.s. VIII (1954), 83–93.
間野潛龍　明代の家規について　　東方學
Merton, Robert K., *Social Theory and Social Structure* (Glencoe, Ill., 1949).
Mizutani Kunichi, *Shina ni okeru kazoku seido* (Dairen, 1928).
水谷國一　支那に於ける家族制度
Moriya Mitsuo, *Kandai kazoku no keitai ni kansuru kōsatsu* (Tokyo, 1954).
守屋美都雄　漢代家族の形態に關する考察
Morohashi Tetsuji, *Shina no kazoku sei* (Tokyo, 1943).
諸橋轍次　支那の家族制
MSSHK: Min shang shih hsi-kuan tiao-ch'a pao-kao lu, originally published in 1930, reprinted with Japanese translation (Tokyo, 1932).
民商事習慣調査報告錄
Mukerjee, Radhakamal, *The Social Structure of Values* (London, 1949).
Niida Noboru, *Chūgoku no nōson kazoku* (2nd ed., Tokyo, 1954).
仁井田陞　中國の農村家族

Niida Noboru, (ed.), *Chūgoku nōson kankō chōsa*, 4 vols. (Tokyo, 1952–1955).
　　　　中國農村慣行調査
Nishiyama Eikyū, *Shina no seishi to kazoku seido* (Tokyo, 1944).
西山榮久　　支那の姓氏と家族制度
Obata Ryūo, "Mei-dai kyōson no kyōka to saiban," *Tōyōshi kenkyū*, XI, nos. 5 and 6 (1952), 23–43.
小畑龍雄　　明代鄕村の敎化と裁判　　　東洋史硏究
P'an Kuang-tan, "Chia-tsu chih-tu yü hsüan-tse tso-yung," *She-hui-hsüeh chieh* (Peiping), IX (1936), 89–104.
潘光旦　　家族制度與選擇作用　　社會學界
—, "Chung-kuo chia-p'u hsüeh lüeh shih," *Tung-fang tsa-chih*, XXVI, no. 1 (1933), 107–120.
　中國家譜學略史　　東方雜誌
—, *Chung-kuo chih chia-t'ing wen-t'i* (Shanghai, 1926).
　中國之家庭問題
P'an Yü-mei, "I-ke ts'un-chen ti nung-fu," *She-hui-hsüeh-chieh* (Peiping), VI (1932), 261–286.
潘玉梅　　一個村鎭的農婦　　社會學界
Parsons, Talcott, *The Social System* (Glencoe, Ill., 1951).
— and E. A. Shils (ed.), *Toward A General Theory of Action* (Cambridge, Mass., 1951).
Radcliffe-Brown, A. R., *African System of Kinship and Marriage* (London, 1950).
—, *Structure and Function in Primitive Society* (Glencoe, Ill., 1952).
Redfield, Robert, *Peasant Society and Culture* (Chicago, 1956).
Ross, Edward Alsworth, *The Changing Chinese* (New York, 1911).
Shiga Shuzō, *Chūgoku kazoku-ko ron* (Tokyo, 1950).
志賀秀三　　中國家族法論
—, *Shina shakai no kenkyū* (Tokyo, 1947).
　　支那社會の硏究
Shih Kuo-heng, *China Enters the Machine Age* (Cambridge, Mass., 1944).
Shimizu Morimitsu, *Chūgoku kyōson shakai ron* (Tokyo, 1951).
清水盛光　　中國鄕村社會論
—, *Chūgoku zokusan seido kō* (Tokyo, 1949).
　　中國族產制度考
—, *Shina kazoku no kōzō* (Tokyo, 1942).
　　支那家族の構造
Smith, Arthur H., *Chinese Characteristics* (New York, 1894).
—, *Village Life in China* (New York, 1899).
Smythe, Lewis, "The Composition of the Chinese Family," *Nanking Journal*, V (1935), 371–393.
Sogabe Shizuo, "Mei Taiso rokuyu no denshō ni tsuite," *Tōyōshi kenkyū*, XII, no. 4 (1953), 27–36.
曾我部靜雄　　明太祖六諭の傳承について　　東洋史硏究
Soothill, William Edward (tr.), *The Analects* (Yokohama, 1910).

Staunton, Sir George Thomas (tr.), *Ta Tsing Leu Lee: Being the Fundamental Law and a Selection from the Supplementary Statute of the Penal Code of China* (London, 1810).
Sun Pen-wen, *Hsien-tai Chung-kuo she-hui wen-t'i*, 4 vols. (Chungking, 1943).
孫本文　　現代中國社會問題
Ta Ch'ing hui-tien (Peking, 1899).
大清會典
Tachibana Boku, *Shina shakai kenkyū* (Tokyo, 1941).
橘樸　　支那社會研究
T'ao Hsi-sheng, *Hun-yin yü chia-tsu* (Shanghai, 1934).
陶希聖　　婚姻與家族
Tao, L. K., "The Family System in China," *The Sociological Review*, VI (1913).
—, "Some Chinese Characteristics in the Light of the Chinese Family," in *Essays Presented to C. G. Seligman* (London, 1934).
Thomas, W. I., *Primitive Behavior* (New York, 1937).
Valk, M. H. Van der, *An Outline of Modern Chinese Family Law* (Peiping, 1939).
Wada Kiyoshi, "Mei no Taiso no kyoiku chokugo ni tsuite," in *Tōyōshi ronsō* in honor of Dr. Shiratori (Tokyo, 1925).
和田清　　明の太祖の教育勅語に就いて　　東洋史論叢
Weber, Max, *The Religion of China, Confucianism and Taoism*, translated by Hans H. Gerth (Glencoe, Ill., 1951).
Wieger, L., *Moral Tenets and Custom in China* (Peking, 1931).
Westermarck, Edward A., *The Origin and Development of Moral Ideas* (2nd ed., London, 1924–1926).
Wilkinson, H., *The Family in Classical China* (Shanghai, 1926).
Wu Ch'i, *Chung-kuo ch'in-shu fa yüan-li* (Sanghai, 1947).
吳歧　　中國親屬法原理
Yang Lien-sheng, "The Concept of 'Pao' as a Basis for Social Relations in China," in John K. Fairbank (ed.), *Chinese Thought and Institutions* (Chicago, 1957), pp. 291-309.
Yang, Martin C., *A Chinese Village: Taitou, Shantung Province* (New York, 1945).
Yang Shih-jang (ed.), *Ta Ch'ing lü-li hsin-pien* (1906).
楊士讓輯　　大清律例新編
Yang Tien-hsün, "Chung-kuo chia-p'u t'ung-lun," *T'u-shu chi-k'an*, n.s. III, nos. 1 and 2 (1941), 9–35 and n.s. VI, nos. 3 and 4 (1945), 17–39.
楊殿珣　　中國家譜通論　　圖書季刊
Yao Tz'u-ai, "P'o hsi ch'ung-t'u ti chu-yao yüan-yin," *She-hui-hsueh-chieh* (Peiping), VI (June, 1933).
姚慈靄　　婆媳衝突的主要原因　　社會學界

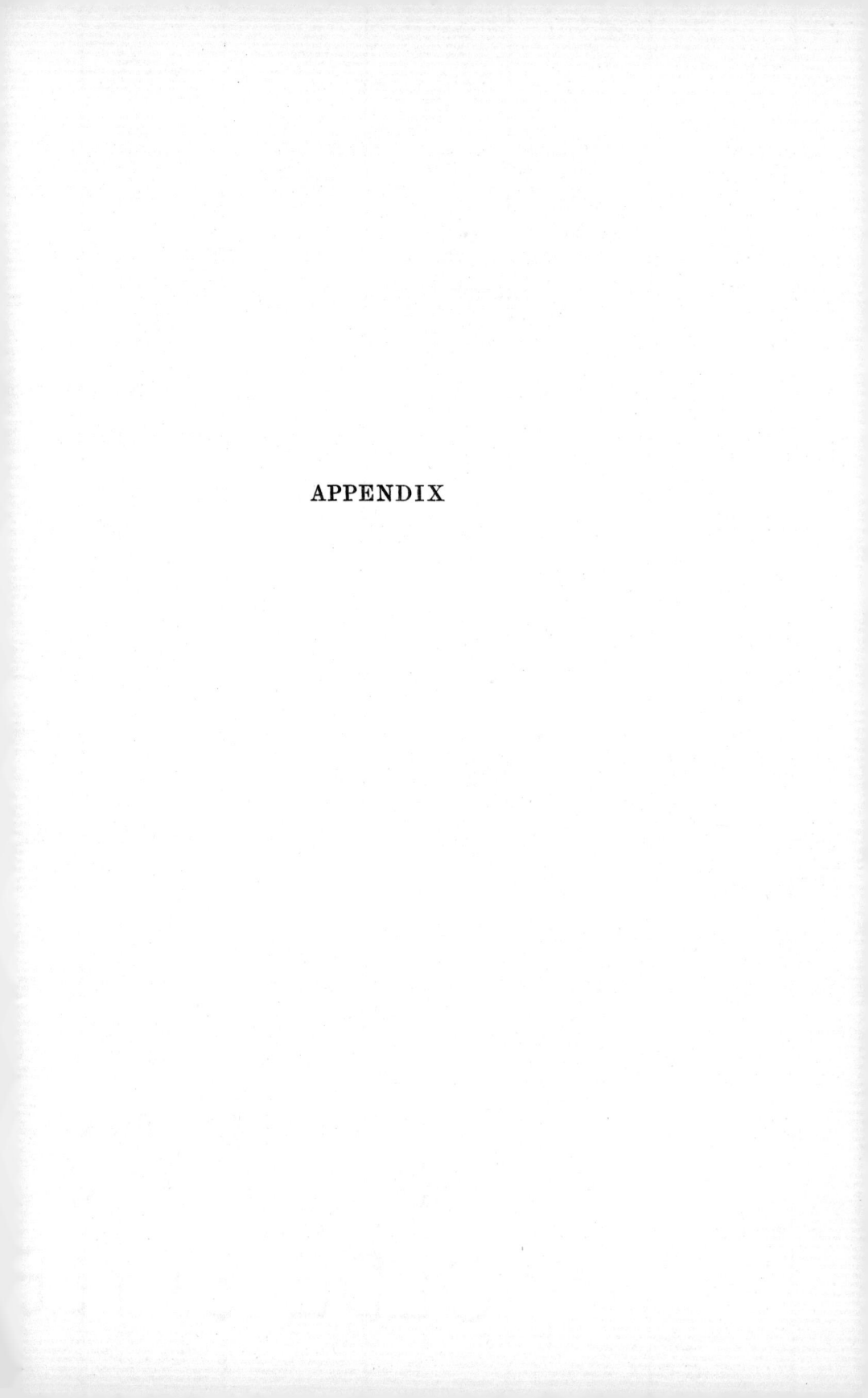

APPENDIX

APPENDIX 211

TABLE 1

GEOGRAPHIC DISTRIBUTION OF THE 151 CLANS
WHOSE RULES ARE UNDER STUDY

Province and locality	Number of clans	Per cent
KIANGSU	83	54.9
Wuchin	26	17.2
Chenkiang	17	11.2
Shanghai	7	4.6
Tanyang	6	4.0
Kiangyin	5	3.3
Soochow	5	3.3
Wusih	5	3.3
Changshu	4	2.6
Kiangtu	2	1.3
Choupu	1	.7
Founing	1	.7
Huat'ang	1	.7
Ihsing	1	.7
Lotien	1	.7
Nanking	1	.7
CHEKIANG	22	14.5
Hsiaoshan	7	4.6
Shaohsing	4	2.6
Tz'uch'i	3	2.0
Ningpo	2	1.3
Hangchow	1	.7
Pukiang	1	.7
Shangyü	1	.7
Tsingtien	1	.7
Wenchow	1	.7
Yüyao	1	.7
ANHWEI	13	8.6
Tungcheng	4	2.6
Hwaining	2	1.3
Kinghsien	1	.7
Chich'i	1	.7
Chuchou	1	.7
Hofei	1	.7
Kucheng	1	.7
Lukiang	1	.7
Taihuhsien	1	.7

TABLE 1 (*continued*)

GEOGRAPHIC DISTRIBUTION OF THE 151 CLANS
WHOSE RULES ARE UNDER STUDY

HUPEH	13	8.6
Huangkang	3	2.0
Wuchang	2	1.3
Chinkouhsiang	1	.7
Hanchwan	1	.7
Hsiaokan	1	.7
Huangpo	1	.7
Loi	1	.7
Mienyang	1	.7
Tungshan	1	.7
Unknown	1	.7
HONAN	7	4.6
Hsiangcheng	2	1.3
Shangchiu	2	1.3
Fukou	1	.7
Hsiuwu	1	.7
Yühsien	1	.7
HUNAN	6	4.0
Hsianghsiang	2	1.3
Pingkiang	2	1.3
Hengyang	1	.7
Shaochen	1	.7
KIANGSI	2	1.3
Nanchang	1	.7
Nanfeng	1	.7
KWANGTUNG	2	1.3
Canton, Hsiangshan, Nanhai and Shunteh	1	.7
Hopu	1	.7
KWANGSI	2	1.3
Kweilin	1	.7
Wuyüan	1	.7
KIANGSU and SHANSI	1	.7
Total	151	100.0

APPENDIX 213

LOCATION OF THE CLANS WHOSE CLAN RULES ARE UNDER STUDY

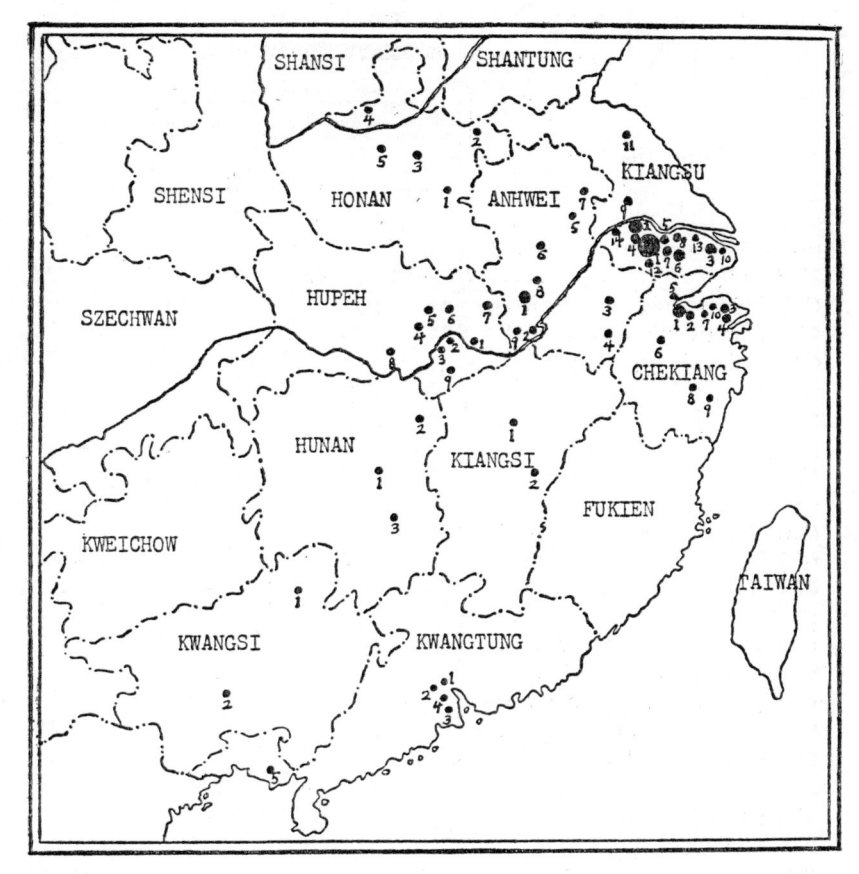

KIANGSU: 1–Wuchin 2–Chenkiang 3–Shanghai 4–Tanyang 5–Kiangyin 6–Soochow 7–Wusih 8–Changshu 9–Kiangtu 10–Choupu 11–Founing 12–Ihsing 13–Lotien 14–Nanking
CHEKIANG: 1–Hsiaoshan 2–Shaohsing 3–Tz'uch'i 4–Ningpo 5–Hangchow 6–Pukiang 7–Shangyü 8–Tsingtien 9–Wenchow 10–Yüyao
ANHWEI: 1–Tungcheng 2–Hwaining 3–Chinghsien 4–Chich'i 5–Chuchou 6–Hofei 7–Kucheng 8–Lukiang 9–Taihuhsien
HUPEH: 1–Huangkang 2–Wuchang 3–Chinkouhsiang 4–Hanchwan 5–Hsiaokan 6–Huangpo 7–Loi 8–Mienyang 9–Tungshan
HONAN: 1–Hsiangcheng 2–Shangchiu 3–Fukou 4–Hsiuwu 5–Yühsien
HUNAN: 1–Hsianghsiang 2–Pingkiang 3–Hengyang
KIANGSI: 1–Nanchang 2–Nanfeng
KWANGTUNG: 1–Canton 2–Nanhai 3–Hsiangshan 4–Shunteh 5–Hopu
KWANGSI: 1–Kweilin 2–Wuyüan

TABLE 2

TABULATION OF THE RULE TITLES IN THE GENEALOGIES OF 151 CLANS
IN RELATION TO COMMON PROPERTY AND PUNISHMENT

Rule title	Number of rules without mention of common property — Without punishment	Number of rules without mention of common property — With punishment	Number of rules with mention of common property — Without punishment	Number of rules with mention of common property — With punishment	Total
Titles beginning with the word *chia* (family)	*80*	*27*	–	*7*	*114*
Chia hsün (family instructions)	47	4	–	1	52
Chia kuei (family regulations) .	16	17	–	4	37
Chia fa (family discipline)	2	2	–	2	6
Chia fan (family standards) ...	5	–	–	–	5
Chia hsün ke-yen (family mottoes)	4	–	–	–	4
Chia li (family proprieties)	2	1	–	–	3
Chia chieh (family injunctions).	1	–	–	–	1
Chia chen (family admonitions).	–	1	–	–	1
Chia chiao (family teachings) ..	–	1	–	–	1
Chia yüeh (family agreement) .	1	–	–	–	1
Chia ch'üan (family advice) ...	1	–	–	–	1
Chia chü (family life)	1	–	–	–	1
Chia i (family decisions)	–	1	–	–	1
Titles with the words *tsu hsün* (ancestors' instructions)	*30*	–	–	–	*30*
Titles beginning with the word *tsu* (clan)	*11*	*5*	*1*	*9*	*26*
Tsu kuei (clan regulations) ...	2	5	–	6	13
Tsu yüeh (clan agreement)....	3	–	–	1	4
Tsu fan (clan standards)......	2	–	–	1	3
Tsu chieh (clan injunctions) ..	1	–	–	–	1
Tsu ch'üan (clan advice)	1	–	–	–	1
Tsu i (clan decisions)	–	–	–	1	1
Tsu hui (clan organization) ...	1	–	1	–	2
Tsu shih-li (clan affairs)	1	–	–	–	1
Titles beginning with the word *tsung* (clan)	*15*	*10*	–	*9*	*34*
Tsung kuei (clan regulations) .	3	5	–	6	14
Tsung yüeh (clan agreement)..	5	2	–	2	9
Tsung hsün (clan instructions)	4	1	–	–	5
Tsung chin (clan restrictions)..	1	1	–	1	3
Tsung fa (clan discipline)	1	–	–	–	1
Tsung chieh (clan injunctions)	1	–	–	–	1
Tsung fan (clan standards)....	–	1	–	–	1

TABLE 2 (continued)

TABULATION OF THE RULE TITLES IN THE GENEALOGIES OF 151 CLANS IN RELATION TO COMMON PROPERTY AND PUNISHMENT

Rule title	Number of rules without mention of common property — Without punishment	Number of rules without mention of common property — With punishment	Number of rules with mention of common property — Without punishment	Number of rules with mention of common property — With punishment	Total
Titles beginning with the word *tz'u* (ancestral hall)	*2*	*9*	*4*	*20*	*35*
Tz'u kuei (an. hall regulations)	2	9	3	15	29
Tz'u t'iao-li (an. hall articles) ..	–	–	–	2	2
Tz'u yüeh (an. hall agreement)	–	–	–	1	1
Tz'u chin (an. hall restriction)	–	–	–	1	1
Tz'u chang (an. hall statues) ..	–	–	–	1	1
Tz'u shih-i (an. hall affairs) ...	–	–	1	–	1
Titles beginning with the word *chi* (sacrifice)	*9*	–	*3*	*1*	*13*
Chi t'iao-kuei (sa. regulations).	9	–	1	1	11
Chi t'ien (ritual land)	–	–	2	–	2
Titles beginning with the words *tsu fen* (ancestral graveyard)	–	*2*	–	–	*2*
Tsu fen chin yüeh (Restrictions for ancestral graveyard)	–	2	–	–	2
Titles beginning with the word *i* (charitable)	–	–	*3*	*4*	*7*
I-chuang kuei-t'iao (charitable estate regulations)	–	–	1	4	5
I-t'ien t'iao-li (charitable land articles)	–	–	1	–	1
I chü (charitable deeds)	–	–	1	–	1
Titles beginning with the word *shu* or *hsüeh* (school) or *shih-kuan* (examination hostel)	*2*	–	*1*	*1*	*4*
Shu t'iao-li (school articles) ...	1	–	–	–	1
Hsueh-t'ien chang-ch'eng (school land statutes)	1	–	1	–	2
Shih-kuan kuei-t'iao (examination hostel regulations)	–	–	–	1	1
Titles beginning with the word *p'u* (genealogy)	*4*	*8*	–	*2*	*14*
P'u li (general rules)	3	2	–	–	5
P'u kuei (genealogy regulations)	–	3	–	2	5
P'u chieh (genealogy injunction)	1	–	–	–	1
P'u chin (genealogy restriction)	–	1	–	–	1

TABLE 2 (*continued*)

TABULATION OF THE RULE TITLES IN THE GENEALOGIES OF 151 CLANS IN RELATION TO COMMON PROPERTY AND PUNISHMENT

Rule title	Number of rules without mention of common property		Number of rules with mention of common property		Total
	Without punishment	With punishment	Without punishment	With punishment	
P'u pu shu (omissions from genealogy)	–	2	–	–	2
Titles with the word mottoes ...	7	–	–	–	7
Titles in miscellaneous wording ..	21	7	1	1	30
Total	181	68	13	54	316*

*The grand total of rule titles exceeds that of the number of clans (151) because many clans have more than one kind of rules in their genealogies.

TABLE 3

CLASSIFICATION OF SUBJECT-MATTER WITH AND WITHOUT PROHIBITION OF MISBEHAVIOR IN THE RULES OF 151 CLANS

Subject-matter	Without prohibition of misbehavior	With prohibition of misbehavior	Total number of clans
Intra-family relations and behavior			
Children toward parents (filial piety)	47	71	118
Parents toward children:			
Education of children	111	–	111
Discipline of children	52	43	95
Protection of children	–	30	30
Inheritance and adoption of an heir	9	51	60
Relations and behavior between brothers	9	97	106
Marriage matches	8	76	84
Marital relations and behavior:			
Harmony and differentiation of roles between husband and wife	19	–	19
Wife's role and conduct	4	58	62
Husband's treatment of wife	–	17	17
Concubinage	10	28	38
Widowhood and treatment of widow:			
Role and conduct of a widow	–	9	9
Remarriage of a widow	7	2*	9
Reward and assistance of a widow	50	–	50
Protection of a widow	–	25	25
Sex segregation	–	32	32
Seclusion of women	–	44	44
Intra-clan relations and activities			
Clan organization and its functionaries	49	26	75
Clan common property:			
Sources and kinds of common property	114	–	114
Management of common property	60	–	60
Protection of common property	4	89	93
Clan continuity:			
Establishment of ancestral hall	109	–	109
Maintenance of ancestral graveyard	80	–	80
Compilation of genealogy	45	–	45
Performance of ancestral rites	50	59	109
Clan relief and aid of needy members	75	–	75

TABLE 3 (*continued*)

CLASSIFICATION OF SUBJECT-MATTER WITH AND WITHOUT PROHIBITION OF MISBEHAVIOR IN THE RULES OF 151 CLANS

Subject-matter	Without prohibition of misbehavior	With prohibition of misbehavior	Total number of clans
Commendation of exemplray members	35	–	35
Control of relations and behavior of clan members toward one another	–	106	106
Extra-clan relations and behavior			
Relations with non-clan relatives	4	15	19
Relations with teachers	28	11	39
Relations with friends	37	35	72
Relations with neighbours and community people	15	35	50
Relations with any outsider	–	9	9
Relations with the ruler of the state	24	–	24
Duty and conduct of clan members in official career	28	9	37
Tax payment and labor service to government	–	53	53
Litigation under the government	5	100*	105
Beliefs and values of the individual			
Religions and beliefs:			
Belief in Buddhism and Taoism	9	40*	49
Belief in Christianity	–	3*	3
Belief in heterodox religious sects	–	7*	7
Belief in geomancy	2	28	30
Belief in sorcery and magics	1	11*	12
Belief in demons and gods	–	8*	8
Belief in prayers for cure of illness	–	9*	9
Belief in fortune-telling	1	1*	2
Belief in ways of Heaven or Nature	4	–	4
Belief in fate	19	–	19
Belief in reward of unostentatious virtue	34	–	34
Care for animal life	9	–	9
Moral values:			
Cautiousness of speech	34	–	34
Courtesy or modesty	26	–	26

APPENDIX

TABLE 3 (*continued*)

CLASSIFICATION OF SUBJECT-MATTER WITH AND WITHOUT PROHIBITION OF MISBEHAVIOR IN THE RULES OF 151 CLANS

Subject-matter	Without prohibition of misbehavior	With prohibition of misbehavior	Total number of clans
Forbearance and conciliation	26	–	26
Uprightness in mind	15	–	15
Benevolence and love	12	–	12
Honesty and sincerity	24	–	24
Forgiveness	10	–	10
Reasonableness	6	–	6
Regard for public welfare	4	–	4
Serenity and tranquility	4	–	4
Propriety, righteousness and sense of shame	19	–	19
Vocational values:			
Attentiveness in vocation	75	–	75
Industriousness and thrift	93	–	93
Studying as preferential vocation	128	–	128
Farming as preferential vocation	111	–	111
Trade as preferential vocation	91	–	91
Craft or industry as preferential vocation	91	–	91
Miscellaneous vocations allowable	14	–	14
Prohibition of loafing and base vocations	–	90	90
Misdemeanors and criminal offenses of the individual			
Gambling	–	84*	84
Drunkenness and disorderliness	–	45*	45
Opium-smoking	–	12*	12
Brutality and fighting	–	20*	20
Sex misbehavior	–	57*	57
Illegal profiteering	–	30*	30
Offenses against private property	–	32*	32
Offenses against human rights and life	–	9*	9
Offenses against the state	–	20*	20
Violation of the law (unspecified)	–	15*	15

* The clans took a negative attitude towards the behavior under the subject-matter.

TABLE 4

CLASSIFICATION OF MISBEHAVIOR SUBJECT TO PROHIBITION WITH AND WITHOUT PUNISHMENT IN THE RULES OF 151 CLANS

Category of misbehavior	Prohibition without mention of punishment	Prohibition with mention of punishment	Total number of clans
Unfilial behavior of children	8	63	71
Parents' lack of discipline of children	38	5	43
Parents' lack of protection of children	12	18	30
Improper adoption and inheritance	26	25	51
Unbrotherly conduct	56	41	97
Misbehavior of wife	33	25	58
Misbehavior of husband toward wife	5	12	17
Misbehavior in regard to concubinage	19	9	28
Misbehavior of a widow	2	7	9
Misbehavior against a widow	12	13	25
Misbehavior in marriage matches	50	26	76
Misbehavior in violating sex segregation	29	3	32
Improper social contact of women	37	7	44
Misbehavior of clan functionaries	1	25	26
Misbehavior against clan common property	24	65	89
Misbehavior in regard to ancestral rites	16	43	59
Misbehavior against fellow clan members	44	62	106
Misbehavior toward non-clan relatives	15	–	15
Misbehavior toward teachers	11	–	11
Misbehavior in making friends and toward friends	22	13	35
Misbehavior toward neighbours	32	3	35
Misbehavior in connection with any outsider	4	5	9
Misbehavior of clan members in official career	4	5	9
Misbehavior in tax payment and labour service	44	9	53
Misbehavior in connection with litigation	59	41	100
Improper religions and beliefs:			
Belief in Buddhism and Taoism	38	2	40
Belief in Christianity	3	–	3
Joining heterodox religious sects	6	1	7
Superstitious belief in geomancy	26	2	28
Belief in sorcery and magics	11	–	11
Superstitious belief in demons and gods	8	–	8

TABLE 4 (*continued*)

CLASSIFICATION OF MISBEHAVIOR SUBJECT TO PROHIBITION WITH AND WITHOUT PUNISHMENT IN THE RULES OF 151 CLANS

Category of misbehavior	Prohibition without mention of punishment	Prohibition with mention of punishment	Total number of clans
Belief in prayers for cure of illness	9	–	9
Belief in fortune-telling	1	–	1
Loafing and taking improper or base vocations	40	50	90
Gambling	52	32	84
Being drunk and disorderly	27	18	45
Opium-smoking	10	2	12
Being brutal and fighting	8	12	20
Sex misbehavior	29	28	57
Illegal profiteering	10	20	30
Offenses against private property	3	29	32
Offenses against human rights and life	2	7	9
Offenses against the state	3	17	20
Violation of the law (unspecified)	2	13	15

TABLE 5

PROHIBITION AND PUNISHMENT OF UNFILIAL BEHAVIOR IN THE RULES OF 71 CLANS

Prohibition and punishment	Favoring wife and children	Living separately			Non-support or inadequate support					Contravention					Hurting feelings	Insulting or cursing			Battery			Neglect of burial or sacrifice			Filial impiety (unspecified)				
		In general	First offense	Repeated offense	In general	Light offense	Grave offense	First offense	Repeated offense	In general	Light offense	Grave offense	First offense	Repeated offense		In general	First offense	Repeated offense	In general	First offense	Repeated offense	In general	Light offense	Grave offense	In general	Light offense	Grave offense	First offense	Repeated offense Incorrigible
Prohibition without mention of punishment	11	1			1																				3				
Clan punishment:																													
Oral censure (admonition or reproof)			1					2																	2 1		3 1	1	1
Penalty to be decided	1		1							1	1																		
Monetary fine	1		1		1	1			1	1			1			1									3 2	3 2	2 2	2	1
Castigation					1																				7 3		9 1	1
Corporal punishment (flogging or equivalent)																												
Forfeit of clan ration													1							1					1	1	1	
Non-participation in commensal meals																									1			
Non-participation in sacrificial rites																									1			
Non-participation in clan affairs, "expelled" written on the back of tablet and no biography in genealogy after death																									1			
Exclusion of tablet from ancestral hall												1											1		1		1	
Exclusion from ancestral hall																									1		1 2	
Exclusion or expunction from genealogy			2				1																		2 1		1	
Expulsion from clan group																									1			
Exclusion from genealogy and clan group							1		1				2	2			1	1			1			1	2	7	8 3	2
Government punishment according to law																									1		1	
Government and clan punishment:																												
Punishment by law and exclusion from ancestral hall																									1		1	
Punishment by law and exclusion from genealogy																												
Total	13	1	2 2		2 1	1	1 2	2	2	2 2	2 2	2	2 2	2	1	2 1	1	1	1	1	1	1	1	1	26 8	8	17	17 3

TABLE 6

PROHIBITION AND PUNISHMENT OF FATHER OR ELDER BROTHER FOR LACK OF DISCIPLINE OF YOUNGSTERS IN THE RULES OF 43 CLANS

Prohibition and punishment	Doting or spoiling youngsters — In general	Light offense	Grave offense	Shielding misbehaving youngsters	No schooling at proper age when family has means	No vocational training at proper age
Prohibition without mention of punishment	40					
Clan punishment:						
Oral censure (admonition or reproof)................	1					
Penalty to be decided				1		
Monetary fine (5–50 silver dollars)		1				
Corporal punishment				1		
Forfeit of clan ration	1					
Exclusion from ancestral hall					1	1
Exclusion from ancestral hall and genealogy			1			
Total	42	1	1	2	1	1

TABLE 7

PROHIBITION AND PUNISHMENT OF PARENTS' MISBEHAVIOR TOWARD THEIR CHILDREN IN THE RULES OF 30 CLANS

Prohibition and punishment	Mistreatment of children (unspecified)	Mistreating patrilocal fiancee of son — In general	Mistreating patrilocal fiancee of son — Light offense	Mistreating patrilocal fiancee of son — Grave offense	Confinement or expulsion of sons by legal wife	Giving away one of many sons to other person	Giving away children to Buddhist or Taoist temples	Marrying off daughter to be concubine	Selling daughter into prostitution	Selling children as indentured servants	Infanticide (mostly female)
Prohibition without mention of punishment	1	2	1		1	1	2			4	6
Clan punishment:											
Penalty to be decided					1		2	1		2	1
Castigation											1
Non-participation in clan affairs, "expelled" written on the back of the tablet and no biography in the genealogy									2	1	
Exclusion of tablet from ancestral hall										2	
Exclusion from ancestral hall										1	
Exclusion or expunction from genealogy								1		2	
Expulsion from clan group				1						1	
Expulsion from ancestral hall and clan group after corporal punishment										1	
Expulsion from clan and local district											
Government punishment according to law										1	2
Government punishment and expunction from genealogy											
Total	1	2	1	1	2	1	4	2	2	15	10

APPENDIX

TABLE 8

PROHIBITION AND PUNISHMENT OF MISBEHAVIOR IN ADOPTION AND INHERITANCE IN THE RULES OF 51 CLANS

Prohibition and punishment	Clan members disputing adoption and inheritance — In general	Clan members disputing adoption and inheritance — First offense	Clan members disputing adoption and inheritance — Disobeying clan order	Adoption by own preference from clan	Widow privately adopting an heir	Illegitimate son as heir	Adopting matrilocal son-in-law as heir	Adoption not from closest kin in clan	Adoption not from proper generation in clan — In general	Adoption not from proper generation in clan — First offense	Adoption not from proper generation in clan — Disobeying clan order	Adoption not from one's clan — In general	Adoption not from one's clan — First offense	Adoption not from one's clan — Disobeying clan order	Clan members adopted by other clan
Prohibition without mention of punishment	5			4	1		6	14	19			21			4
Clan punishment:															
Oral censure										1		3			3
Non-recognition by clan group												2			1
Forfeit of clan ration												1			2
Castigation		1										1			
Corporal punishment												1			
Exclusion of tablet from ancestral hall									1			4			
Exclusion from ancestral hall						1			1			1			
Exclusion or expunction from genealogy							1								
Expunction from genealogy and forfeit of clan ration									1			2			
Expunction from genealogy and forfeit of property							1					1			
Expulsion from clan group							1					3			
Expulsion from clan and forfeit of property												1			
Exclusion from ancestral hall and genealogy															
Exclusion from genealogy and clan group and forfeit of property															
Government order to rejoin original clan															1
Government punishment according to law													2	2	
Total	5	1	1	4	1	1	9	14	21	1	1	41	2	2	11

TABLE 9

PROHIBITION AND PUNISHMENT OF UNBROTHERLY BEHAVIOR IN THE RULES OF 97 CLANS

Prohibition and punishment	Discord between brothers due to wives' influence — In general	Discord — First offense	Discord — Repeated offense	Dispute for property	Quarreling and fighting — In general	Quarreling — Light offense	Quarreling — Grave offense	Quarreling — First offense	Quarreling — Incorrigible	Mistreating younger brother — Light offense	Mistreating younger brother — Grave offense	Contravention of elder brother — In general	Contravention — Light offense	Contravention — Grave offense	Insulting or cursing elder brother	Beating elder brother or his wife	Unbrotherly behavior (unspecified) — In general	Unbrotherly — Light offense	Unbrotherly — Grave offense	Unbrotherly — First offense	Unbrotherly — Repeated offense
Prohibition without mention of punishment	55			54	5					5		2			1		4	2		2	1
Clan punishment:																		3		1	1
Oral censure					2	1				1			1							1	1
Penalty to be decided								2												3	1
Monetary fine					2				1				1				4			4	1
Castigation																	2				
Corporal punishment																				1	
Forfeit of clan privileges																	1				1
Non-participation in commensal meals									1								1				1
Non-participation in sacrificial rites			1														1				
Non-participation in clan affairs, "expelled" written on the back of the tablet and no biography in genealogy																	1				
Exclusion or expunction from genealogy														1		1					7
Expulsion from clan group		1	1	1			1														
Exclusion from genealogy and clan group				1							1										
Government punishment according to law																					
Total	56	1	1	56	9	1	1	2	2	6	1	4	1	1	3	1	10	5	5	12	12

APPENDIX   227

TABLE 10

PROHIBITION AND PUNISHMENT OF MISBEHAVIOR OF WIFE IN THE RULES OF 52 CLANS

Prohibition and punishment	Meddling outside affairs	Taking man's role	Hoarding family property privately	Disobeying husband's instruction	Being a termagant	Sowing family discord	Offending seniors in family or clan	Jealousy (opposing husband's taking a concubine for begetting an heir) - In general	Jealousy - First offense	Jealousy - Repeated offense Incorrigible	Discord with sisters-in-law - In general	Discord with sisters-in-law - First offense	Discord with sisters-in-law - Incorrigible	Unfilial behavior toward husband's parents - In general	Unfilial - First offense	Unfilial - Incorrigible	Subject to seven traditional grounds for divorce* - In general	Subject - First offense	Subject - Incorrigible	Licentiousness and disgrace	Elopement	Incest
Prohibition without mention of punishment	12	15	3	8	7	14	7	7			19			11								
Clan punishment:																						
Oral censure	1	1		1					1			1					1					
Penalty to be decided					1			1	2			3			2							
Castigation																						
Corporal punishment								1		2					1			1		1		
Exclusion of tablet from ancestral hall																						
Exclusion from ancestral hall													1			1			1	1		2
Exclusion or expunction from genealogy																1				3	1	
To be divorced										2												
Government punishment according to law																						
Government punishment plus clan punishment:																						
Government punishment and exclusion from ancestral hall																						
Government punishment and to be divorced																						
Total	13	16	3	9	8	14	7	9	2	2	22	1	1	13	3	3	5	1	1	5	1	2

* The seven traditional reasons for divorcing a wife are: no son, adultery, disobedience to husband's parents, bitter tongue, stealing, envy, and evil disease.

TABLE 11
PUNISHMENT OF HUSBAND FOR WIFE'S MISBEHAVIOR IN THE RULES OF 10 CLANS

Punishment	Meddling outside affairs	Licentiousness and disgrace	Sowing family discord	Quarreling with sisters-in-law	Unfilial behavior toward husband's parents — In general	Unfilial behavior toward husband's parents — First offense	Unfilial behavior toward husband's parents — Incorrigible	Offending seniors in family or clan — In general	Offending seniors in family or clan — First offense	Offending seniors in family or clan — Incorrigible
Clan punishment:										
Oral censure			1	1		2		1		
Monetary fine				1	3	1		1	2	
Castigation		1		2				1		
Corporal punishment	1									
Forfeit of clan privileges										
Exclusion or expunction from genealogy							1			1
Exclusion from ancestral hall									1	
Government punishment according to law					1					
Government punishment and exclusion from ancestral hall										
Total	1	1	1	4	3	2	2	2	2	2

TABLE 12

PROHIBITION AND PUNISHMENT OF HUSBAND'S MISBEHAVIOR TOWARD WIFE IN THE RULES OF 17 CLANS

Prohibition and punishment	Divorcing wife for her looks or family poverty	Divorcing wife without sufficient reasons	Confinement of wife	Making wife a prostitute	Mistreating wife for favoring concubine — In general	Mistreating wife for favoring concubine — Light offense	Mistreating wife for favoring concubine — Grave offense	Mistreatment resulting in suicide	Selling wife because of poverty or no reason — In general	Selling wife because of poverty or no reason — Light offense	Selling wife because of poverty or no reason — Grave offense
Prohibition without mention of punishment	2	4		1	11				1		
Clan punishment:											
Penalty to be decided		1	1		1						
Monetary fine						1					
Castigation										1	
Corporal punishment					2				1		
Exclusion of tablet from ancestral hall		1									
Exclusion from ancestral hall		1							1		
Exclusion or expunction from genealogy				1					1		
Expulsion from clan group									2		
Exclusion from ancestral hall and genealogy								1			
Exclusion from genealogy and clan group									1		
Government punishment according to law								1			1
Government punishment and expunction from genealogy									1		
Total	2	7	1	2	14	1	1	1	8	1	1

TABLE 13

PROHIBITION AND PUNISHMENT OF MISBEHAVIOR IN REGARD TO CONCUBINAGE IN THE RULES OF 28 CLANS

Prohibition and punishment	Taking concubines					Treatment of concubines							Misbehavior of concubine	
	Taking more than one concubine	Taking concubine when one is very old	Taking concubine before 40 years old	Taking concubine when one has a son	Taking concubine without any reason	Favoring concubine and mistreating wife	Allowing concubine to emulate wife	Promoting concubine as a wife	Mistreating concubine: In general	Mistreating concubine: Light offense	Mistreating concubine: Grave offense	Making concubine a prostitute	Offending legal wife	Being shrewish
Prohibition without mention of punishment	2	2			1	8	16	7	1				1*	
Clan punishment:														
Oral censure			1	1		1				1				
Penalty to be decided				2		1		2	1		1	1		
Monetary fine						2								
Corporal punishment														
Exclusion or expunction from genealogy														
Exclusion from genealogy and ancestral hall														1*
Dismissal														
Total	2	2	1	3	1	12	16	9	2	1	1	1	1	1

* Husband to be punished for concubine's misbehavior.

TABLE 14

PROHIBITION AND PUNISHMENT OF WIDOW'S MISBEHAVIOR IN THE RULES OF 9 CLANS

Prohibition and punishment	Being a termagant	Disgraceful behavior	Disposing privately property of late husband	Taking a son-in-law as heir	Remarrying	Remarrying while retaining property of husband
Prohibition without mention of punishment						2
Clan punishment:						
Oral censure	1	1	1		1	
Monetary fine						
Expunction of surname from genealogy						
To remarry by clan order				1		1
Exclusion from ancestral hall and genealogy				1		1
Expulsion from clan group		1	1		1	1
Forfeit of property and expulsion from clan						
To be sold by government order						
Total	1	2	2	2	2	5

TABLE 15

PROHIBITION AND PUNISHMENT OF MISBEHAVIOR AGAINST WIDOW IN THE RULES OF 25 CLANS

Prohibition and punishment	Slandering a widow — In general	Slandering a widow — First offense	Slandering a widow — Repeated offense	Insulting a widow — In general	Insulting a widow — First offense	Insulting a widow — Repeated offense	Scheming for her property — In general	Scheming for her property — Light offense	Scheming for her property — Grave offense	Remarrying her by pressure	Selling her into servitude by pressure	Inducing her loss of chastity	Causing her suicide by persecution — Light offense	Causing her suicide by persecution — Grave offense
Prohibition without mention of punishment	1			9			6			3		1		
Clan punishment:														
Penalty to be decided		1		2			1	1		1	1			
Castigation	1			2			2			2		1		
Corporal punishment		1		1	1								1	
Exclusion from ancestral hall and genealogy			1	1		1			1	1				1
Government punishment according to law														
Total	2	1	1	15	1	1	9	1	1	7	1	2	1	1

APPENDIX

TABLE 16
PROHIBITION AND PUNISHMENT OF MISBEHAVIOR IN REGARD TO BETROTHAL AND MARRIAGE IN THE RULES OF 76 CLANS

Prohibition and punishment	Improper Betrothal Behavior: Betrothal in childhood	Improper Betrothal Behavior: Breaking betrothal for contempt of poverty	Improper behavior of marriage: Marriage of younger brother before elder	Improper behavior of marriage: Marriage during mourning period	Improper behavior of marriage: Marriage by elopement	Improper behavior of marriage: Adultery before marriage	Improper Hypergamy: Marriage for wealth and power	Improper Hypergamy: Marrying off daughter as concubine for money	Improper hypogamy: Marrying a widow	Improper hypogamy: Marrying a woman of unknown background	Improper hypogamy: Marrying a prostitute	Improper hypogamy: Marrying servant's daughter	Improper hypogamy: Marrying female servant — In general	Improper hypogamy: Marrying female servant — First offense Disobeying clan order	Improper hypogamy: Marrying a low class person (unspecified)	Cross-cousin marriage	Improper marriage with non-clan kin or possible kin: Marrying fiancée of elder brother — In general	Improper marriage with non-clan kin or possible kin: First offense Disobeying clan order	Improper marriage with non-clan kin or possible kin: Marrying a person with same surname	Improper marriage with family or clan member: Marrying widow of younger brother — In general	Improper marriage with family or clan member: First offense Disobeying clan order	Improper marriage with family or clan member: Marrying elder brother's widow	Improper marriage with family or clan member: Incestuous marriage
Prohibition without mention of punishment	12	3	1	6			59	3	1		1		1		4	3	2		10	2		2	2
Clan punishment:																							
Penalty to be decided		1			1		1								1		1		1		1		1
Forfeit of clan ration													1		1								
Castigation												1											
Corporal punishment													1						1	1			1
Exclusion from sacrificial rites						1		1	1	1	1		1				1		1		1	1	1
Exclusion of tablet from ancestral hall															2				1				
Exclusion or expunction from genealogy															1				1		1	1	
Exclusion from ancestral hall and genealogy														1	1		1		1		1	1	1
Expulsion from clan group																						1	
Exclusion from genealogy and clan group																						1	
Divorce or nullification of engagement																	1		2	1		2	2
Nullification of engagement, punishing parents and expunction from genealogy																							
Government punishment according to law																			1	1	1		
Government punishment and divorce																			1	1			
Total	12	4	1	6	1	1	60	4	1	1	2	1	4	1	11	3	3	1	17	6	1	7	7

233

TABLE 17

PROHIBITION AND PUNISHMENT OF MISBEHAVIOR VIOLATING SEX SEGREGATION IN THE RULES OF 32 CLANS

Prohibition and punishment	Violation of sex segregation (unspecified)	Handing things directly between sister-in-law and brother-in-law	Handing things directly to opposite sex	Women eating at same table with own brothers	Mixed seating at banquet or other occasions	Common toilet for both sexes	Teasing opposite sex	Gambling and card game in mixed company	Religious activities in mixed company	Row with opposite sex	Male servants entering inner court and house	Male adult entering young woman's bedroom	Divulging women's secrets
Prohibition without mention of punishment	11	4	3	5	13	7	2	3	3	1	10		2
Clan punishment:													
Castigation												1	1
Corporal punishment												1	1
Total	11	4	3	5	13	7	2	3	3	1	10	2	4

APPENDIX 235

TABLE 18

PROHIBITION AND PUNISHMENT OF WOMEN'S MISBEHAVIOR AND IMPROPER SOCIAL CONTACT IN THE RULES OF 44 CLANS

Prohibition and punishment	Walking in darkness alone or without light	Reading profane literature	Loafing and gossiping	Flirting	To call in jewelers	To call in beauticians	To call in nuns and service women*	Receiving neighborhood women	Befriending remarried women	Pledging sworn sisterhood or adopted relatives	Frequent visits from relatives	Girls accompanying mother to visit her relatives	Married woman visiting own home after death of parents	Married woman visiting own home where a member is nun or monk	Visiting homes of sisters-in-law	Staying overnight away from home	Spring outing and public celebrations	Visiting theatrical performance or festival gatherings	Visiting Buddhist or Taoist temples
Prohibition without mention of punishment	12	3	2	1	1	2	15			2	1	2	3	2	2	2	9	15	22
Clan punishment:																			
Oral censure			1§					1	2§	1									1
Penalty to be decided				1§												1			1
Monetary fine (1–20 silver dollars)																	1§		
Monetary fine and denunciatory notice posted on gate by clan																			1§
Castigation																			
Corporal punishment																			
Total	12	3	3	2	1	2	15	1	2	3	1	2	3	2	2	3	10	16	26

* Buddhist nuns, Taoist nuns, female fortune-tellers, female brokers, match-makers, soceresses, bewitchers, medical women, and midwives.

§ Husband or son to be punished for woman's misbehavior.

TABLE 19

PROHIBITION AND PUNISHMENT OF MISBEHAVIOR OF CLAN FUNCTIONARIES IN THE RULES OF 26 CLANS

Prohibition and punishment	Clan Head — Avoiding responsibility of arbitration	Clan Head — Receiving bribe and favoritism	Clan Head — Degrading his status by being indentured servant	Clan Head — Grave transgressions	Manager or Officer in Charge — Absence from clan meeting without excuse	Manager or Officer in Charge — Failure of summoning a clan meeting promptly to deal with dispute	Manager or Officer in Charge — Neglect to record births of clan members	Manager or Officer in Charge — Neglect to keep ancestral hall clean and locked	Manager or Officer in Charge — Neglect to repair ancestral hall regularly	Manager or Officer in Charge — Misuse of ancestral hall fund and articles	Manager or Officer in Charge — Default of duty	Embezzlement of clan fund and property — In general	Embezzlement of clan fund and property — First offense	Embezzlement of clan fund and property — Repeated offense
Prohibition without mention of punishment	1	1			1									
Clan punishment:														
Denunciation by clan members		1												
Oral censure		1												
Penalty to be decided												2	1	
Restitution												1		
Provision of banquet												1		
Monetary fine							1	1				1		
Non-participation in commensal meal														
Restitution and non-participation in clan affairs												2	1	
Castigation						1						1		
Castigation and restitution												1		
Dismissal											1	2	1	
Dismissal and restitution														
Dismissal and non-participation in commensal meal												1		
Dismissal and non-participation in clan affairs										1				
Corporal punishment												1	1	
Corporal punishment and chanting liturgy for remorse												1		
Non-participation in clan affairs, "expelled" written on the back of tablet and no biography in genealogy														
Expulsion from clan group					3							5		2
Government punishment according to law														
Total	1	4	1	3	1	1	1	1	1	1	1	19	3	3

236 THE TRADITIONAL CHINESE CLAN RULES

TABLE 20

PUNISHMENT OF MISBEHAVIOR IN MANAGING COMMON FUND IN THE RULES OF 20 CLANS

Punishment	Misappropriation	Embezzlement In general	Embezzlement First offense	Embezzlement Repeated offense
Clan punishment:				
Oral censure (admonition or reproof)		1		
Penalty to be decided		1		
Restitution	3			
Monetary fine and restitution		1		
Forfeit of executive right forever and restitution		2	1	
Castigation	1	3		
Castigation and restitution		1		
Corporal punishment and chanting liturgy		1		
Dismissal and non-participation in commensal meal		1		
Non-participation in clan affairs, "expelled" written on the back of tablet and no biography in genealogy		2		
Exclusion from ancestral hall forever		1		
Government punishment according to law	1	2		4
Total	5	13	4	4

238   THE TRADITIONAL CHINESE CLAN RULES

TABLE 21

PROHIBITION AND PUNISHMENT OF MISUSE OF ANCESTRAL HALL IN THE RULES OF 44 CLANS

Prohibition and punishment	Opening door illicitly	Use for private banquet	Running a private school	Use for processing cotton	Illicit entering of tablet	Storing farming tools	Storing goods or coffin, or making coffin — In general	Storing goods or coffin, or making coffin — First offense	Storing goods or coffin, or making coffin — Repeated offense	Use or rent as living quarters — In general	Use or rent as living quarters — First offense	Use or rent as living quarters — Repeated offense	Renting rooms by pressure	Chess, game or gambling	Allowing animals inside	Causing damage — In general	Causing damage — First offense	Causing damage — Repeated offense
Prohibition without mention of punishment	3	3	3		2	6	9	1		15	1			1		2		
Clan punishment: Penalty to be decided	1					6	6	1						2	3	2		
Restitution							1			1						1		
Providing ancestral offerings				1			1											
Providing theatrical play				1	1		1			1	1			1				
Forfeit or destroying property involved							1							1		1		
Monetary fine						1	1											
Monetary fine and restitution																		
Monetary fine and forfeit of property involved						1			1			1	1					1
Castigation																		
Corporal punishment																		
Corporal punishment and chanting liturgy																		
Exclusion from ancestral hall																		
Eviction by government order																	1	
Government punishment according to law																		
Total	4	3	3	2	3	14	21	1	1	17	1	1	1	6	3	6	1	1

TABLE 22

PROHIBITION AND PUNISHMENT OF MISBEHAVIOR WITH REGARD TO PROPERTY IN ANCESTRAL HALL IN THE RULES OF 33 CLANS

Prohibition and punishment	Illicit borrowing of utensils or furniture	Damaging trees — In general	Damaging trees — Light offense	Damaging trees — Grave offense	Damaging trees — First offense	Damaging trees — Repeated offense	Damaging or smearing walls — In general	Damaging or smearing walls — Light offense	Damaging or smearing walls — Grave offense	Stealing property — Light offense	Stealing property — Grave offense	Illicit selling or mortgage of ritual utensils or other property	Illicit selling or mortgage of property deeds and other documents
Prohibition without mention of punishment	14	1											
Clan punishment:													
Penalty to be decided	1												
Providing candles and bogus money to be burned for ancestral spirits	1												
Providing theatrical play							1						
Restitution	8	1					1						
Monetary fine	3												
Monetary fine and restitution			1										
Monetary fine and forfeit of executive right of clan affairs forever												1	
Castigation										1			
Corporal punishment				1				1					
Dismissal, monetary fine and restitution		1											
Expunction from genealogy and exclusion from sacrificial rites													1
Government punishment					1					1	1		
Total	27	2	1	1	1		1	1	1	1	1	2	1

TABLE 23

PROHIBITION AND PUNISHMENT OF MISBEHAVIOR WITH REGARD TO ANCESTRAL GRAVEYARD IN THE RULES OF 49 CLANS

Prohibition and punishment	Pasturing or allowing animals to tramp — In general	Pasturing — First offense	Pasturing — Repeated offense	Encroachment or illicit cultivation	Illicit excavation	Temporary burial — First offense	Temporary burial — Disobeying clan order	Burial on top of old grave	Illicit burial without permission — In general	Illicit burial — Light offense	Illicit burial — Grave offense	Illicit burial — First offense	Illicit burial — Disobeying clan order	Illicit selling or mortgage — In general	Illicit selling — Light offense	Illicit selling — Grave offense	Illicit selling — First offense	Illicit selling — Disobeying clan order
Prohibition without mention of punishment	3			2	1				3					4				
Clan punishment:																		
Oral censure	5	1		1					1	1								
Penalty to be decided	1								1	1								
Ordered removal of coffin from graveyard	1			1					2									
Providing theatrical play				1					1									
Monetary fine																		
Monetary fine and restitution																		
Monetary fine and ordered removal of coffin	1			3		1			4	1	1	1						
Castigation									1			3						
Corporal punishment												1						
Corporal punishment and removal of coffin																		
Corporal punishment and providing banquet																		
Non-participation in clan affairs, "expelled" written on the back of tablet and no biography in genealogy														2				
Exclusion or expunction from genealogy	1			3	1	1	1	1	1	1	4		6	2	1	1		2
Exclusion from genealogy and non-participation in sacrificial rites									3			3		1				
Exclusion from ancestral hall and graveyard	1																	
Government punishment according to law	1								1					1				
Government punishment and removal of coffin																		
Government punishment and expulsion from clan																		
Total	12	1	1	11	2	1	1	1	18	4	4	6	6	11	1	1	2	2

TABLE 24

PROHIBITION AND PUNISHMENT OF MISBEHAVIOR WITH REGARD TO TREES OF THE ANCESTRAL GRAVEYARD IN THE RULES OF 43 CLANS

Prohibition and punishment	Illicit wood and leaves gathering — In general	Illicit wood and leaves gathering — First offense	Illicit wood and leaves gathering — Repeated offense	Felling trees illicitly — In general	Felling trees illicitly — Light offense	Felling trees illicitly — Grave offense	Felling trees illicitly — First offense	Felling trees illicitly — Repeated offense	Selling trees illicitly — In general	Selling trees illicitly — First offense	Selling trees illicitly — Repeated offense
Prohibition without mention of punishment.				12					1		
Clan punishment:											
Penalty to be decided	3	1		6			1				
Providing theatrical play				1							
Monetary fine				1							
Monetary fine and restitution	1										
Castigation				3			1		1		
Castigation and restitution				2			1				
Corporal punishment							2			1	
Corporal punishment and forfeit of property involved				1							
Expunction from genealogy and non-participation in sacrificial rites				2							
Government punishment according to law		1		5	1		4		1		
Government punishment and expulsion from clan				2							
Total	4	1	1	35	1	1	4	4	2	1	1

TABLE 25

PROHIBITION AND PUNISHMENT OF MISBEHAVIOR INFRINGING UPON COMMON LAND PROPERTY IN THE RULES OF 20 CLANS

Prohibition and punishment	Illicit pasturing	Encroachment	Usurping cultivation — In general	Usurping cultivation — First offense	Usurping cultivation — Disobeying clan order	Suggesting its sale	Selling donated land by donor's descendants	Forcing clan to buy one's inferior land	Illicit selling or mortgage — In general	Illicit selling or mortgage — Light offense	Illicit selling or mortgage — Grave offense
Prohibition without mention of punishment							2		1		
Clan punishment:											
Penalty to be decided	1								1		
Restitution		1									
Monetary fine and restitution			1								
Castigation				1		1		1			
Corporal punishment				1					1		
Non-participation in commensal meals		1									
Corporal punishment and forfeit of property									1		
Non-participation in clan affairs forever and restitution									1		
Non-participation in clan affairs, "expelled" written on the back of the tablet and no biography in genealogy after death									2		
Exclusion from ancestral hall									1		
Exclusion from ancestral hall after corporal punishment									1		
Exclusion or expunction from genealogy									1		
Expulsion from clan group									2		1
Exclusion from ancestral hall and genealogy after corporal punishment							1				
Government punishment according to law			2	2				1	4		
Government punishment plus clan punishment:											
Government punishment and expulsion from clan									1		
Government punishment, forfeit of property and exclusion from sacrificial rites									1		
Total	1	2	3	2	2	1	3	2	17	1	1

APPENDIX 243

TABLE 26

PROHIBITION AND PUNISHMENT OF AGGRESSIVE AND DISREGARDFUL BEHAVIOR TOWARD FELLOW CLAN MEMBERS IN THE RULES OF 76 CLANS

Prohibition and punishment	Failing to greet members en route	Neglect to congratulate or condole members	Indifference toward member in distress	Unkindness toward fellow members	Slandering fellow members	Cursing and fighting clan members	Allowing servants to insult clan members	Settling matters arbitrarily by power — In general	Settling matters arbitrarily by power — First offense	Settling matters arbitrarily by power — Disobeying clan order	Insulting members by relying on prestige — In general	Insulting members by relying on prestige — First offense	Insulting members by relying on prestige — Repeated offense	Abusing orphans, widows or helpless members — In general	Abusing orphans, widows or helpless members — First offense	Abusing orphans, widows or helpless members — Repeated offense	Majority oppressing minority — In general	Majority oppressing minority — First offense	Majority oppressing minority — Repeated offense	Powerful members oppressing weak ones — In general	Powerful members oppressing weak ones — First offense	Powerful members oppressing weak ones — Repeated offense	Wealthy and honored oppressing the poor and inferior — In general	Wealthy and honored oppressing the poor and inferior — First offense	Wealthy and honored oppressing the poor and inferior — Repeated offense
Prohibition without mention of punishment	11	1	1		3	3	8				5			18			5			21			40		
Clan punishment:																									
Oral censure (admonition or reproof)	1	1		1	1	1	1		1			1		1	1		1	1		3			1	1	1
Penalty to be decided				1			1										1			1			2	1	
Monetary fine						4								1	3			2		2				1	
Castigation						1					1		1		1								2	1	1
Corporal punishment																									
Forfeit of clan privileges for 1–5 years										1	1									1			1		
Exclusion from ancestral hall																									
Exclusion or expunction from genealogy																									
Expulsion from clan group																	3		3			4			2
Government punishment according to law																						1			
Government punishment and exclusion from genealogy																									
Total	12	2	1	3	4	9	10	1	1	1	7	1	1	24	4	4	6	4	4	28	5	5	47	3	3

TABLE 27

PROHIBITION AND PUNISHMENT OF MISBEHAVIOR OF JUNIOR MEMBERS IN VIOLATION OF GENERATION-AGE ORDER IN THE RULES OF 83 CLANS

Prohibition and punishment	Seating as equals of seniors	Addressing seniors improperly	Disrespect of senior members — In general	Disrespect — Light offense	Disrespect — Grave offense	Disrespect — First offense	Disrespect — Repeated offense	Contravening senior members — In general	Contravening — Light offense	Contravening — Grave offense	Contravening — First offense	Contravening — Repeated offense	Insulting or humiliating seniors — In general	Insulting — First offense	Insulting — Repeated offense	Assault of senior member
Prohibition without mention of punishment	1	13	38													
Clan punishment:																
Oral censure		1	1			4					2					
Penalty to be decided	1		2	1		1										
Providing ancestral offerings								2								
Castigation		1	8			1							2	1		1
Corporal punishment			10			1	2	2				2	1			1
Exclusion from ancestral hall			1										1			
Expulsion from clan group						1	2	2				2	1		1	
Government punishment according to law																
Total	2	15	60	1	1	6	6	2	2	2	2	2	4	1	1	2

TABLE 28

PROHIBITION AND PUNISHMENT OF AGGRESSIVE BEHAVIOR AGAINST FELLOW CLAN MEMBERS INVOLVING MONEY OR PROPERTY IN THE RULES OF 24 CLANS

Prohibition and punishment	Borrowing by threat or pressure	Unreasonable demand by using age and poverty as pressure — First offense	Unreasonable demand by using age and poverty as pressure — Repeated offense	Deliberate dispute or trespassing member's property — In general	Deliberate dispute or trespassing member's property — First offense	Deliberate dispute or trespassing member's property — Repeated offense	Monopolizing public welfare	Defraudation and extortion of members — In general	Defraudation and extortion of members — First offense	Defraudation and extortion of members — Repeated offense
Prohibition without mention of punishment	3			4				9		
Clan punishment:										
Penalty to be decided	1	1						2	1	
Castigation				1	1			1	3	
Corporal punishment				1				1		
Exclusion or expunction from genealogy			1			1	1			4
Government punishment according to law							1			
Total	4	1	1	5	1	1	1	13	4	4

APPENDIX 245

TABLE 29

PROHIBITION AND PUNISHMENT OF MISBEHAVIOR OF SENIOR MEMBERS IN ABUSING GENERATION-AGE STATUS AGAINST JUNIOR MEMBERS IN THE RULES OF 38 CLANS

Prohibition and punishment	Insulting and Mistreating junior members			Cursing and beating juniors
	In general	First offense	Repeated offense	
Prohibition without mention of punishment	21			2
Clan punishment:				
Oral censure	4	1		
Penalty to be decided	1			
Providing banquet for apology				1
Castigation	7			
Corporal punishment		1		
Government punishment according to law			2	
Total	33	2	2	3

TABLE 30

PROHIBITION AND PUNISHMENT OF INCEST BETWEEN CLAN MEMBERS IN THE RULES OF 26 CLANS

Prohibition and punishment	In general	Light offense	Grave offense	First offense	Repeated offense
Prohibition without mention of punishment	2				
Clan punishment:					
Oral censure				1	
Penalty to be decided	1				1
Castigation	1			1	
Corporal punishment	1	1		1	
Exclusion of tablet from ancestral hall	1				
Exclusion from ancestral hall	1				
Exclusion or expunction from genealogy	2		1		
Expulsion from clan group	3				
Exclusion from ancestral hall after corporal punishment	1				
Expulsion from clan group after corporal punishment	1				
Exclusion from clan group and genealogy	1			1	
Exclusion from ancestral hall and genealogy, and expulsion from local district after corporal punishment	1				
Government punishment according to law	3				2
Government punishment plus clan punishment:					
Government punishment and expunction from genealogy	2				
Government punishment and exclusion from clan group and genealogy					1
Total	21	1	1	4	4

TABLE 31

PROHIBITION AND PUNISHMENT OF MISBEHAVIOR IN DUTY FOR ANCESTRAL WORSHIP IN THE RULES OF 17 CLANS

Prohibition and punishment	Neglecting duty to clean ancestral hall and prepare fortnightly rites	Neglecting sacrifice for saving expenses	Falsifying account of sacrificial rites	Evading one's turn for preparing sacrifices
Prohibition without mention of punishment			2	6
Clan punishment:				
Penalty to be decided	1	1	2	2
Chanting liturgy in remorse			1	
Corporal punishment				2
Corporal punishment and monetary fine				1
Exclusion from sacrificial ceremony				1
Total	1	1	5	12

APPENDIX 249

TABLE 32

PROHIBITION AND PUNISHMENT OF MISBEHAVIOR DURING SACRIFICIAL RITES AND ENSUING ACTIVITIES IN THE RULES OF 59 CLANS

Prohibition and punishment	Sacrificial rites							Commensal meal and sharing of sacrificial meat	
	Not in proper dress	Late arrival	Absence without excuse	Ritual impropriety*	Illicit presence of women	Maid-servants entering ancestral hall	Participation without permission	Being drunk and quarrelsome
Prohibition without mention of punishment	6		11	7	2			4
Clan punishment:								
Being ordered to leave ancestral hall	1				1			2
Oral censure			1	2				2
Penalty to be decided	1		10	9		1§		6
Forfeit of clan ration			1					
Monetary fine			6	2				
Kneeling in ancestral hall	2			5				2
Providing ancestral offerings								1
Providing candles for rites			1				1	
Providing bogus money burned for the dead	1							
Reducing share of sacrificial meat			1					
Forfeit of share of sacrificial meat	1		2					
Non-participation in the commensal meal	1	2						
Non-participation in the sacrificial rites	1							
Castigation			3	4				1
Corporal punishment			1	2	1§	1		2
Government punishment according to law								1
Total	14	2	37	31	4	2	1	21

* Ritual impropriety denotes misbehavior such as haughty manner, overstepping one's rank, quarreling, and clamoring.

§ Husband to be punished for wife's misbehavior and master for maid's misbehavior.

TABLE 33

PROHIBITION AND PUNISHMENT OF MISBEHAVIOR TOWARD AND IN MAKING FRIENDS IN THE RULES OF 35 CLANS

Prohibition and punishment	Improper Attitude toward Friends							Making Improper Friends																
	Intimacy and disrespect	Playfulness	Boastfulness and conceitedness	Excessive joking	Excessive reproof or demand	Making many friends indiscriminately	Befriending wealthy and powerful persons by flattery	Befriending brokers and profiteering agents	Befriending habitual litigator	Befriending licentious persons	Befriending unscrupulous persons	Befriending treacherous persons	Befriending foolhardy persons: In general	First offense	Repeated offense	Befriending bad elements (unspecified): In general	Light offense	Grave offense	First offense	Incorrigible	Befriending secret society members: In general	Light offense	Grave offense
Prohibition without mention of punishment	3	10	3	1	1	7	10	3	2	1	9	2	2			17	1	1	1		1		
Clan punishment:																							
Oral censure														1		1						1	
Castigation																1		1				1	
Corporal punishment																1							
Exclusion from ancestral hall																							
Exclusion or expunction from genealogy																1							
Exclusion from clan affairs and ancestral graveyard															1	3				1			1
Government punishment according to law																							1
Government punishment and exclusion from ancestral hall, genealogy, and graveyard																							
Total	3	10	3	1	1	7	10	3	2	1	9	2	2	1	1	25	1	1	1	1	1	2	2

TABLE 34

PROHIBITION AND PUNISHMENT OF MISBEHAVIOR TOWARD NEIGHBORS IN THE RULES OF 35 CLANS

Prohibition and punishment	Unfriendliness and disregard	Mutual dislike due to children's fight	Addressing neighbors improperly (neglect of generation-age order)	Charging neighbors illicit usury	Allowing children or animals to trample neighbor's field or yard	Scheming for neighbor's geomantic sites	Disputing boundary or water sources	Quarreling or litigation	Insulting by relying on one's prestige
Prohibition without mention of punishment		4	1	1	4	1	5	14	23
Clan punishment:									
Penalty to be decided	1								
Monetary fine	1								1
Providing ancestral offerings								1	
Corporal punishment									
Total	2	4	1	1	4	1	5	15	24

APPENDIX 251

TABLE 35

PROHIBITION AND PUNISHMENT OF AGGRESSIVE BEHAVIOR INVOLVING NON-CLAN MEMBERS IN THE RULES OF 9 CLANS

Prohibition and punishment	Wrangling with other clan by relying on clan influence	Protecting lawless outsiders by relying upon influence	Conspiring with outsiders against clan members		
			In general	Light offense	Grave offense
Prohibition without mention of punishment			4		
Clan punishment:					
Oral censure	1		1		
Castigation			1		
Corporal punishment			2		
Expulsion from clan group					1
Government punishment according to law		1			1
Total	1	1	6	2	2

TABLE 36

PROHIBITION AND PUNISHMENT OF MISBEHAVIOR OF CLAN MEMBERS IN OFFICIAL CAREER IN THE RULES OF 9 CLANS

Prohibition and punishment	Neglecting duty	Playing favoritism	Being avaricious	Being cruel toward the people	Imposing illicit tax upon the people	Bending the law to suit private interest	Becoming a traitor for private interest
Prohibition without mention of punishment		2	5	1		1	
Clan punishment:							
Penalty to be decided	1						
Exclusion of tablet from ancestral hall			1				
Exclusion or expunction from genealogy			1				1
Exclusion from genealogy and of tablet from ancestral hall			1				
Exclusion from ancestral hall and genealogy			1				
Appealing to the higher court of government for investigation					1		
Total	1	2	9	1	1	1	1

TABLE 37

PROHIBITION AND PUNISHMENT OF MISBEHAVIOR IN REGARD TO TAX PAYMENT AND LABOR SERVICE IN THE RULES OF 53 CLANS

Prohibition and punishment	Tax arrears — In general	Tax arrears — First offense	Tax arrears — Repeated offense	Refusal to pay tax	Tax evasion by hiding property	Dodging labor service	Labor service evasion by misrepresenting property ownership	Tax or labor service evasion by bribery	Fraud and extortion when in charge of tax collection and remittance
Prohibition without mention of punishment	44			1		5	3	8	4
Clan punishment:									
Penalty to be decided	1	1			1	1			
Castigation	1	1							
Corporal punishment	1								
Exclusion from ancestral hall			1						
Government punishment according to law				1			1		1
Government punishment and forfeit of tax-defaulting land					1				
Total	47	1	1	2	1	6	4	8	5

254   THE TRADITIONAL CHINESE CLAN RULES

TABLE 38

PROHIBITION AND PUNISHMENT OF MISBEHAVIOR IN REGARD TO LITIGATION IN THE RULES OF 100 CLANS

Prohibition and punishment	Resort to litigation in general	Being litigious	Litigation against non-clan members while oneself in the wrong	Litigation between brothers or between nephew and uncle	Litigation against clan elders	Helping non-clan persons in litigation against clan members	Litigation by false accusation	Litigation by defying clan arbitration	Litigation without clan arbitration: In general	First offense	Repeated offense	Conduct litigation for others	Inciting litigation between others: In general	Light offense	Grave offense	First offense	Disobeying clan order
Prohibition without mention of punishment	57	10	7				1		8			4	10	1	1		
Clan punishment:																	
Oral censure			1	1					1			1	1	1	1	1	
Penalty to be decided									3								
Forfeit of right to stay in clan hostel in city																	
Castigation						1			5				2				
Corporal punishment		1	1	1					6	1		1	3			1	
Exclusion from ancestral hall									1								
Exclusion from ancestral hall after corporal punishment																	
Exclusion or expunction from genealogy		1			1	1	1	1	1		1		2		1		2
Exclusion from ancestral hall and genealogy									1				1				
Expulsion from clan group																	
Government punishment according to law																	
Government punishment plus clan punishment:																	
Government punishment and expunction from genealogy			1										1		1		
Government punishment and exclusion from ancestral hall, genealogy, and graveyard																	
Total	57	12	9	2	1	2	2	1	26	1	1	7	20	2	2	2	2

APPENDIX 255

TABLE 39

PROHIBITION AND PUNISHMENT OF MISBEHAVIOR IN REGARD TO RELIGIONS AND BELIEFS IN THE RULES OF 67 CLANS

Prohibition and punishment	Religions and religious activities											Folk beliefs and superstitions								Improper burial or removal of remains because of geomancy		
	Belief in Christianity	Belief in Buddhism, Taoism, or other heterodox religions	Hiring Buddhist monks to chant in funeral service	Worshipping Buddha and feeding monks	Women joining religious groups and listening to sermons in mixed company	Women visiting Buddhist or Taoist temples	Giving away sons to temples	Joining heterodox religious groups	To be monk, Taoist or nun	Belief in fortune-telling	Belief in astrology for betrothal	Belief in curing illness by prayer	Superstitious belief in demons and gods	Belief in sorcery and magic charms	Superstitious belief in geomancy	Postponing burial because of geomancy	In general	First offense	Disobeying clan order
Prohibition without mention of punishment	3	18	20	2	3	22	2	6	7	1	1	9	8	11	6	15	5		
Clan punishment																			
Oral censure				1		1*			1									1	
Penalty to be decided						2	2		2										
Monetary fine									2										
Castigation																			
Castigation and correction of burial																1			
Corporal punishment				1		1*		1											
Exclusion of tablet from ancestral hall																			
Exclusion or expunction from genealogy																			1
Expulsion from district and destroying offender's house																			
Government punishment according to law																			
Total	3	18	20	3	3	26	4	7	13	1	1	9	8	11	6	16	5	1	1

* Husband to be punished for wife's misbehavior.

TABLE 40

PROHIBITION AND PUNISHMENT OF IMPROPER VOCATIONS IN THE RULES OF 90 CLANS

Prohibition and punishment	Broker or middleman	Herb doctor	Fortune-teller	Astrologer	Buddhist or Taoist priest	Sorcerer or sorceress	Sedan chair bearer	Butcher	Indictment drafter	Conductor of lawsuit	Government clerk	Soldier	Lictor or official servant	Household servant: In general	Household servant: First offense	Household servant: Repeated offense	Indentured servant	Boxer or pugilist	Traveling singer	Performer or dancer of vulgar ballad	Musician	Actor or player	Prostitute	Improper vocation (unspecified): In general	Improper vocation (unspecified): First offense	Improper vocation (unspecified): Incorrigible	Low class vocation (unspecified): In general	Low class vocation (unspecified): First offense	Low class vocation (unspecified): Incorrigible	Loafing without proper vocation: In general	Loafing without proper vocation: First offense	Loafing without proper vocation: Incorrigible
Prohibition without mention of punishment	1	3	3	4	7	1		4	3	18	6	3	17	1			1	2	1	3		6	7		1 2		2	1		34		
Clan punishment: Oral censure					1	1		1		1										1		1		1	1						3	
Penalty to be decided					1								2				1					1		3	1					2	2	
Forfeit of clan ration																	1					1	1*	1	1		1			4	4	1
Castigation					2					1			3				1					1								5		2
Corporal punishment					2								1				2	2				2	1	2								
Non-participation in sacrificial rites and commensal meals																						1										
Exclusion of tablet from ancestral hall											1		1				1					1										
Exclusion from ancestral hall										1						1						1		2								
Exclusion or expunction from genealogy										1			2	2																		
Expunction from genealogy after corporal punishment																						1									1	
Exclusion from sacrificial rites and genealogy forever																						1										
Exclusion from genealogy and of tablet from ancestral hall													1	1								1	2				2					
Exclusion from ancestral hall and genealogy													2	1			1					1	1				3					
Expulsion from clan group													1				1					1	1				1			1	1	
Expulsion from clan group after corporal punishment								1					1							1		1	1	1								
Exclusion from genealogy and clan group																																
Exclusion from ancestral hall and clan							1																									
Government punishment according to law																								1	2					1		
Total	1	3	3	4	13	2	2	6	4	22	7	4	30	7	1	1	7	4	2	6	1	21	13	9	3	3	9	1	1	46	4	4

*Father or elder brother to be punished for girl's misbehavior.

TABLE 41

PROHIBITION AND PUNISHMENT OF GAMBLING
IN THE RULES OF 84 CLANS

Prohibition and punishment	In general	Light offense	Grave offense	First offense	Incorrigible
Prohibition without mention of punishment	52				
Clan punishment:					
Oral censure	2		4		
Forfeit of clan ration.......................			1		
Castigation	11	1		1	1
Corporal punishment	2	2		4	1
Exclusion from ancestral hall and genealogy ...			1		
Expulsion from clan group..................	1				1
Government punishment according to law	3		1		7
Government punishment and exclusion from ancestral hall, genealogy, and ancestral graveyard			1		
Total	71	3	3	10	10

TABLE 42

PROHIBITION AND PUNISHMENT OF BEING DRUNK AND DISORDERLY
IN THE RULES OF 45 CLANS

Prohibition and punishment	In general	Light offense	Grave offense	First offense	Incorrigible
Prohibition without mention of punishment	27				
Clan punishment:					
Oral censure				2	
Castigation	5	1		1	1
Corporal punishment	3	3		1	1
Exclusion or expunction from genealogy	1				
Exclusion from ancestral hall and genealogy ...			1		
Government punishment according to law	1		2		2
Government punishment and exclusion from ancestral hall, genealogy, and ancestral graveyard			1		
Total.........................	37	4	4	4	4

TABLE 43

PROHIBITION AND PUNISHMENT OF BRUTALITY AND FIGHTING
IN THE RULES OF 20 CLANS

	Brutality					Fighting savagely					Fighting with weapons
Prohibition and punishment	In general	Light offense	Grave offense	First offense	Incorrigible	In general	Light offense	Grave offense	First offense	Incorrigible	
Prohibition without mention of punishment	1					8					1
Clan punishment:											
Oral censure			2								
Penalty to be decided			1								
Castigation	1					1	1				
Corporal punishment	1		1			2	1		1		
Government punishment according to law			1	4				2		1	
Total	2	1	4	4		11	2	2	1	1	1

TABLE 44

PROHIBITION AND PUNISHMENT OF OPIUM-SMOKING
IN THE RULES OF 12 CLANS

Prohibition and punishment	In general	First offense	Incorrigible
Prohibition without mention of punishment	10		
Clan punishment:			
Corporal punishment		1	
Government punishment according to law	1		1
Total	11	1	1

APPENDIX   259

TABLE 45

PROHIBITION AND PUNISHMENT OF SEX MISBEHAVIOR IN THE RULES OF 57 CLANS

Prohibition and punishment	Visiting prostitute					Being licentious					Adultery				
	In general	Light offense	Grave offense	First offense	Incorrigible	In general	Light offense	Grave offense	First offense	Incorrigible	In general	Light offense	Grave offense	First offense	Incorrigible
Prohibition without mention of punishment	21					18					7				
Clan punishment:															
Oral censure	1			1											
Penalty to be decided	2					1					1	2		1	
Castigation	1	1	1	1	1	2	1		1		2				
Corporal punishment						1					1				
Exclusion of tablet from ancestral hall	1					1									
Exclusion or expunction from genealogy									1	1	1			1	1
Exclusion from genealogy and ancestral hall	1							1							
Expulsion from clan group	1	1			1	1			1		1	2	1	
Exclusion from genealogy and clan group						2				1	1		2	1	
Exclusion from ancestral hall and clan group	1									1					
Government punishment according to law															
Government punishment and exclusion from genealogy															
Government punishment and exclusion from genealogy and clan group															
Total	28	1	1	2	2	26	1	1	2	2	14	2	2	2	2

TABLE 46

PROHIBITION AND PUNISHMENT OF CRIMINAL OFFENSES
AGAINST HUMAN RIGHTS AND LIFE IN THE RULES OF 9 CLANS

Prohibition and punishment	Decoying or kidnapping women — In general	First offense	Disobeying clan	Trading human beings	Murder for money
Prohibition without mention of punishment	2				
Clan punishment:					
Corporal punishment	1				
Exclusion or expunction from genealogy					1
Expulsion from clan group			1		
Ordered suicide					1
Government punishment according to law	2	1		1	
Government punishment and expunction from genealogy	1			1	
Total	6	1	1	2	2

TABLE 47

PROHIBITION AND PUNISHMENT OF ILLEGAL PROFITEERING IN THE RULES OF 30 CLANS

Prohibition and punishment	Sacrificing public interest for personal gain	Selling falsified medicine	Illicit usury - In general	Illicit usury - First offense	Illicit usury - Incorrigible	Forgery of seals or credentials - In general	Forgery of seals or credentials - Light offense	Forgery of seals or credentials - Grave offense	Counterfeiting money - In general	Counterfeiting money - Light offense	Counterfeiting money - Grave offense	Swindling and defrauding - In general	Swindling and defrauding - Light offense	Swindling and defrauding - Grave offense	Swindling and defrauding - First offense	Swindling and defrauding - Incorrigible	Harbouring prostitutes	Selling opium - Light offense	Selling opium - Grave offense	Operating opium den - In general	Operating opium den - First offense	Operating opium den - Incorrigible	Making and selling gambling instruments	Making loan for gambling	Operating gambling den - In general	Operating gambling den - Light offense	Operating gambling den - Grave offense	Operating gambling den - First offense	Operating gambling den - Incorrigible
Prohibition without mention of punishment	5	1	1						1			5													2				
Clan punishment:																													
Oral censure				1		1				1			2		2			1			1		1			1		1	
Castigation	1					1			1						2		1			1					3				1
Corporal punishment						1						2	1																
Exclusion or expunction from genealogy												1													2				
Expulsion from clan group					1			1			1			2		2			1	1		1		1	4		2	2	1
Government punishment according to law																													
Total	6	1	1	1	1	2	1	1	2	1	1	9	2	2	2	2	1	1	1	2	1	1	1	1	11	2	2	1	1

APPENDIX 261

TABLE 48

PROHIBITION AND PUNISHMENT OF CRIMINAL OFFENSES
AGAINST PRIVATE PROPERTY IN THE RULES OF 32 CLANS

Prohibition and punishment	Theft or burglary — In general	Light offense	Grave offense	First offense	Incorrigible	Robbery or plunder — In general	Light offense	Grave offense	First offense	Repeated offense	Arson
Prohibition without mention of punishment.	4					3					
Clan punishment:											
Castigation	2	3	1			1					
Corporal punishment	1	1		3		1					
Non-participation in sacrificial rites forever	1										
Exclusion of tablet from ancestral hall	1										
Exclusion from ancestral hall				1					1		
Exclusion or expunction from genealogy	3			1		2					1
Exclusion of tablet from ancestral hall and expunction from genealogy	1										
Exclusion from ancestral hall and genealogy					1						
Expulsion from clan group	4			1					1		
Exclusion from ancestral hall and clan	1	2									
Ordered suicide						1					
Government punishment according to law	2	1	3	1		1	1	2			
Government punishment plus clan punishment:											
Government punishment and expunction from genealogy	2										
Government punishment and exclusion from genealogy and clan group					1						
Total	22	5	5	5	5	8	2	2	1	1	1

TABLE 49

PROHIBITION AND PUNISHMENT OF OFFENSES AGAINST THE STATE
IN THE RULES OF 20 CLANS

Prohibition and punishment	Treason — In general	Treason — Light offense	Treason — Grave offense	Treason — First offense	Treason — Disobeying clan order	Harbouring criminals — In general	Harbouring criminals — Light offense	Harbouring criminals — Grave offense
Prohibition without mention of punishment	2					1		
Clan punishment:								
Monetary fine						1		
Castigation		1				2	2	
Corporal punishment	1		2					
Exclusion or expunction from genealogy	1							
Exclusion from ancestral hall and genealogy				1				
Ordered suicide						1		
Put to death						1		
Government punishment according to law					1	4		2
Government punishment plus clan punishment:								
Government punishment and exclusion from genealogy and clan group					1			
Government punishment and exclusion from ancestral hall and genealogy and forfeit of property						1		
Total	4	1	2	1	2	11	2	2

TABLE 50

PROHIBITION AND PUNISHMENT OF OFFENSES AGAINST THE LAW
IN THE RULES OF 15 CLANS

Prohibition and punishment	In general	First offense	Incorrigible
Prohibition without mention of punishment	2		
Clan punishment:			
Oral censure	1	1	
Forfeit of clan ration	1		
Castigation		1	
Non-participation in clan affairs, "expelled" written on the back of the tablet and no biography in genealogy	1		
Exclusion or expunction from genealogy	1		
Exclusion from ancestral hall and genealogy			1
Expulsion from clan group	3		1
Expulsion from clan group after corporal punishment	2		
Exclusion from ancestral hall and clan	1		
Government punishment according to law	1		
Total	13	2	2

MONOGRAPHS OF THE ASSOCIATION FOR ASIAN STUDIES

I. *Money Economy in Medieval Japan.* A Study in the Use of Coins, by DELMER M. BROWN. 1951. viii, 128 pages, bibliography. Cloth $2.50.

II. *China's Management of the American Barbarians.* A Study of Sino-American Relations, 1841–1861, with documents, by EARL SWISHER. 1951. xxi, 844 pages. Glossary, bibliography. Cloth $7.50.

III. *Leadership and Power in the Chinese Community of Thailand,* by G. WILLIAM SKINNER. Cornell University Press, Ithaca, N.Y., 1958. xvii, 363 pages. 9 charts. Cloth $6.50.

IV. *Siam under Rama III, 1824–1851,* by WALTER F. VELLA. 1957. viii, 180 pages. 2 illustrations, 4 maps, appendix, bibliography, index. Cloth $5.00.

V. *The Rise of the Merchant Class in Tokugawa Japan, 1600–1868.* An Introductory Survey, by CHARLES DAVID SHELDON. 1958. ix, 206 pages. Glossary, bibliography, index. Cloth $5.00.

VI. *Chinese Secret Societies in Malaya.* A Survey of the Triad Society from 1800–1900, by L. F. COMBER, B.A., F.R.A.S. 1959. viii, 324 pages. 15 illustrations, 1 map in color, 5 maps, bibliography, index. Cloth $6.50.

VII. *The Traditional Chinese Clan Rules,* by HUI-CHEN WANG LIU. 1959. x, 264 pages. 1 illustration, 50 tables, bibliography. Cloth $5.50.

VIII. *A Comparative Analysis of the Jajmani System,* by THOMAS O. BEIDELMAN. 1959. iv, 86 pages, bibliography, index. Cloth $2.50.

IX. *Colonial Labor Policy and Administration 1910–1941,* by J. NORMAN PARMER. 1959. appr. 336 pages. 2 maps. *In press.*

Editorial Board

JOHN F. CADY   MARIUS B. JANSEN
F. HILARY CONROY FREDERICK W. MOTE
HOLDEN FURBER   LAURISTON SHARP
NORTON GINSBURG   ALEXANDER C. SOPER
STEPHEN N. HAY   JOSEPH E. SPENCER
DANIEL H. H. INGALLS
L. CARRINGTON GOODRICH, *Editor*

Distributed by

J. J. AUGUSTIN PUBLISHER, LOCUST VALLEY, NEW YORK